Evolution

&

Decline of

Hinduism

Dr. Anil Chadah 'Samarth'

Made with ❤ on the notionpress.com platform

Contents

Preface

The partition of India in 1947 was a pivotal event that shaped the country's political landscape. The division of British India into Hindu-majority India and Muslim-majority Pakistan led to massive displacement, violence, and widespread social upheaval. The estimated displacement due to partition was estimated as 14-17 million people. It was the largest mass migration in history. The refugees faced immense hardship, poverty, and trauma.

There was widespread violence and bloodshed and it is estimated that 200,000 to 2 million people were killed. There were large scale communal riots, massacres, and genocide. Cities like Lahore, Delhi, and Calcutta witnessed brutal violence. The families were torn apart, separated by newly drawn borders and the communities were disrupted and social networks were destroyed. The psychological trauma had lasting impact on individuals and society.

Large scale refugee camps with inadequate aid and sanitation had to be set up to rehabilitate the people. There were disease outbreaks, malnutrition, and starvation which had lasting impact on physical and mental health.

The creation of two nation-states India and Pakistan resulted in division of assets, infrastructure, and resources. There was disruption of trade, commerce, and industry which had long-term economic impacts on both the countries. The partition was a transformative event that profoundly impacted the country's political, social, and economic landscape.

The legacy of partition was ongoing conflicts (Kashmir, border disputes) and had its impact on social, economic, and cultural values. The then leaders had to focus on nation building, integrating princely state, addressing refugee crises and managing communal tensions.

Following India's partition in 1947, the country has struggled to manage its religious diversity and promote social cohesion. Though the partition of India was on the basis of religion, not all the Muslims, who had demanded a separate nation on the basis of religion migrated to newly created Pakistan and stayed in India. Approximately, 25% of India pre-partition Muslim population (around 35 million) stayed back in India. Some people consider it as a mistake of the then leaders, but in retrospect it appears to be a calculated move since though the partition was religion-centric and Pakistan declared itself an Islamic State, India was not declared a Hindu State despite majority of Hindus. This resulted in persistent communal tensions, identity politics and Hindu-Muslim divide.

As Indian democracy evolved, vote bank politics emerged and politicians began to recognize the importance of appealing to specific voter groups. This led to religious and caste-based politics, polarization, vote bank mobilization and identity-based politics. The politicians began to focus on minority groups, particularly Muslims, to secure votes. This was driven by demographic significance as (i) Muslims constituted around 14% of India's population; (ii) there were Muslim concentrations in key states like Uttar Pradesh, Bihar, and West Bengal; and (iii) partition-related grievances and perceived injustices arose. Some argue that politicians in India prioritized minority interests, particularly Muslims, to secure votes.

The then major political party started giving preference to minority community of Muslims and it started taking appeasement steps after independence. But, initially the motive was not clear and the public could not understand it; the largest crunch of population being uneducated and the remaining either under the influence of the British legacy or were busy in settling down in life after the nightmare of partition. If the political parties in existence at that time intended to make India a Hindu State, nothing could stop it. However, ignoring the Hindu sentiment, politics of appeasement started to take shape for reasons best known to everyone.

Though the population could not understand the appeasement policy for whatever reasons, but neo-politicians quickly understood this formula and grabbed it. They started winning elections by appeasement of Muslims and Hindus were left with no support of their own in their own country. Some Hindus felt that they were marginalized and perceived minority appeasement as detrimental to Hindu interests. They also felt that they were being disenfranchised and that their concerns were being neglected.

This resulted in emergence of Hindu nationalist movements and emergence of BJP as the major Hindu Party. Even now, the politicians try to devise ways and means to appease the Muslims and win their votes. In spite of the nationalist movement engineered by the BJP, the present state of affairs for Hindus is very grave and, therefore, it prompted me to write this book, which may serve as an eye opener for many.

Sources:

[1] University of Oxford - Faculty of History: Why was British India Partitioned in 1947?

[2] Wikipedia: Partition of India

Dr.Anil Chadah 'Samarth'
anilkr112@gmail.com

Part – I

Evolution

Of

Hinduism

Chapter 1

Introduction to Hinduism

Hinduism is one of the world's oldest and largest religions, with a rich and diverse history spanning over 4,000 years. The term "Hinduism" is derived from the Indus River, which was known as the Sindhu River in ancient times. The Persians, who invaded India in the 6th century BCE, referred to the people living east of the river as "Hindus." Hinduism is a way of life, a philosophy, and a religion that originated in the Indian subcontinent. It is based on the Vedic civilization, which dates back to the Bronze Age. The Vedas, the oldest sacred texts of Hinduism, contain hymns, prayers, and philosophical discussions that form the foundation of Hindu thought.

Hindu Dharma and Hinduism are often used interchangeably, but some scholars and practitioners make a distinction between the two:

Hindu Dharma:

-Refers to the eternal and universal principles of the universe, beyond human constructs.

-Emphasizes the natural order (Rita) and the cosmic law (Dharma) that governs the universe.

-Focuses on the individual's duty (Swadharma) and their role in maintaining the cosmic order.

-Encompasses the philosophical and spiritual aspects of the Vedic tradition.

Hinduism:

-Refers to the specific religious and cultural practices of the Hindu community.

-Includes the various traditions, customs, and beliefs of Hindu society.

-Encompasses the rituals, sacraments, and festivals that are unique to Hinduism.

-Often associated with the institutionalized religion and its various denominations.

In essence, Hindu Dharma represents the timeless and universal principles, while Hinduism represents the specific cultural and religious expression of those principles.

However, it's important to note that this distinction is not universally accepted, and many use the terms interchangeably or have different understandings of the nuances between them.

It is a complex and multifaceted faith that encompasses a wide range of beliefs, practices, and traditions and some key aspects of Hinduism, in brief, are given as under:

Core Beliefs:

1.**Brahman:The ultimate reality and universal consciousness.**

In Hinduism and Vedanta philosophy, Brahman refers to the ultimate reality and universal consciousness that pervades the universe. It is considered the unchanging, all-pervading, and eternal essence of the universe, beyond human comprehension.

Brahman is often described as the uncaused cause, the ultimate source of everything, and the essence of all existence. It is beyond human attributes, qualities, and limitations, and is often referred to as the Absolute, the Infinite, or the Unbounded.

The concept of Brahman is closely tied to the idea of Atman, the individual self or soul, which is seen as a spark of Brahman within each being. The ultimate goal of Hinduism and Vedanta is to realize the unity of Atman and Brahman, achieving liberation (Moksha) from the cycle of birth and death.

Brahman is often described as having three aspects:

1.Sat (Existence):The ultimate reality that exists beyond human perception.
2.Chit (Consciousness):The universal consciousness that pervades all existence.
3.Ananda (Bliss):The eternal joy and happiness that is inherent in Brahman.

The concept of Brahman is complex and multifaceted, and its nature is explored in various Hindu scriptures, such as the Upanishads and the Bhagavad Gita.

2.Atman:The individual self or soul

In Hinduism and Vedanta philosophy, Atman (Sanskrit: आत्मन्) refers to the individual self or soul, which is considered a spark of the ultimate reality, Brahman. Atman is the essence of who you are, beyond your physical body, mind, and emotions.

Here are some key aspects of Atman:

1.Individuality:Atman is the unique, personal self that distinguishes you from others.
2.Imortality:Atman is eternal, existing beyond the birth and death of the physical body.
3.Consciousness:Atman is considered a conscious entity, aware of its surroundings and experiences.
4.Spiritual essence:Atman is the spiritual core of a person, beyond their material possessions, accomplishments, and relationships.
5.Potential for realization:Atman has the potential to realize its true nature, achieving liberation (Moksha) from the cycle of rebirth and death.

The concept of Atman is closely tied to the idea of self-discovery and spiritual growth. The ultimate goal is to realize the true nature of Atman, which is considered to be identical to Brahman, the ultimate reality. This realization is known as Self-Realization or Atman-Brahman union.

The Upanishads, ancient Hindu scriptures, explore the concept of Atman in depth, offering insights and guidance for those seeking spiritual understanding and liberation.

Some key questions related to Atman include:

-Who am I, beyond my physical existence?

-What is my purpose in life?
-How can I realize my true nature and achieve spiritual liberation?

Contemplating these questions can lead to a deeper understanding of Atman and the ultimate reality, Brahman.

3.**Karma:The law of cause and effect, where actions influence future lives**

Karma is a fundamental concept in Eastern philosophies!

Karma (Sanskrit: कर्म) refers to the law of cause and effect, which governs the universe and governs the consequences of an individual's actions. It is a central concept in Hinduism, Buddhism, and Jainism, among other Eastern philosophies.

Here are the key aspects of Karma:

1.Cause and Effect:Every action (thought, word, or deed) has consequences, which affect the individual and the world around them.
2.Universal Justice:Karma ensures that the universe maintains balance and justice, without bias or prejudice.
3.Personal Responsibility:Individuals are responsible for their actions, and their karma determines their future experiences.
4.Reincarnation:Karma influences the circumstances of an individual's rebirth, shaping their next life's experiences.
5.Three Types of Karma:

-Sanchita Karma:Accumulated karma from past lives, influencing current life circumstances.

-Prarabdha Karma:Karma currently being experienced, shaping current life events.

-Agami Karma:Karma being created in the present, affecting future experiences.

6.Karma's Purpose:Karma aims to teach individuals valuable lessons, promoting spiritual growth, self-improvement, and eventual liberation from the cycle of rebirth.

The law of Karma encourages individuals to:

-Reflect on their actions and their consequences
-Take responsibility for their choices
-Strive for self-improvement and personal growth
-Cultivate positive actions and thoughts, leading to a more harmonious life

By understanding Karma, individuals can navigate life's challenges with a deeper sense of purpose and awareness, ultimately seeking to break free from the cycle of cause and effect and achieve spiritual liberation.

Reincarnation, the cycle of birth, death, and rebirth

Reincarnation, also known as Samsara or Punarjanma, is the belief that the soul, or consciousness, is reborn into a new body after death. This cycle of birth, death, and rebirth is a central tenet of several Eastern religions and philosophies, including Hinduism, Buddhism, Jainism, and Sikhism.

The key aspects of reincarnation are:

1.The Soul's Journey: The soul, or Atman, is reborn into a new body, carrying with it the accumulated karma from past lives.
2.Cycle of Birth and Death: The soul experiences multiple births, lives, and deaths, bound by the laws of karma.
3.Rebirth: The soul is reborn into a new body, influenced by its past karma, and continues its spiritual journey.
4.Karma's Influence: Karma from past lives determines the circumstances of the next birth, including the family, social status, and life experiences.
5.Three Realms: In Hinduism and Buddhism, the soul can be reborn in one of three realms:
- -Heaven (Swarga):A realm of pleasure and happiness.
- -Hell (Naraka):A realm of suffering and pain.
- -Earth (Bhu-loka):The human realm, where the soul can work out its karma.

6.Goal of Liberation (Moksha): The ultimate goal is to break free from the cycle of reincarnation through spiritual liberation (Moksha or Nirvana), achieving union with the ultimate reality (Brahman or Nirvana).
7.Reincarnation's Purpose:Reincarnation allows the soul to:
- -Work out past karma.
- -Learn valuable lessons.
- -Evolve spiritually.
- -Eventually achieve liberation.

Reincarnation is a complex and multifaceted concept, with varying interpretations across different cultures and belief systems. It offers a profound perspective on the nature of existence, the soul's journey, and the pursuit of spiritual growth and liberation.

4.**Dharma:Righteous living, duty, and morality**

Dharma, the natural order of the universe:

Dharma (Sanskrit: धर्म) refers to the natural order of the universe, encompassing the principles and laws that govern the cosmos, human society, and individual behavior. It is a central concept in Hinduism, Buddhism, Jainism, and Sikhism, among other Eastern philosophies.

The key aspects of Dharma are:

1.Universal Principle:Dharma is the underlying principle that sustains the universe, maintaining harmony and balance.
2.Natural Order:Dharma governs the natural world, including the laws of physics, the cycles of nature, and the interconnectedness of all living beings.
3.Social Order:Dharma also governs human society, providing the framework for social norms, ethics, and morality.
4.Personal Duty:Dharma is an individual's duty to fulfill their role in society, following their personal principles and values.
5.Righteousness:Dharma is associated with righteousness, justice, and morality, guiding individuals to lead a virtuous life.
6. Three Aspects:

Sanatana Dharma: The eternal and universal principles that govern the universe. Sanatana Dharma (Sanskrit: सनातन धर्म) refers to the eternal and universal principles that govern the universe, transcending time and space. It is the essence of the Vedic tradition, encompassing the eternal truths and natural laws that sustain the cosmos and guide human behavior.

Sanatana Dharma is characterized by:

1.Eternality:Timeless and unchanging principles, applicable to all beings and situations.
2.Universality:Applicable to all aspects of life, encompassing spiritual, social, and personal dimensions.
3.Natural Law: Aligns with the natural order of the universe, reflecting the intrinsic nature of reality.
4.Dharma Shastra:The scriptures and texts that expound Sanatana Dharma, including the Vedas, Upanishads, and Bhagavad Gita.
5.Four Pillars:
-Dharma (Righteousness): Fulfilling one's duties and responsibilities.
-Artha (Wealth):Acquiring wealth and resources through ethical means.
-Kama (Pleasure):Enjoying life's pleasures in a lawful and harmonious manner.
-Moksha (Liberation):Seeking spiritual liberation and self-realization.
6.Three Gunas:The three fundamental qualities of nature (Sattva, Rajas, and Tamas) that influence human behavior and the world.
7.Karma and Reincarnation:The understanding that actions have consequences, and the soul reincarnates to experience the effects of past actions.

Sanatana Dharma offers a profound and holistic understanding of the universe, human nature, and the path to spiritual growth and self-realization. It is a rich and complex philosophy that has shaped Indian thought and culture for millennia.

Varnashrama Dharma:The social and personal duties related to one's position in society. Varnashrama Dharma (Sanskrit: वर्णाश्रम धर्म) refers to the social and personal duties related to one's position in society, as outlined in the Vedic tradition. It is a key aspect of Sanatana Dharma, emphasizing the importance of social harmony and individual fulfillment.

Varnashrama Dharma consists of:

1.Four Varnas (Social Classes):
 -Brahmins (Priests and Scholars): Pursue knowledge and spiritual growth.
 -Kshatriyas (Warriors and Rulers): Govern and protect society.
 -Vaishyas (Merchants and Traders): Engage in commerce and agriculture.
 -Shudras (Laborers): Provide service and support.
2.Four Ashramas (Stages of Life):
 -Brahmacharya (Student Life):Study and learn.
 -Grihastha (Householder Life):Build a family and career.
 -Vanaprastha (Retired Life):Focus on spiritual growth and service.
 -Sannyasa (Renunciate Life):Embrace spiritual liberation and self-realization.
3.Duties and Responsibilities:Each varna and ashrama has specific duties, such as:
 -Following a specific occupation.
 -Performing rituals and sacraments.
 -Practicing self-control and self-discipline.
 -Cultivating spiritual growth and self-awareness.

Varnashrama Dharma aims to:

-Maintain social harmony and order.
-Ensure individual fulfillment and growth.
-Promote spiritual development and self-realization.

By understanding and fulfilling one's role in society, individuals can contribute to the well-being of all and achieve their full potential.

Swadharma:An individual's unique duty, aligned with their personal nature and talents.

Goal of Dharma:Dharma is a rich and complex concept, encompassing various aspects of human life and the natural world. It offers a profound perspective on the interconnectedness of all things and the importance of living in harmony with the natural order of the universe.

The ultimate goal is to fulfill one's Dharma, achieving spiritual growth, personal fulfillment, and contributing to the well-being of society and the universe.

The ultimate goal of Dharma is to achieve spiritual growth, self-realization, and liberation (Moksha) from the cycle of birth and death (Samsara). By fulfilling one's duties and responsibilities, an individual can:

1.Attain Spiritual Growth:Develop a deeper understanding of the self and the universe.
2.Realize Self-Actualization:Fulfill one's potential and purpose in life.

3.Experience Inner Peace:Cultivate a state of inner calm, contentment, and joy.
4.Achieve Liberation:Break free from the cycle of rebirth and attain union with the ultimate reality (Brahman).
5.Enjoy Supreme Bliss:Experience the highest form of happiness and fulfillment (Ananda).

The goal of Dharma is not just to follow rules or norms but to:

-Cultivate a sense of purpose and meaning
-Develop a strong moral character
-Embody compassion, empathy, and kindness
-Embrace self-discipline and self-control
-Seek spiritual knowledge and wisdom

By fulfilling one's Dharma, an individual can lead a life of purpose, happiness, and spiritual fulfillment.

Hinduism is also known for its diverse deities, rituals, and practices, such as yoga, meditation, and puja (worship).

5.**Moksha:Liberation from the cycle of rebirth, achieving unity with Brahman.**

Moksha is a central concept in Hinduism, representing the ultimate goal of spiritual liberation. Here's a deeper dive into Moksha:

What is Moksha?

Moksha is the release from the cycle of birth, death, and rebirth (samsara), achieving unity with the ultimate reality, Brahman. It's the state of freedom from the bondage of karma, desires, and ego.

Types of Moksha:

1.Kaivalya:Liberation from the cycle of rebirth, achieving isolation from the material world.

2.Sarupya:Attaining a form similar to the deity or Brahman.

3.Sayujya:Merging with Brahman, losing individual identity.

4.Salokya:Residing in the same realm as Brahman.

Paths to Moksha:

1.Jnana Yoga:The path of knowledge, understanding the true nature of reality.

2.Bhakti Yoga:The path of devotion, surrendering to a personal deity.

3.Karma Yoga:The path of selfless action, performing duties without attachment.

4.Raja Yoga:The path of meditation, controlling the mind and senses.

Characteristics of Moksha:

1.Eternal bliss:Experiencing infinite happiness and peace.

2.Freedom from karma:No longer bound by the law of cause and effect.

3.Unity with Brahman:Merging with the ultimate reality.

4.End of rebirth:No longer trapped in the cycle of samsara.

Achieving Moksha:

Moksha is achieved through a combination of spiritual practices, self-inquiry, and devotion. It requires:

1.Discernment:Understanding the true nature of reality.

2.Detachment:Letting go of worldly attachments and desires.

3.Self-control:Mastering the mind and senses.

4.Surrender: Submitting to a higher power or Brahman.

Remember, Moksha is a complex and multifaceted concept, and its interpretation may vary across different Hindu traditions and philosophies.

Key Deities:

1.Brahma:The creator

2.Vishnu:The preserver

3.Shiva:The destroyer

4.Devi:The goddess, representing feminine power

Sacred Texts:

1.Vedas:Ancient scriptures containing hymns, prayers, and rituals.

2.Upanishads:Philosophical texts exploring the nature of reality.

3.Bhagavad Gita:A key scripture teaching spiritual growth and selfless action.

Practices:

1.Puja:Worship and offerings to deities.

2.Yoga:Physical, mental, and spiritual disciplines.

3.Meditation:Focusing the mind to achieve inner peace.

4.Festivals:Celebrating various gods, goddesses, and spiritual events.

Philosophical Schools:

1.Advaita Vedanta:Non-dualism, emphasizing the unity of Brahman and Atman.

2.Vishishtadvaita:Qualified non-dualism, recognizing the distinctness of individual souls.

3.Dvaita:Dualism, separating the individual self from the ultimate reality.

Chapter 2

Evolution of Hinduism

A brief overview of the evolution of Hinduism!

Hinduism has evolved over thousands of years, shaping a rich and diverse religious and cultural heritage. The condensed timeline, as under, of its evolution will give a brief picture.

Indus Valley Civilization (3300 BCE - 1300 BCE):

Around 6000 BC, some wanderers, later believed to be Dravidians, settled alongside Indus River in the mountains and developed villages for their living. They started cultivating barley and wheat. They built their houses with mudbricks and started living in those houses. After about ten centuries, around about 5000 BC, the climate started changing bringing about more rains. Therefore, the people, who had settled alongside the Indus River, started growing different crops for feeding the growth in their population. They also started rearing up domestic animals, like, cows, sheep, goats, etc.

After an interval of around another ten centuries, i.e., around about 4,000 BC, they began trade with far off places of Central Asia as also western parts of Khyber Pass. They learnt the use of bronze and other metals for the purpose of trading. With the passage of time, they started spreading in greater areas with development of cities having beautiful architectural buildings constructed with pucca bricks. The cities also had elaborate sewage disposal systems and streets paved with stones or concrete.

Mohenjo-Daro is one of the largest and most well-known cities of the Indus Valley Civilization (IVC), which existed around 4300-1300 BCE. It's located in modern-day Pakistan, in the province of Sindh, near the Indus River.

Some fascinating facts about Mohenjo-Daro are:

-Sophisticated urban planning:Mohenjo-Daro had advanced city planning, with a grid-like street pattern, public baths, and a sophisticated drainage system.

-Advanced architecture:The city featured impressive architecture, including the Great Bath, a large public bath made of brick and stone.

-Trade and commerce:Mohenjo-Daro was an important center of trade and commerce, with connections to other IVC cities and regions.

-Unique writing system:The IVC had a distinct writing system, which has not yet been fully deciphered.

-Decline and abandonment:Mohenjo-Daro was eventually abandoned around 1900 BCE, due to climate change, drought, or invasions.

-UNESCO World Heritage Site:Mohenjo-Daro was designated a UNESCO World Heritage Site in 1980, recognizing its cultural and historical significance.

(a)**Early roots of Hinduism in the Indus Valley Civilization:**

The Indus Valley Civilization (3300 BCE - 1300 BCE) was a sophisticated urban culture that flourished in the northwestern region of the Indian subcontinent. While the civilization's religious practices are not fully understood, archaeological evidence suggests that many Hinduisms' early roots can be traced back to this period.

Some key similarities and possible influences include:

1.**Worship of goddesses**:The Indus Valley Civilization worshipped female deities, similar to the Hindu goddesses Lakshmi, Saraswati, and Kali.

The people of the Indus Valley Civilization worshipped a diverse pantheon of goddesses, gods, and natural phenomena, reflecting their connection with nature and the cycles of life. Some notable examples include:

Goddesses:

-Mother Goddess (similar to Hinduism's Adi Parashakti)

Mother Goddess (source: google)

-Goddess of fertility and prosperity (similar to Lakshmi)

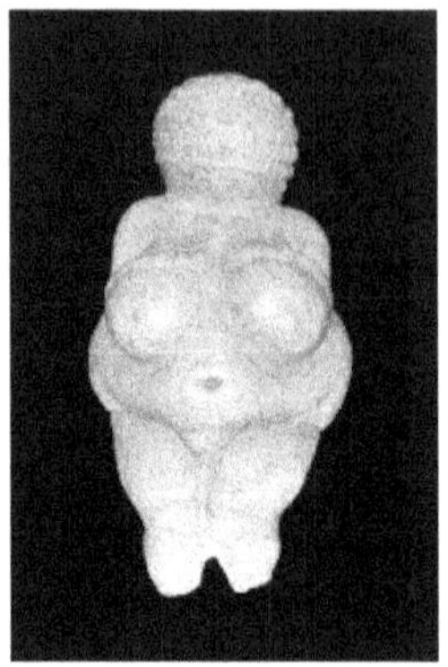

Goddess of Fertility (source: google)

-Goddess of war and protection (similar to Durga)

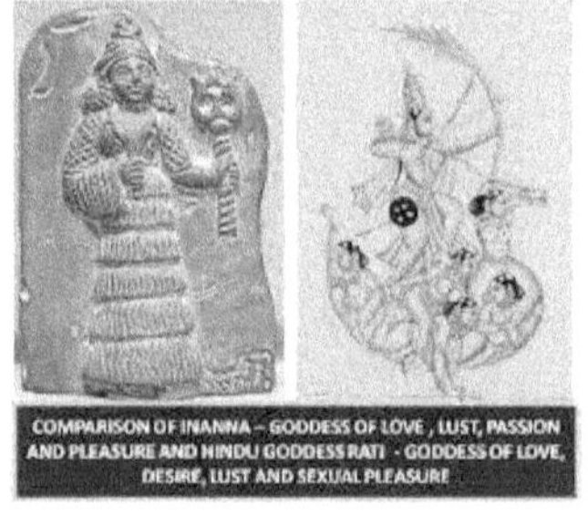

Goddess of war & protection (source: google)

<u>Gods:</u>

-Male deity with a horned headdress (similar to Shiva)

God of Indus Valley Civilization (source: google)

-God of the sky and thunder (similar to Indra)

God of the sky and thunder (source: google)

-God of the sun and light (similar to Surya)

God of the sun and light (source: google)

Natural Phenomena:

-Sacred trees (like the pipal tree, considered sacred in Hinduism)

-Animals (like the humped bull, elephant, and peacock)

-Water and rivers (like the Saraswati River, considered sacred in Hinduism)

-Mountains and hills (like the Himalayas, considered sacred in Hinduism)

Worship practices involved:

-Ritual bathing and purification

-Offerings and sacrifices

-Chanting and music

-Dance and performance

-Symbolic representations (like seals and figurines)

This worship of goddesses, gods, and natural phenomena reflects the civilization's emphasis on fertility, prosperity, protection, and the cycles of nature, which would later influence Hinduism's diverse pantheon and reverence for the natural world.

2.**Phallic symbols**:The civilization's use of phallic symbols, like the lingam, is reminiscent of the Hindu worship of Shiva.

The Indus Valley Civilization's use of phallic symbols, such as the lingam, is a notable aspect of their religious and cultural practices. These symbols were associated with fertility, prosperity, and the worship of male deities.

The lingam, in particular, is a symbol that has been interpreted in various ways:

-Fertility symbol:Representing the male reproductive organ, it may have symbolized fertility, virility, and the power of creation.

-Shiva worship:The lingam is a central symbol in Hinduism's Shaivism tradition, representing Shiva, the destroyer and transformer.

-Cosmic pillar:Some scholars see the lingam as a symbol of the cosmic axis, connecting heaven and earth.

The presence of phallic symbols in Indus Valley Civilization suggests:

-A focus on fertility and prosperity

-A connection to ancient Hinduism's Shaivism tradition

-A possible link to ritual practices and ceremonies

These symbols demonstrate the civilization's emphasis on the cycles of nature and the human experience, which would later influence Hinduism's diverse traditions and symbolism.

3.**Yoga and meditation**:The Indus Valley Civilization's depictions of figures in meditative postures suggest early roots of yoga and meditation practices.

The Indus Valley Civilization (3300 BCE - 1300 BCE) shows evidence of yoga and meditation practices, which were integral to their religious and spiritual beliefs. Excavations have revealed:

i)Figurines in meditative postures: Terracotta figurines depict individuals in yoga-like poses, suggesting a focus on mindfulness and spiritual growth.

ii)Seals with yogic symbols:Seals feature symbols similar to the Hinduism's "Om" (Aum) and the "Chakra" (wheel), indicating a connection to yogic philosophies.

iii)Ritualistic bathing platforms:Large bathing platforms, like the Great Bath at Mohenjo-Daro, may have been used for ritual purification and meditation.

iv)Sacred spaces for contemplation:The civilization's architecture includes spaces for quiet reflection and contemplation, such as the "Hall of the Pillars" at Mohenjo-Daro.

These findings suggest that yoga and meditation were practiced in the Indus Valley Civilization, for:

a)Spiritual growth and self-realization

b)Ritual purification and cleansing

c)Mental and physical well-being

d)Connection with the divine and nature

The emphasis on yoga and meditation in this ancient civilization highlights the importance of mindfulness and spiritual practices in their daily lives, which would later influence Hinduism's emphasis on yoga, meditation, and spiritual growth.

4.**Ritual bathing**:The civilization's elaborate bathing platforms and drains indicate a focus on ritual purification, similar to Hinduism's emphasis on bathing in sacred rivers.

Ritual bathing was a significant practice in the Indus Valley Civilization, reflecting their emphasis on purification, cleanliness, and spiritual growth. The civilization's elaborate bathing platforms and drains suggest a sophisticated understanding of hygiene and public health.

Ritual bathing played a role in:

i)Religious purification:Cleansing the body and soul for religious rituals and ceremonies.

ii)Spiritual renewal:Bathing as a symbol of spiritual rebirth and regeneration.

iii)Community bonding:Public bathing areas fostering social connections and community bonding.

iv)Therapeutic benefits:Bathing for health and wellness, using water from sacred sources like rivers and wells.

The Great Bath at Mohenjo-Daro, a massive public bathing platform, is a testament to the importance of ritual bathing in this ancient civilization. This practice later influenced Hinduism's emphasis on ritual bathing in sacred rivers and temples, like the Ganges River and the Kumbh Mela festival.

Ritual bathing in the Indus Valley Civilization demonstrates their advanced understanding of urban planning, public health, and spiritual practices, which would continue to shape Indian culture and Hinduism for millennia to come.

5.**Sacred animals**:The reverence for animals like the humped bull (similar to Shiva's Nandi) and the elephant (associated with Ganesh) suggests early connections to Hindu symbolism.

The Indus Valley Civilization revered certain animals as sacred, reflecting their connection with nature and the divine. Some of these animals include:

i)Humped Bull (similar to Shiva's Nandi): Symbolizing strength, fertility, and prosperity.

ii)Elephant (associated with Ganesh): Representing wisdom, good fortune, and remover of obstacles.

iii)Peacock (connected to Krishna): Embodiment of beauty, grace, and divine love.

iv)Tiger (associated with Durga): Symbolizing power, courage, and protection.

v)Fish (connected to Vishnu): Representing spiritual growth, transformation, and salvation.

These sacred animals were revered for their:

a)Symbolic significance:Representing various aspects of human life and the natural world.

b)Economic importance:Providing food, transportation, and other essential resources.

c)Cultural significance:Featuring in art, literature, and religious rituals.

The reverence for sacred animals in the Indus Valley Civilization later influenced Hinduism's emphasis on animal worship, symbolism, and the protection of all living beings (Ahimsa).

6.**Agricultural cycles**:The civilization's agricultural practices and festivals may have influenced Hinduism's emphasis on seasonal cycles and fertility rituals.

The Indus Valley Civilization's agricultural practices were deeply connected to their religious and cultural beliefs. They recognized the importance of agricultural cycles and the fertility of the land, which influenced their religious rituals and festivals.

Some key aspects of agricultural cycles in this civilization include:

i)Seasonal festivals:Celebrations like the spring festival (Vasant) and the autumn harvest festival (Sharad) honored the cycles of nature.

ii)Fertility rituals:Rituals like the "Marriage of the Goddess" ensured fertility and prosperity in the land and people.

iii)Agricultural deities:Goddesses like Annapurna (the goddess of grain) and gods like Varuna (the god of rain) were revered for their role in agricultural cycles.

iv)Crop rotation and irrigation:Advanced agricultural practices like crop rotation and sophisticated irrigation systems ensured fertile land and abundant harvests.

The Indus Valley Civilization's emphasis on agricultural cycles and fertility later influenced Hinduism's emphasis on:

a)Worship of nature:Recognizing the divine in the natural world.

b)Seasonal festivals:Celebrating the cycles of nature and the harvest.

c)Agricultural symbolism:Using agricultural imagery in religious rituals and symbolism.

The connection between agriculture, religion, and culture in the Indus Valley Civilization demonstrates their profound respect for the natural world and its cycles.

7.**Mystical symbols**:The Indus Valley Civilization's use of symbols like the swastika, the pipal tree, and the conch shell are still revered in Hinduism today.

The Indus Valley Civilization used various mystical symbols, which were imbued with spiritual and religious significance. Some of these symbols include:

i)Swastika (or Svastika):A symbol of good fortune, prosperity, and spiritual growth.

ii)Pipal Tree (or Ashvattha):Representing the connection between heaven and earth.

iii)Conch Shell (or Shankha):Symbolizing the sound of the universe and spiritual awakening.

iv)Chakra (or Wheel):Representing the cycles of life, death, and rebirth.

v)Yoga and Meditation Symbols:Symbols like the "Om" (Aum) and the "Chakra" (wheel) indicate a focus on spiritual practices.

These mystical symbols were used in various contexts, including:

a)Religious rituals:Used in ceremonies and worship.

b)Art and architecture:Featured in pottery, seals, and building designs.

c)Personal adornments:Used in jewelry and other personal items.

d)Spiritual practices:Used in meditation, yoga, and other spiritual disciplines.

The use of mystical symbols in the Indus Valley Civilization demonstrates their deep connection to spirituality, religious beliefs, and the mysteries of the universe. These symbols would later influence Hinduism's rich tradition of symbolism and spiritual practices.

While the Indus Valley Civilization's religious practices were distinct, these similarities suggest that early Hinduism may have borrowed and evolved from this ancient culture.

Chapter 3

Vedic Period (1500 BCE - 500 BCE)

(a) Composition of the Vedas, the oldest Hindu scriptures

The Vedas, the oldest Hindu scriptures, were composed over a period of several centuries by ancient Indian sages and seers. The composition of the Vedas is attributed to the following stages:

1.Revelation (1500 BCE - 1200 BCE):The Vedas were revealed to the rishis (sages) through divine inspiration.

2.Oral Tradition (1200 BCE - 800 BCE):The revealed knowledge was passed down orally through generations of rishis and brahmins (priests).

3.Compilation (800 BCE - 500 BCE):The oral traditions were compiled into written texts by scholars and priests.

4.Redaction (500 BCE - 200 BCE):The compiled texts were edited and revised to create the final versions of the Vedas.

The four Vedas, in the order of their composition, are:

(i)Rigveda (1500 BCE - 1200 BCE):The oldest Veda, containing hymns and prayers.
(ii)Yajurveda (1200 BCE - 900 BCE): Contains rituals and sacrificial formulas.
(iii)Samaveda (1200 BCE - 800 BCE): Focuses on melodies and chants.
(iv)Atharvaveda (800 BCE - 500 BCE): Includes spells, incantations, and rituals for specific purposes.

The Vedas are considered apaurusheya, or "not created by humans," and are revered as the ultimate authority in Hinduism.

(b)<u>Emergence of the caste system and Brahminical traditions in ancient India</u>

The caste system, a complex social hierarchy, evolved over time, with the Brahmins (priests and scholars) at the top. The four main castes (varnas) are:

1.Brahmins (priests, teachers, and scholars)
2.Kshatriyas (rulers, warriors, and administrators)
3.Vaishyas (merchants, traders, and farmers)
4.Shudras (labourers and service workers)

The Brahmins, considered the purest and most superior, developed and maintained the Vedic traditions, performing rituals and sacrifices. They also developed the concept of "varnashrama dharma," which emphasized social duty and the four stages of life:

1.Brahmacharya (student life)
2.Grihastha (householder life)
3.Vanaprastha (retired life)
4.Sannyasa (renunciate life)

Brahminical traditions include:

1Vedic rituals and sacrifices
2.Study and teaching of the Vedas
3.Maintenance of social order and hierarchy
4.Development of Hindu philosophy and theology

The emergence of the caste system and Brahminical traditions shaped Indian society, influencing social, cultural, and religious practices for centuries to come. While the caste system has been criticized for its rigidity and inequality, the Brahminical traditions have contributed significantly to India's rich cultural heritage.

Chapter 4

Epic Period (500 BCE - 500 CE)

The Epic Period in Indian history, spanning from 500 BCE to 500 CE, is a fascinating era marked by significant cultural, philosophical, and literary developments.

Key Features:

1.**Epic Literature:**This period saw the composition of iconic epics like the Ramayana and Mahabharata, which shaped Indian thought, values, and identity.

2.**Hinduism and Jainism:**Both religions evolved and spread, influencing art, architecture, and society.

3.**Buddhism:**Emerged in the 6th century BCE, emphasizing spiritual growth, non-violence, and enlightenment.

4.**Mahajanapadas:**16 powerful kingdoms, including Magadha, Kosala, and Gandhara, vied for dominance.

5.**Persian and Greek Influences:**India interacted with Western powers, leading to cultural exchange and conflicts.

6.**Philosophical Developments:**Six orthodox schools of Hindu philosophy (Shad Darshanas) emerged, along with heterodox traditions like Buddhism and Jainism.

7.**Art and Architecture:**Sculpture, painting, and temple construction flourished, showcasing Indian craftsmanship.

Notable Figures:

1.Gautama Buddha:Founder of Buddhism

2.Mahavira:Founder of Jainism

3.Panini:Renowned grammarian and scholar

4.Chanakya (Kautilya):Statesman and author of the Arthashastra

5.Ashoka the Great:Emperor who spread Buddhism and established a vast empire

Timeline:

-500 BCE:Emergence of Buddhism and Jainism

-400 BCE:Composition of the Ramayana and Mahabharata epics

-300 BCE:Rise of the Mauryan Empire under Chandragupta Maurya

-250 BCE:Ashoka's reign and the spread of Buddhism

-100 CE:Rise of the Kushan Empire and Greek influences

-500 CE:Decline of the Epic Period and the beginning of the Puranic Period

The Epic Period sets the stage for exploring the rich cultural, philosophical, and literary heritage of ancient India.

(a)Composition of the Epics (Ramayana and Mahabharata)

The Ramayana and Mahabharata, two of the most revered Epics in Hinduism, were composed over a period of several centuries. Here's a brief overview:

Ramayana-

-Composed by Valmiki (400 BCE - 200 BCE);

-Originally consisted of 6 chapters (khands);

-Later additions and interpolations expanded it to 7 chapters;

-Story revolves around Rama's journey, exile, and battle against Ravana;

-Teaches ideals of dharma, loyalty, victory of good over evil and duty.

Mahabharata-

-Composed by Vyasa (400 BCE - 200 BCE);

-Originally consisted of 8 chapters (parvas);

-Later additions and interpolations expanded it to 18 chapters;

-Story revolves around the Pandavas and Kauravas' struggle for the throne;

-Teaches ideals of dharma, duty, and the nature of reality.

Both Epics were composed in Sanskrit and were passed down orally before being reduced to writing. These epics were influenced by Vedic philosophy and mythology and shaped Indian thought, culture, and society.

These Epics have had a profound impact on Indian literature, art, and culture, and still continue to inspire and guide millions of people around the world.

(b)<u>Development of the Bhakti movement (devotional worship)</u>

The Bhakti movement, which emerged in the 1st millennium CE, emphasized devotional worship and personal experience of the divine. The key aspects were:

-Emphasis on love and devotion (bhakti) over ritual and doctrine;

-Focus on the individual's personal relationship with the divine;

-Use of music, dance, and art to express devotion;

-Rise of vernacular languages (e.g., Tamil, Hindi, Marathi) for devotional literature;

-Importance of saints and mystics (e.g., Mirabai, Kabir, Tukaram) who shared their experiences;

-Popularization of pilgrimage sites and temples;

-Inclusivity and accessibility for all, regardless of caste or social status.

The Bhakti movement influenced Hinduism in many ways, including:

-Shifting focus from rituals to personal devotion;

-Encouraging emotional expression and spiritual experience;

-Democratizing access to the divine;

-Inspiring some of India's most beloved devotional literature and music;

-Shaping the development of various Hindu traditions and sects.

The Bhakti movement's emphasis on personal devotion and experience has made it a vital part of Hinduism's rich spiritual heritage, continuing to inspire millions of devotees to this day.

Chapter 5

Puranas and Tantra (500 CE - 1500 CE)

The period spanning from 500 CE to 1500 CE is considered as the period of "Puranas and Tantra" in Indian history. A brief overview of this period is given hereunder:

Key Features:

1.Puranic Literature:Composed during this period, the Puranas are ancient texts that expanded on Hindu mythology, legends, and genealogies.

2.Tantric Practices:Tantra emerged as a distinct philosophical and spiritual movement, emphasizing ritual practices, yoga, and devotion.

3.Hindu Revival:A resurgence of Hinduism occurred, with the rise of devotional (Bhakti) movements and the construction of grand temples.

4.Decline of Buddhism and Jainism:The influence of Buddhism and Jainism waned, while Hinduism became more dominant.

5.Islamic Invasions:Muslim invasions began in the 8th century CE, leading to the establishment of Islamic rule in parts of India.

6.Regional Kingdoms:Various regional kingdoms, such as the Pallavas, Cholas, and Vijayanagara Empire, rose and fell.

7.Artistic and Architectural Developments: Temple architecture, sculpture, and painting flourished, showcasing Indian artistic excellence.

Notable Figures:

1.Adi Shankara:Philosopher and theologian who systematized Advaita Vedanta

2.Ramanuja:Philosopher and theologian who developed Vishishtadvaita Vedanta

3.Madhva:Philosopher and theologian who founded Dvaita Vedanta

4.Jayadeva:Poet and composer of the Gita Govinda

5.Kabir:Mystic poet and saint who blended Hindu and Islamic influences

Timeline:

-500 CE:Puranic literature and Tantric practices emerged;

-600 CE:Bhakti movements gained momentum;

-800 CE:Islamic invasions began;

-1000 CE:Vijayanagara Empire rose;

-1200 CE:Delhi Sultanate established;

-1500 CE:Puranic and Tantric period resulted in transitions into the Bhakti and Sufi period.

This period saw significant developments in Hinduism, the emergence of Tantra, and the impact of Islamic invasions on Indian society.

Puranas (500 CE - 1500 CE):

The Puranas are a collection of sacred texts in Hinduism, comprising stories, legends, mythology, and historical accounts. They are considered Smriti texts, meaning "remembered" or "traditional" knowledge, as opposed to Shruti texts, which are "revealed" knowledge.

Key Features:

1.Mythology and Legends:Puranas contain stories of gods, goddesses, heroes, and demons, exploring themes like creation, destruction, and rebirth.

2.Genealogies and Histories:They provide accounts of royal dynasties, sages, and historical events.

3.Philosophical and Spiritual Teachings: Puranas convey Hindu philosophical concepts, spiritual practices, and devotional traditions.

4.Rituals and Practices:They describe various rituals, ceremonies, and practices, such as worship, sacrifices, and festivals.

5.Geography and Cosmology:Puranas contain descriptions of the universe, earth, and sacred geography.

Major Puranas:

1. Brahma Purana

2. Padma Purana

3. Vishnu Purana

4. Shiva Purana

5. Markandeya Purana

6. Bhagavata Purana (also known as the Srimad Bhagavatam)

Impact and Significance:

1.Hindu Tradition:Puranas have shaped Hindu beliefs, practices, and culture.

2.Influence on Art and Literature:They have inspired countless works of art, literature, and performance.

3.Devotional Movements:Puranas have fueled Bhakti movements and devotional practices.

Timeline:

-500 CE:Composition of early Puranas begins

-1000 CE:Major Puranas take shape

-1500 CE:Puranic period transitions into the Bhakti and Sufi period

The Puranas are a rich and diverse collection of texts, offering insights into Hindu mythology, philosophy, and culture. The Puranas are ancient texts that narrate the history of the universe and gods. There are 18 major Puranas and several minor ones that contain stories, myths, and legends of Hindu beliefs and practices. They focus on the trimurti (Brahma, Vishnu, Shiva) and their roles in creation and destruction and describe the avatars (incarnations) of Vishnu and the lives of saints and sages. The Puranas play an important and pivotal role in providing guidance on dharma, rituals, and spiritual practices.

The Puranas

The Puranas are ancient Hindu texts that narrate the history of the universe, gods, and goddesses. They are considered the sacred history of the Hindu universe, covering creation, preservation, and destruction. The 18 major Puranas include:

1. Brahma Purana
2. Padma Purana
3. Vishnu Purana
4. Shiva Purana
5. Bhagavata Purana
6. Naradeya Purana
7. Markandeya Purana
8. Agni Purana
9. Bhavishya Purana
10. Brahmavaivarta Purana
11. Linga Purana
12. Varaha Purana
13. Skanda Purana
14. Vamana Purana
15. Kurma Purana
16. Matsya Purana
17. Garuda Purana
18. Brahmanda Purana

These texts explore various themes, including:

-Creation of myths

-Gods and goddesses

-Avatars (incarnations) of Vishnu

-Cosmology and the universe's cycles

-Dharma and moral principles

-Rituals and spiritual practices

-The lives of saints and sages

The Puranas offer insights into Hindu philosophy, mythology, and culture, making them a rich and fascinating part of India's spiritual heritage.

Tantra (500 CE - 1500 CE):

Tantra is a complex and multifaceted movement that emerged in ancient India, emphasizing spiritual growth, self-realization, and union with the divine. It encompasses a wide range of practices, rituals, and philosophies, often misunderstood or misrepresented in popular culture.

Key Features:

1.Spiritual Practices:Tantra involves various practices, such as yoga, meditation, and rituals, aimed at attaining spiritual liberation.

2.Rituals and Worship:Tantric rituals often involve the use of mantras, yantras, and sacred geometry, honoring deities and the divine feminine.

3.Philosophical Teachings:Tantra explores concepts like the nature of reality, consciousness, and the universe.

4.Energy and Kundalini:Tantra focuses on harnessing and balancing energy, particularly the Kundalini force, believed to reside within the human body.

5.Sacred Sexuality:Tantra views sexuality as a sacred and potent force, often incorporating ritualized sexual practices.

Tantric Traditions:

1.Hindu Tantra:Emphasizes union with the divine through devotion and rituals.

2.Buddhist Tantra:Focuses on achieving enlightenment through tantric practices and rituals.

3.Jain Tantra:Combines tantric practices with Jain principles and ethics.

Influence and Legacy:

1.Hinduism and Buddhism:Tantra has significantly influenced both Hindu and Buddhist traditions.

2.Art and Iconography:Tantric symbolism and imagery have inspired Indian art and iconography.

3.Spiritual Movements:Tantra has influenced modern spiritual movements and Western esotericism.

Timeline:

-500 CE:Tantric practices and texts emerged

-1000 CE:Tantra became a distinct movement

-1500 CE:Tantra's influence peaked, eventually declining

Tantra was a rich and complex movement that shaped Indian spirituality and culture. It emerged as a philosophical and ritualistic tradition that emphasized the union of opposites (Shiva-Shakti) and focused on the feminine divine and the power of the goddess. The practices included yoga, meditation, and rituals to balance the energies of the body and mind and emphasized on the importance of the guru-disciple relationship. It developed tantric art, architecture, and literature. It was a philosophical and ritualistic tradition that flourished in India and beyond!

The key aspects of emphasis of Tantra on the union of opposites (Shiva-Shakti) and the feminine divine can be categorized as under:

1.Duality:Union of male and female principles, consciousness and energy.

2.Devi:The feminine divine, worshipped as the ultimate reality.

3.Yoga:Practices like Kundalini Yoga, Hatha Yoga, and Tantra Yoga.

4.Rituals:Sacred rituals, like Puja (worship) and Homa (fire ceremonies).

5.Mantras:Sacred sounds and chants, like the famous Tantric mantra, "Om Shakti".

6.Guru-disciple:The importance of the guru-disciple relationship.

7.Spiritual growth:Emphasis on personal transformation and self-realization.

Tantra influenced various aspects of Indian culture, including:

1.Art:Tantric art, architecture, and iconography.

2.Literature:Tantric texts, like the Tantrasara and the Kularnava Tantra.

3.Music:Tantric music and dance, like the Odissi tradition.

4.Philosophy:Tantric philosophy, which influenced Hinduism and Buddhism.

Tantra's impact extends beyond India, with influences seen in:

1.Buddhism:Tantric Buddhism, practiced in Tibet, Nepal, and Bhutan.

2.Jainism:Tantric influences on Jain philosophy and practices.

3.Sikhism:Tantric influences on Sikh philosophy and practices.

Tantra's rich and complex legacy continues to inspire spiritual seekers and scholars alike.

The Hindu thought and practice was influenced by both Puranas and Tantra. They shaped the development of Hindu traditions and sects and contributed to the rich cultural and spiritual heritage of India. It continues to inspire and guide millions of Hindus around the world.

These texts and traditions have had a profound impact on Hinduism, offering insights into the nature of the universe, the divine, and human consciousness.

Chapter 6

Medieval Period (1500 CE - 1800 CE)

The key developments towards the evolution of Hinduism during the Medieval Period (1500 CE - 1800 CE) can be summarized as under:

1.**Bhakti Movement**:Devotional movements like Bhakti, led by saints like Mirabai, Kabir, and Chaitanya, emphasized personal devotion and love for a personal deity.

2.**Puranic Hinduism**:The influence of Puranas continued, with a focus on mythology, rituals, and temple worship.

3.**Tantric Practices**:Tantra continued to evolve, with a focus on esoteric rituals and spiritual practices.

4.**Philosophical Debates**:Scholars like Adi Shankara's followers and others engaged in debates on Advaita Vedanta, Vishishtadvaita, and Dvaita philosophies.

5.**Islamic Influence**:Islamic rule in parts of India led to cultural exchange, syncretism, and the emergence of new traditions like Sufi-Hindu fusion.

6.**Vernacular Languages**:Regional languages like Hindi, Marathi, and Bengali emerged, facilitating the spread of Hindu scriptures and devotional literature.

7.**Temple Architecture**:Temple construction continued, with notable examples like the Konark Sun Temple and the Meenakshi Amman Temple.

Notable Figures:

1.Chaitanya Mahaprabhu:Bengali saint and founder of Gaudiya Vaishnavism.

2.Mirabai:Rajasthani princess and devotee of Krishna, known for her poetry and devotion.

3.Kabir:Mystic poet and saint who blended Hindu and Islamic influences.

4.Tukaram:Marathi poet and saint who composed devotional songs.

Regional Traditions:

1.**Vaishnavism**:Flourished in Bengal, Orissa, and Gujarat, with a focus on Krishna and Vishnu worship.

Vaishnavism is a significant tradition within Hinduism that focuses on the worship of Vishnu, one of the principal deities in Hinduism, as the ultimate reality or supreme being. It is one of the four main sects of Hinduism, alongside Shaivism, Shaktism, and Smartism.

Vaishnavism emphasizes devotion (bhakti) to Vishnu and his various incarnations, particularly Rama and Krishna. The tradition believes in the concept of avatar, where Vishnu descends to earth in various forms to restore cosmic order and righteousness.

Some key aspects of Vaishnavism include:

-Puja (worship) and bhakti (devotion) to Vishnu and his avatars

-Study of sacred texts like the Bhagavad Gita and the Puranas

-Importance of guru-shishya parampara (teacher-disciple lineage)

-Emphasis on ahimsa (non-violence) and compassion

Vaishnavism has various sub-traditions, such as:

-Sri Vaishnavism (southern India)

-Gaudiya Vaishnavism (Bengal region)

-Pushtimarg (western India)

Each sub-tradition has its unique practices, philosophies, and interpretations.

2.**Shaivism**:Predominant in South India, with a focus on Shiva worship and Tamil Shaiva Siddhanta.

Shaivism is a major tradition within Hinduism that focuses on the worship of Shiva, one of the principal deities in Hinduism, as the ultimate reality or supreme being. It is one of the four main sects of Hinduism, alongside Vaishnavism, Shaktism, and Smartism.

Shaivism encompasses a broad range of philosophical and devotional traditions, including:

1.Dualistic (Dvaita) and non-dualistic (Advaita) approaches

2.Devotional (bhakti) and meditative (yoga) practices

3.Worship of Shiva in various forms, such as:

-Linga (symbolic form)

-Nataraja (cosmic dancer)

-Pashupati (lord of animals)

-Mahadeva (great god)

Some key aspects of Shaivism include:

-Emphasis on the cyclical nature of time and the universe

-Recognition of the individual self (jiva) and the ultimate reality (Brahman)

-Importance of rituals, such as puja and abhisheka (libations)

-Study of sacred texts like the Shiva Purana and the Tirumurai

Shaivism has various sub-traditions, including:

-Shaiva Siddhanta (Southern India)

-Kashmir Shaivism (Kashmir region)

-Lingayatism (Western India)

-Nathism (esoteric tradition)

Each sub-tradition has its unique practices, philosophies, and interpretations.

3.**Shaktism**:Emerged in Eastern India, emphasizing the worship of the divine feminine.

Shaktism is a tradition within Hinduism that focuses on the worship of the Goddess, known as Devi or Shakti, as the ultimate reality or supreme being. It is one of the four main sects of Hinduism, alongside Vaishnavism, Shaivism, and Smartism.

Shaktism emphasizes the feminine aspect of the divine and recognizes the Goddess as the embodiment of power, energy, and creativity. The tradition encompasses various forms of the Goddess, such as:

1.Durga (invincible goddess)

2.Kali (transformative goddess)

3.Lakshmi (goddess of prosperity)

4.Saraswati (goddess of knowledge)

5.Parvati (goddess of love and fertility)

Some key aspects of Shaktism include:

-Worship of the Goddess through rituals, such as puja and havan (fire offerings)

-Recognition of the divine feminine in all aspects of life

-Emphasis on the importance of feminine energy and power

-Study of sacred texts like the Devi Mahatmyam and the Tantras

Shaktism has various sub-traditions, including:

-Srikula (family of Sri, the goddess of prosperity)

-Kalikula (family of Kali, the transformative goddess)

-Shakta Pithas (sacred sites of the Goddess)

Shaktism also influences other Hindu traditions, such as Vaishnavism and Shaivism, which recognize the importance of the feminine aspect of the divine.

Chapter 7

Modern Period (1800 CE – present)

An overview of the influence of Western ideas, reform movements, and globalization on Hinduism from 1800 CE to present is as under: -

Western Ideas (1800-1947):

(i)Exposure to Western education, science, and philosophy led to:

(a)Modernization and rationalization of Hindu thought-

Modernization and rationalization of Hindu thought (1800-1947) involved:

1.Reinterpretation of scriptures:Reformers reexamined ancient texts, emphasizing rationality and monotheism.

2.Critique of traditional practices:Social evils like sati, child marriage, and caste rigidity were challenged.

3.Emphasis on reason and science:Hindu thinkers incorporated Western scientific methods and ideas.

4.Revival of classical philosophy:Interest in ancient Indian philosophy, like Vedanta and Yoga, was renewed.

5.Development of Neo-Hinduism:A modern, inclusive, and universalistic form of Hinduism emerged.

Key figures:

1.Raja Ram Mohan Roy (1772-1833): Advocated for social reform and monotheistic worship.

2.Swami Vivekananda (1863-1902): Popularized Advaita Vedanta and Hinduism globally, emphasizing reason and science.

3.Dayananda Saraswati (1824-1883): Founder of Arya Samaj, promoted Vedic rituals and social reform.

4.Aurobindo Ghosh (1872-1950): Integrated Western philosophy and Indian spirituality, advocating for human evolution.

5.Sarvepalli Radhakrishnan (1888-1975): Interpreted Hindu philosophy in modern terms, emphasizing reason and experience.

This period saw a significant transformation of Hindu thought, making it more inclusive, rational, and globally relevant.

(b)Emergence of Hindu reform movements-

The emergence of Hindu reform movements (1800-1947) was a response to:

1.Social and cultural stagnation

2.Western colonialism and Christian missionary activities

3.Critique of traditional practices and superstitions

Key movements and their focus areas:

1.Brahmo Samaj (1828)

-Monotheism

-Social reform (sati, child marriage, caste)

-Women's rights

2.Arya Samaj (1875)

-Vedic rituals and practices

-Social reform (caste, women's rights)

-Education and self-improvement

3.Ramakrishna Mission (1897)

-Spiritual revival

-Social service (education, healthcare)

-Women's empowerment

4.Prarthana Samaj (1867)

-Social reform (caste, women's rights)

-Education and intellectual pursuits

5.Theosophical Society (1875)

-Revival of Eastern spirituality

-Esoteric knowledge and mysticism

These movements aimed to:

i)Modernize Hinduism

ii)Remove social evils

iii)Promote education and intellectual growth

iv)Revitalize spirituality

v)Unify Hindu society

Key figures:

1.Raja Ram Mohan Roy (Brahmo Samaj)

2.Swami Dayananda Saraswati (Arya Samaj)

3.Ramakrishna Paramahamsa and Swami Vivekananda (Ramakrishna Mission)

4.Atmaram Pandurang (Prarthana Samaj)

5.Helena Blavatsky and Henry Steel Olcott (Theosophical Society)

These reform movements transformed Hindu society, paving the way for modernization and social change.

(c)Critique of traditional practices and social hierarchy

The key figures were:

-Raja Ram Mohan Roy (1772-1833): Founder of Brahmo Samaj, advocated for social reform and monotheism

-Swami Vivekananda (1863-1902): Popularized Advaita Vedanta and Hinduism globally

Reform Movements (1800-1947):

-Brahmo Samaj (1828):Emphasized monotheism, social reform, and women's rights

-Arya Samaj (1875): Focused on Vedic rituals, social reform, and education

-Ramakrishna Mission (1897):Combined spirituality with social service

-Indian National Congress (1885):Political movement that drew on Hindu symbolism and ideology

Globalization (1947-present):

Hinduism's global spread through:

-Migration and diaspora communities

-International organizations like ISKCON (1966) and Sai Baba movement

-Digital media and online platforms

Contemporary issues:

-Hindu nationalism and politics

-Debates on caste, gender, and social justice

-Interfaith dialogue and comparative spirituality

The key figures were:

-Mahatma Gandhi (1869-1948):Led India's independence movement, emphasized non-violence and Hindu-Muslim unity

-Swami Chinmayananda (1916-1993): Popularized Vedanta and Hindu spirituality globally

-Amma (1953-present):Renowned spiritual leader and humanitarian

This period has seen significant transformations in Hinduism, from modernization and reform to globalization and diversification.

Chapter 8
The Caste System

The caste system is a complex and ancient social hierarchy that has shaped Indian society for centuries. It is a system of social stratification based on occupation, rank, and family lineage. The caste system has influenced Hinduism and has been influenced by it, with both supporting and challenging its existence. The four main varnas (categories) of the caste system are:

Brahmins (priests, teachers, and scholars):

Brahmins are a varna (social class) in Hinduism, traditionally considered the highest of the four varnas. They have played a significant role in Hindu society, religion, and culture. Here are some key aspects of Brahmins:

Traditional Roles:

1.Priests:Brahmins have traditionally served as priests, performing rituals, ceremonies, and sacrifices.
2.Teachers:They have been teachers, sharing knowledge of Hindu scriptures, philosophy, and culture.
3.Scholars:Brahmins have been scholars, studying and interpreting Hindu texts, and contributing to Hindu philosophy.

Social Status:

1.Highest Varna:Brahmins have traditionally been considered the highest varna, with a high social status.

2.Respect and Authority:They have been accorded respect and authority in Hindu society, due to their knowledge and spiritual leadership.

Rituals and Practices:

1.Puja (Worship): Brahmins perform pujas, offering prayers, flowers, and offerings to deities.
2.Yajna (Sacrifices):They perform yajnas, sacred fires, for spiritual growth, purification, and community well-being.
3.Samskaras (Life-Cycle Rituals):Brahmins perform samskaras, rituals marking important life events, like birth, initiation, marriage, and death.

Modern Roles:

1.Cultural Preservation:Brahmins continue to play a crucial role in preserving Hindu culture, traditions, and values.
2.Spiritual Leadership:They provide spiritual guidance, counseling, and leadership in Hindu communities.
3.Academic and Professional Contributions: Brahmins have made significant contributions in various fields, including academia, science, literature, and politics.

Legacy:

1.Hindu Tradition:Brahmins have been instrumental in shaping and preserving Hindu tradition, philosophy, and culture.
2.Social and Cultural Impact:They have had a profound impact on Hindu society, influencing social norms, values, and practices.

3.Continued Relevance:Brahmins continue to play an essential role in modern Hindu society, adapting to changing times while preserving tradition.

Kshatriyas (rulers, warriors, and administrators):

Kshatriyas are a varna (social class) in Hinduism, traditionally associated with ruling, warrior, and administrative roles. Here are some key aspects of Kshatriyas:

Traditional Roles:

1.Rulers:Kshatriyas have historically held positions of power, ruling kingdoms and empires.
2.Warriors:They have been warriors, defending their territories and upholding justice.
3.Administrators:Kshatriyas have also served as administrators, governing and managing public affairs.

Values and Qualities:

1.Courage:Kshatriyas are expected to embody courage, bravery, and strength.
2.Leadership:They are trained to lead, command, and inspire others.
3.Dharma:Kshatriyas are expected to uphold dharma (righteousness, duty, and justice).

Historical Significance:

1.Ancient Kingdoms:Kshatriyas established and ruled ancient Indian kingdoms, such as the Vedic period kingdoms and the Mauryan Empire.

2.Warrior Tradition:They have a long tradition of martial excellence, producing legendary warriors like Arjuna and Bhishma.
3.Administrative Legacy:Kshatriyas have contributed to India's administrative systems, including the development of laws, taxation, and governance.

Modern Roles:

1.Leadership:Kshatriyas continue to hold leadership positions in various fields, including politics, business, and social organizations.
2.Public Service:They are often found in public service roles, such as government administration, law enforcement, and defense.
3.Entrepreneurship:Kshatriyas have also excelled in entrepreneurship, starting businesses and driving innovation.

Legacy:

1.Hindu Polity:Kshatriyas have shaped Hindu polity, influencing political systems, laws, and governance.
2.Cultural Heritage:They have contributed to India's cultural heritage, including literature, art, and architecture.
3.Continued Relevance:Kshatriyas remain relevant in modern times, adapting to changing circumstances while upholding their traditional values.

Vaishyas (merchants, traders, and farmers):

Vaishyas are a varna (social class) in Hinduism, traditionally associated with mercantile, trading, and agricultural activities. Here are some key aspects of Vaishyas:

Traditional Roles:

1.Merchants:Vaishyas have historically been involved in trade, commerce, and entrepreneurship.
2.Traders:They have traded goods, commodities, and services, facilitating economic exchange.
3.Farmers:Vaishyas have also been farmers, cultivating land, and producing agricultural products.

Values and Qualities:

1.Entrepreneurship:Vaishyas are known for their entrepreneurial spirit, innovation, and risk-taking.
2.Business Acumen:They possess business acumen, financial management, and negotiation skills.
3.Hard Work:Vaishyas are expected to be hardworking, diligent, and dedicated to their profession.

Historical Significance:

1.Economic Growth:Vaishyas have contributed significantly to India's economic growth, trade, and commerce.
2.Urbanization:They have played a crucial role in urbanization, establishing trade centers, markets, and cities.
3.Agricultural Development:Vaishyas have also driven agricultural development, introducing new farming techniques and technologies.

Modern Roles:

1.Business Leaders:Vaishyas continue to excel in business, leading companies, and driving innovation.

2.Entrepreneurs:They start new ventures, create jobs, and stimulate economic growth.
3.Professionals:Vaishyas are also found in various professions, such as finance, law, and management.

Legacy:

1.Economic Development:Vaishyas have shaped India's economic development, trade policies, and commercial practices.
2.Cultural Contributions:They have contributed to Indian culture, supporting arts, literature, and education.
3.Continued Relevance:Vaishyas remain relevant in modern times, adapting to changing economic landscapes and technologies.

Shudras (labourers and service workers):

Shudras are a varna (social class) in Hinduism, traditionally associated with labor and service roles. Here are some key aspects of Shudras:

Traditional Roles:

1.Laborers: Shudras have historically worked as laborers, engaging in manual labor and physical work.
2.Service Workers: They have also served as service workers, providing support and assistance to other varnas.
3.Artisans:Shudras have been skilled artisans, crafting goods and providing services like blacksmithing, carpentry, and weaving.

Values and Qualities:

1.Hard Work:Shudras are expected to be hardworking, diligent, and dedicated to their work.
2.Loyalty:They are valued for their loyalty, commitment, and dedication to their employers and community.
3.Skillfulness:Shudras are skilled in various trades, crafts, and services, contributing to the economy and society.

Historical Significance:

1.Economic Backbone:Shudras have been the economic backbone of Indian society, providing essential labor and services.
2.Social Support:They have played a crucial role in supporting other varnas, enabling them to pursue their duties and responsibilities.
3.Cultural Contributions:Shudras have contributed to Indian culture, developing folk arts, music, and literature.

Modern Roles:

1.Blue-Collar Workers:Shudras continue to work in blue-collar jobs, driving economic growth and development.
2.Service Industry:They are employed in the service industry, providing essential services like healthcare, hospitality, and transportation.
3.Entrepreneurs:Shudras are also becoming entrepreneurs, starting small businesses and creating jobs.

Legacy:

1.Social Mobility:Shudras have experienced social mobility, improving their economic and social status over time.

2.Cultural Preservation:They have preserved traditional skills, crafts, and customs, enriching Indian cultural heritage.
3.Continued Relevance:Shudras remain essential to Indian society, contributing to its economic, social, and cultural fabric.

Outside the varna system are the Dalits (untouchables) and Adivasis (indigenous peoples), who have faced historical oppression and discrimination. The caste system has been supported by some Hindu texts and traditions, but also challenged by others. Hindu reform movements and modern Indian law have sought to abolish the caste system, but it remains a significant social issue. Key issues related to the caste system include:

Social inequality and discrimination:

Social inequality and discrimination have been persistent issues in Indian society, despite efforts to address them. Here are some key aspects:

Historical Context:

1.Caste System:The caste system has been a major driver of social inequality, with certain castes facing discrimination and exclusion.
2.Colonial Legacy:British colonial rule perpetuated and reinforced existing social inequalities, creating new ones.
3.Social and Economic Disparities:India's economic growth has exacerbated social and economic disparities, widening the gap between the rich and the poor.

Forms of Discrimination:

1.Caste-Based Discrimination:
Discrimination against lower castes, Dalits, and tribals continues, despite legal protections.

2.Gender Discrimination:Women face discrimination in various forms, including unequal access to education, employment, and healthcare.
3.Religious and Minority Discrimination: Religious and minority groups, such as Muslims, Christians, and Sikhs, face discrimination and violence.
4.Class-Based Discrimination:Economic inequality leads to discrimination against the poor and marginalized.

Effects of Discrimination:

1.Social Exclusion:Discrimination leads to social exclusion, limiting access to education, employment, and healthcare.
2.Economic Disadvantage:Discrimination perpetuates economic disadvantage, reducing opportunities and social mobility.
3.Mental Health Impact:Discrimination affects mental health, leading to anxiety, depression, and trauma.
4.Social Unrest:Discrimination can lead to social unrest, protests, and violence.

Initiatives for Change:

1.Legal Protections:India has enacted laws to protect marginalized groups, such as the Scheduled Castes and Tribes (Prevention of Atrocities) Act.
2.Affirmative Action:Initiatives like reservation policies aim to promote social inclusion and equality.

3.Social Movements:Grassroots movements, like the Dalit rights movement, advocate for social change and equality.
4.Education and Awareness:Efforts to educate people about discrimination and promote empathy and understanding.

Occupational and economic restrictions:

Occupational and economic restrictions have been a significant aspect of social inequality in India, particularly in the context of the caste system. Here are some key points:

Occupational Restrictions:

1.Caste-based occupations:Certain castes were traditionally restricted to specific occupations, such as:
 -Brahmins:priests, teachers, and scholars
 -Kshatriyas:warriors, rulers, and administrators
 -Vaishyas:merchants, traders, and farmers
 -Shudras:laborers, service workers, and artisans
2.Limited access to education and training: Lower castes faced restrictions on accessing education and training, limiting their career prospects.
3.Segregation in workplaces:Even in modern times, workplaces may be segregated based on caste, with lower castes facing discrimination.

Economic Restrictions:

1.Limited access to resources and credit: Lower castes faced restrictions on accessing resources, credit, and markets, limiting their economic mobility.

2.Wage disparities:Lower castes often received lower wages for the same work, perpetuating economic inequality.
3.Limited entrepreneurship opportunities: Lower castes faced restrictions on starting businesses, limiting their economic empowerment.

Impact:

1.Perpetuation of poverty: Occupational and economic restrictions perpetuated poverty among lower castes.
2.Limited social mobility: Restrictions limited social mobility, making it difficult for individuals to improve their socio-economic status.
3.Social and economic inequality: Occupational and economic restrictions contributed to social and economic inequality, perpetuating the caste system.

Initiatives for Change:

1.Affirmative action policies:Initiatives like reservation policies aim to promote social inclusion and equality.
2.Vocational training and education: Programs providing vocational training and education can help bridge the skill gap and promote economic mobility.
3.Microfinance and entrepreneurship support:Initiatives supporting microfinance and entrepreneurship can empower lower castes to start businesses and improve their economic status.

Endogamy and marriage restrictions:

Endogamy and marriage restrictions have been significant aspects of the caste system in India, perpetuating social inequality and limiting social mobility. Here are some key points:

Endogamy:

1.Marriage within the caste:Endogamy refers to the practice of marrying within one's own caste or sub-caste.
2.Preservation of caste purity:Endogamy aimed to preserve the perceived purity of the caste by preventing inter-caste marriages.

Marriage Restrictions:

1.Prohibition on inter-caste marriages: Marriages between individuals from different castes were prohibited or discouraged.
2.Arranged marriages:Marriages were often arranged by families to ensure that the couple belonged to the same caste.
3.Social ostracism:Couples who married outside their caste faced social ostracism, exclusion, and even violence.

Impact:

1.Limited social mobility:Endogamy and marriage restrictions limited social mobility, making it difficult for individuals to improve their socio-economic status.
2.Perpetuation of caste system:These practices perpetuated the caste system, reinforcing social inequality and discrimination.
3.Restriction on choice and autonomy: Endogamy and marriage restrictions denied individuals the right to choose their partners, limiting their autonomy and agency.

Initiatives for Change:

1.Legislative reforms:Laws like the Hindu Marriage Act (1955) and the Special Marriage Act (1954) aimed to promote inter-caste marriages and challenge endogamy.
2.Social awareness campaigns:Campaigns and initiatives raising awareness about the harms of endogamy and promoting inter-caste marriages.
3.Empowerment through education: Education and economic empowerment can help individuals make informed choices about their marriages and challenge caste-based restrictions.

Purity and pollution rituals:

Purity and pollution rituals have been an integral part of the caste system in India, perpetuating social inequality and reinforcing social hierarchies. Here are some key aspects:

Purity Rituals:

1.Upanayana (thread ceremony):A ritual marking a boy's transition to manhood, symbolizing purity and Brahminical status.
2.Purification rituals:Rituals like bathing, fasting, and chanting to maintain individual and communal purity.
3.Worship and offerings:Rituals to appease deities, maintain cosmic order, and ensure purity.

Pollution Rituals:

1.Funerary rites:Rituals to manage death's impurity, including cremation and post-cremation rituals.

2.Menstrual taboos:Restrictions on women during menstruation, considering them impure.
3.Untouchability practices:Rituals and practices to maintain distance from and exclude "impure" castes.

Impact:

1.Reinforced social hierarchies:Purity and pollution rituals reinforced social hierarchies, solidifying caste divisions.
2.Perpetuated social inequality:These rituals perpetuated social inequality, limiting access to resources, spaces, and opportunities.
3.Internalized oppression:Members of lower castes internalized their perceived impurity, perpetuating self-exclusion and social exclusion.

Initiatives for Change:

1.Social reform movements:Movements like the Bhakti movement and the Dalit rights movement challenged purity and pollution rituals.
2.Legislative reforms:Laws like the Untouchability (Offences) Act (1955) aimed to eradicate untouchability practices.
3.Education and awareness:Initiatives promoting education, awareness, and critical thinking can help challenge and dismantle purity and pollution rituals.

Caste-based violence and oppression:

Caste-based violence and oppression have been a tragic reality in India, perpetuating social inequality and causing immense human suffering. Here are some key aspects:

Forms of Violence:

1.Physical violence:Assaults, murders, and massacres targeting individuals or communities based on their caste.
2.Sexual violence:Rape and sexual assault of women and girls from lower castes.
3.Psychological violence:Emotional abuse, harassment, and humiliation.

Oppression:

1.Discrimination:Denial of basic rights, opportunities, and services based on caste.
2.Segregation:Forced segregation in housing, education, and public spaces.
3.Exploitation:Economic exploitation, including forced labor and low wages.

Impact:

1.Human rights violations:Caste-based violence and oppression constitute severe human rights violations.
2.Trauma and fear:Survivors and communities experience trauma, fear, and anxiety.
3.Perpetuation of inequality:Caste-based violence and oppression maintain social inequality and perpetuate the caste system.

Initiatives for Change:

1.Legislative reforms:Laws like the Scheduled Castes and Tribes (Prevention of Atrocities) Act (1989) aim to prevent and punish caste-based violence.

2.Social movements:Movements like the Dalit rights movement and anti-caste organizations challenge caste-based oppression.
3.Education and awareness:Initiatives promoting education, awareness, and empathy can help dismantle caste-based violence and oppression.

The caste system is a complex and controversial aspect of Hinduism and Indian society, requiring understanding, dialogue, and reform.

Chapter 9
The Ruling and Ruled Classes

In Hinduism, the concept of ruling and ruled classes has been a significant aspect of social hierarchy and power dynamics. The ruling classes, comprising kings, nobles, and aristocrats, held political power and authority, while the ruled classes, including commoners and subjects, were expected to obey and serve. The ruling classes were often associated with the Kshatriya varna, while the ruled classes were associated with the Vaishya and Shudra varnas. However, this was not always a rigid division, and individuals could move between classes based on merit, wealth, or circumstances. Key aspects of the ruling and ruled classes include:

Political power and authority:

The concepts of ruling and ruled classes, political power, and authority are fundamental to understanding social dynamics, governance, and relationships between groups. Some of the key aspects are as under:

Ruling Class:

1.Holds power and authority
2.Makes decisions for the society or organization
3.Often holds wealth, influence, and privilege
4.Can be composed of various groups (e.g., aristocracy, politicians, corporations)
5.May maintain power through coercion, persuasion, or manipulation

Ruled Class:

1.Subject to the decisions and authority of the ruling class
2.Often has limited power, influence, and access to resources
3.May experience oppression, exploitation, or marginalization
4.Can be composed of various groups (e.g., common people, workers, minorities)
5.May resist or challenge the ruling class through various means (e.g., protest, activism, revolution)

Political Power:

1.Ability to influence or control decisions and actions
2.Can be held by individuals, groups, or institutions
3.Often linked to authority, legitimacy, and coercion
4.Can be exercised through various means (e.g., laws, policies, social norms)
5.Can be challenged or contested by other groups or individuals

Authority:

1.Legitimized power, often based on social norms, institutions, or traditions
2.Can be derived from various sources (e.g., law, morality, expertise)
3.Often associated with leadership, governance, or decision-making
4.Can be exercised through persuasion, coercion, or manipulation

5.Can be challenged or delegitimized if abused or perceived as unjust

These concepts are complex and interconnected. Understanding their dynamics can help us analyze social structures, political systems, and relationships between groups, ultimately informing strategies for positive change and social justice.

Social status and prestige:

Here are the key aspects of ruling and ruled classes related to social status and prestige:

Ruling Class:

1.High social status and prestige due to power, wealth, and influence
2.Often associated with elite education, exclusive social clubs, and high-end cultural events
3.May use prestige to legitimize their power and authority
4.Can maintain status through strategic marriages, business deals, and political alliances
5.Often shape cultural norms, values, and social standards to reinforce their position

Ruled Class:

1.Generally lower social status and prestige compared to the ruling class
2.May experience social exclusion, marginalization, or stigma
3.Often have limited access to elite education, social networks, and high-status cultural events

4.May challenge the ruling class's prestige through counter-cultural movements or social activism
5.Can develop alternative status hierarchies and prestige systems within their own communities

Key factors influencing social status and prestige in the ruling and ruled classes:

1.Wealth and economic power
2.Education and credentials
3.Family background and connections
4.Occupational status and career advancement
5.Cultural capital (e.g., knowledge, taste, and preferences)
6.Social networks and relationships
7.Political power and influence
8.Media representation and public image

Understanding the dynamics of social status and prestige in the ruling and ruled classes can help us:

1.Analyze social inequalities and power imbalances
2.Recognize the role of cultural capital in maintaining social hierarchies
3.Identify strategies for social mobility and empowerment
4.Develop more inclusive and equitable social policies and practices

Economic control and wealth:

Here are the key aspects of ruling and ruled classes related to economic control and wealth:

Ruling Class:

1.Concentration of wealth and economic power
2.Control over means of production, distribution, and exchange
3.Ownership of land, resources, and capital
4.Access to lucrative business opportunities and investments
5.Influence over economic policies and regulations
6.Ability to accumulate and pass down wealth through generations
7.Often use economic power to maintain political influence and social status

Ruled Class:

1.Limited access to economic resources and opportunities
2.Dependence on the ruling class for employment, income, and benefits
3.Often subjected to exploitation, low wages, and poor working conditions
4.Limited social mobility and wealth accumulation
5.May experience poverty, debt, and economic insecurity
6.Often excluded from decision-making processes around economic policies and resource allocation
7.May resist or challenge economic control through labor movements, activism, or alternative economic models

Key factors influencing economic control and wealth in the ruling and ruled classes:

1.Ownership and control of productive assets
2.Access to credit, finance, and investment opportunities
3.Education and skills training

4.Labor market dynamics and unionization
5.Government policies and regulations (e.g., taxation, trade, and labor laws)
6.Globalization and international trade agreements
7.Technological advancements and automation

Understanding the dynamics of economic control and wealth in the ruling and ruled classes can help us:

1.Analyze economic inequalities and power imbalances
2.Recognize the role of economic systems in maintaining social hierarchies
3.Identify strategies for economic empowerment and social mobility
4.Develop more equitable economic policies and practices

Cultural patronage and influence:

Here are the key aspects of ruling and ruled classes related to cultural patronage and influence:

Ruling Class:

1.Patronage of arts, literature, and culture to promote their values and interests
2.Influence over education, media, and cultural institutions
3.Promotion of cultural norms, values, and beliefs that legitimize their power
4.Support for cultural events, festivals, and traditions that reinforce their status
5.Often use cultural patronage to shape public opinion and ideology
6.May appropriate or commodify cultural practices from the ruled class for their own benefit

7.Can dictate what is considered "high culture" or "refined taste"

Ruled Class:

1.Often have their cultural practices, traditions, and values marginalized or suppressed
2.May resist or challenge dominant cultural narratives through counter-cultural movements
3.Develop alternative cultural institutions, media, and art forms to express their own experiences and perspectives
4.Can experience cultural appropriation or exploitation by the ruling class
5.May struggle for recognition and validation of their cultural identity and practices
6.Can use cultural expression as a form of resistance, activism, or social commentary
7.Often have to navigate dominant cultural norms and values to access resources and opportunities

Key factors influencing cultural patronage and influence:

1.Access to education and cultural institutions
2.Control over media and communication channels
3.Economic resources and patronage
4.Social networks and relationships
5.Political power and influence
6.Cultural capital (e.g., knowledge, taste, and preferences)
7.Historical and colonial legacies

Understanding the dynamics of cultural patronage and influence can help us:

1.Analyze how culture is used to maintain power and social hierarchies
2.Recognize the importance of cultural diversity and representation
3.Identify strategies for cultural empowerment and resistance
4.Develop more inclusive and equitable cultural policies and practices.

Religious authority and interpretation:

Here are the key aspects of ruling and ruled classes related to religious authority and interpretation:

Ruling Class:

1.Often use religion to legitimize their power and authority
2.Control over religious institutions, clergy, and scripture
3.Interpret religious texts to justify their dominance and policies
4.Use religious authority to shape moral and social norms
5.May suppress or co-opt dissenting religious voices
6.Can use religion to maintain social order and control
7.Often have privileged access to religious education and resources

Ruled Class:

1.May have their religious beliefs and practices marginalized or suppressed
2.Can resist or challenge dominant religious interpretations
3.Develop alternative religious traditions, practices, or interpretations
4.May experience religious oppression or persecution

5.Can use religion as a source of comfort, resistance, or empowerment
6.Often have limited access to religious education and resources
7.May experience internalized oppression or self-doubt due to dominant religious narratives

Key factors influencing religious authority and interpretation:

1.Control over religious institutions and scripture
2.Access to religious education and resources
3.Social and political power dynamics
4.Cultural and historical context
5.Economic interests and patronage
6.Networks of religious leaders and influencers
7.State-church relationships and policies

Understanding the dynamics of religious authority and interpretation can help us:

1.Analyze how religion is used to maintain power and social hierarchies
2.Recognize the importance of religious diversity and inclusivity
3.Identify strategies for religious empowerment and resistance
4.Develop more equitable and just religious policies and practices

The relationship between the ruling and ruled classes has been complex, with both cooperation and conflict throughout history. Hindu texts like the Manusmriti and the

Bhagavad Gita have shaped the norms and expectations of these classes. The impact of colonialism, nationalism, and democracy has significantly altered the dynamics of the ruling and ruled classes in India, with ongoing debates about social justice, equality, and political representation.

Chapter 10

Conclusion

Thus, Hinduism has evolved over 4,000 years, transforming from a complex set of Vedic rituals and philosophies to a diverse, multifaceted faith. Key milestones include:

-Vedic Period (1500 BCE - 500 BCE): Emergence of Vedas, emphasis on rituals and sacrifices.

-Upanishadic Period (800 BCE - 400 BCE): Shift to philosophical inquiry, exploration of ultimate reality (Brahman).

-Epic Period (400 BCE - 500 CE): Composition of epics like Ramayana and Mahabharata, introduction of avatar concept.

-Puranic Period (500 CE - 1500 CE): Development of devotional traditions, worship of deities like Vishnu, Shiva, and Devi.

-Medieval Period (500 CE - 1500 CE): Rise of bhakti movement, emphasis on personal devotion and love.

-Modern Period (1800 CE - present): Influence of Western ideas, reform movements, and globalization.

Throughout its evolution, Hinduism has retained its core principles, such as:

-Karma and rebirth

-Dharma (duty/righteousness)

-Ahimsa (non-violence)

-Moksha (liberation)

Yet, it has adapted and expanded, incorporating diverse traditions, philosophies, and practices, making Hinduism one of the world's most rich and complex faiths.

European Invasions (1505 CE - 1947 CE):

European Invasions (1505 CE - 1947 CE): A period of significant cultural, economic, and political impact on India.

Key events and figures:

1.Vasco da Gama (1505 CE):Portuguese explorer who established trade routes.

2.British East India Company (1600 CE): Trading company that eventually ruled India.

3.Robert Clive (1757 CE): British commander who defeated Siraj-ud-Daula, establishing British rule.

4.Warren Hastings (1773 CE):First British Governor-General of India, impeached for corruption.

5.Lord Curzon (1899 CE): British Viceroy who partitioned Bengal, sparking nationalist movements.

6.Mahatma Gandhi (1915 CE):Led India's non-violent independence movement.

7.Indian Independence Act (1947 CE): Britain granted India independence, partitioning the country into India and Pakistan.

Impact on India:

1.Introduction of Western education, science, and technology.

2.Development of English language and literature.

3.Influence on Indian art, architecture, and culture.

4.Establishment of British colonial rule and administration.

5.Economic exploitation and drain of resources.

6.Impact on Indian industries, like textiles and handicrafts.

7.Emergence of Indian nationalist movements and eventual independence.

This period saw the introduction of Western ideas, education, and technology, but also economic exploitation, cultural destruction, and political oppression, shaping India's struggle for independence and its modern identity.

-Introduced Western education, science, and technology

-Influenced Indian art, literature, and architecture

-Developed English language and literature

-Established British colonial rule and administration

-Impacted Indian economy, politics, and society

Both Islamic and European invasions:

-Shaped Indian history, culture, and society

-Introduced new ideas, technologies, and beliefs

-Challenged traditional Indian values and practices

-Led to cultural exchange and synthesis

-Had a lasting impact on Indian identity and consciousness

These invasions have had a profound and lasting impact on Indian culture, society, and politics, shaping the country's trajectory and identity.

Part – II

Expansion Of Hinduism

Chapter 1

Ancient India (1500 BCE - 500 CE)

During Ancient India (1500 BCE - 500 BCE), Hinduism expanded in the following manner:

I. Vedic Period

(A) Emergence of Vedas and Vedic culture in the Indo-Gangetic Plain:

The emergence of Vedas and Vedic culture in the Indo-Gangetic Plain (1500 BCE - 500 BCE) is a significant period in Hinduism's history. Here's an overview:

Vedic Period:

-This period was the compositional period of the Vedas, the oldest Hindu scriptures;

-During this period Vedic culture, rituals, and practices developed;

-The concept of Brahman (ultimate reality) emerged in this period; and

-The varna system (social hierarchy) emerged in Hinduism during this period.

The key features of the expansion of Hinduism during this period can be categorised as under:

-Vedic rituals and sacrifices (yajnas);

-Development of priestly class (Brahmins);

-Emergence of Sanskrit language;

-Concept of dharma (duty/righteousness); and

-Worship of natural elements (fire, water, sun).

The following Vedas were written in this period which further contributed towards the expansion of Hinduism:

-Rigveda (oldest Veda, 1500 BCE);

-Yajurveda;

-Samaveda;

-Atharvaveda.

Vedic Culture:

(a) Nomadic, pastoral society:Vedic culture (1500 BCE - 500 BCE) was characterized by a nomadic, pastoral society, with:

1.Cattle herding:Cattle were the primary source of wealth and livelihood.

2.Nomadic lifestyle:People moved seasonally with their cattle to find grazing land and water.

3.Tribal organization:Society was organized into tribes (Jana) and clans (gotra).

4.Kinship ties:Family and clan relationships were central to social organization.

5.Simple settlements:Temporary settlements were made of animal hide, wood, and thatch.

The key features of the Vedic pastoral society were:

1.Mobility:Constant movement with cattle allowed for exploration and expansion.

2.Cattle-centric economy:Cattle provided food, clothing, and wealth.

3.Social hierarchy:Emergence of social classes, with Brahmins (priests) and Kshatriyas (warriors) at the top.

4.Gender roles:Men managed cattle and warfare, while women handled domestic duties.

5.Connection with nature:Vedic people had a deep connection with the natural environment.

This nomadic, pastoral society shaped Vedic culture, influencing:

1.Vedic rituals and practices (e.g., cattle sacrifice)

2.Vedic literature (e.g., Rigveda's emphasis on cattle)

3.Social organization and hierarchy

4. Economic systems and trade

5.Worldview and philosophy (e.g., concept of Brahman)

The Vedic pastoral society laid the groundwork for Hinduism's development and spread.

(b)Tribal organization (Jana): In Vedic culture, tribal organization (Jana) referred to the social and political structure of the Vedic people. Here are some key aspects:

Jana (Tribal Organization):

-A Jana was a tribe or clan, typically consisting of several families and clans.

-Janas were often named after their ancestors or geographical locations.

-Each Jana had its own:

-Territory

-Chief or leader (Rajan)

-Council of elders (Sabha)

-Social hierarchy

Key Features:

-Kinship ties: Jana members were connected through blood, marriage, or adoption.

-Shared rituals and practices: Janas had their own Vedic rituals, deities, and traditions.

-Economic cooperation:Janas shared resources, like cattle and land.

-Mutual defence:Janas protected each other from external threats.

-Decision-making:Janas made collective decisions through their Sabha (council).

Examples of Janas:

-Bharatas

-Matsyas

-Yadus

-Turvasas

-Anus

Influence on Vedic Society:

-Jana organization shaped Vedic social structure, politics, and culture.

-Janas played a crucial role in the development of Vedic rituals, practices, and traditions.

-The Jana system influenced the emergence of the varna (social class) system.

The Jana tribal organization was a fundamental aspect of Vedic culture, shaping their social, political, and religious landscape.

(c)Importance of family and clan:In Vedic culture, family and clan played a vital role in shaping individual identity, social structure, and religious practices. Some key aspects are explained hereunder:

Importance of Family (Kula):

-Family was the basic unit of Vedic society;

-Emphasis on patriarchal lineage (gotra);

-Family rituals and ceremonies (e.g., naming, marriage, death);

-Ancestral worship and reverence.

Importance of Clan (Gotra):

- Gotra referred to a group of families tracing their ancestry to a common forefather

-Clans were exogamous (marriage outside the clan)

-Clan identity shaped social status, occupation, and ritual roles

-Gotra pride and loyalty were essential

Key Features:

-Joint family system: Extended families lived together

-Family property and assets:Shared among family members

-Family rituals and ceremonies:Reinforced family bonds and social cohesion

-Clan solidarity:Clans provided support, protection, and a sense of belonging

Influence on Vedic Society:

-Family and clan shaped Vedic social structure, rituals, and practices

-Emphasis on family and clan reinforced patriarchal values and social hierarchy

-Family and clan identity influenced marriage, occupation, and social status

In Vedic culture, family and clan were essential components of individual identity, social organization, and religious practices. The strong emphasis on family and clan reinforced social cohesion, patriarchal values, and tradition.

(d)Beginnings of urbanization:In Vedic culture, the beginnings of urbanization emerged during the Late Vedic Period (800-500 BCE). Here are some key aspects:

(i)Factors contributing to urbanization:

1.Growing population and agricultural surplus

2.Increased trade and commerce

3.Emergence of complex societies and specialized labour

4.Development of new technologies (e.g., iron tools)

(ii)Characteristics of early urban centres:

1.Small in size (typically 1-5 square kilometers)

2.Fortified with walls and gates

3.Centralized administration and governance

4.Specialized labour and crafts (e.g., metallurgy, pottery)

5.Trade networks and marketplaces

(iii)Examples of early urban centres:

1.Hastinapura (near modern-day Meerut)

2.Kausambi (near modern-day Allahabad)

3.Varanasi (one of the oldest continuously inhabited cities)

4.Rajagriha (modern-day Rajgir)

5.Ujjain (an important centre of trade and culture)

(iv)Impact of urbanization:

1.Social changes:Emergence of new social classes, occupations, and cultural practices

2.Economic growth:Increased trade, commerce, and specialized labour

3.Political developments:Centralized administration, kingdoms, and empires

4.Cultural advancements:Development of art, architecture, literature, and philosophy

The beginnings of urbanization marked a significant shift in Vedic culture, laying the groundwork for the development of complex societies, kingdoms, and empires in ancient India.

Influence:

-Shaped Hindu philosophy, rituals, and practices

-Influenced Indian culture, language, and society

-Spread to other regions through migration and trade

Key Figures:

-Vedic seers and sages (e.g., Agastya, Vasistha)

-Ancient Indian rulers (e.g., Manu, Bharata)

This period marked the foundation of Hinduism's scriptural, philosophical, and cultural heritage.

(B) Spread of Vedic rituals and practices:

The spread of Vedic rituals and practices (1500 BCE - 500 BCE) occurred through:

1.Migration and trade: Vedic people moved to new regions, taking their rituals and practices with them.

2.Conquest and expansion:Vedic rulers expanded their territories, imposing their culture and practices on conquered areas.

3.Brahminical influence:Brahmins, the priestly class, played a key role in spreading Vedic rituals and practices.

4.Royal patronage:Rulers supported and promoted Vedic rituals, ensuring their continuation and spread.

5.Oral tradition:Vedic knowledge and practices were transmitted orally, allowing for widespread dissemination.

Regions where Vedic rituals and practices spread:

1.Indo-Gangetic Plain

2.Western India (modern-day Gujarat, Maharashtra)

3.Eastern India (modern-day Bengal, Odisha)

4.Southern India (modern-day Tamil Nadu, Kerala)

5.Central India (modern-day Madhya Pradesh)

Key Vedic rituals and practices that spread:

1. Yajnas (fire sacrifices)

2. Puja (worship)

3. Homa (fire rituals)

4. Samskaras (life-cycle rituals)

5. Study of Vedas and Vedic literature

This spread of Vedic rituals and practices laid the foundation for Hinduism's widespread presence in ancient India.

II. Upanishadic Period (800 BCE - 400 BCE):

(i)Development of philosophical inquiry and spirituality:

The Upanishadic Period (800 BCE - 400 BCE) was a transformative era in ancient India, marked by:

1.Philosophical inquiry:Exploration of fundamental questions about existence, reality, and human nature.

2.Spiritual growth:Development of spiritual practices, such as meditation and yoga, to attain self-realization.

3.Emergence of new ideas:Concepts like Brahman (ultimate reality), Atman (individual self), and Moksha (liberation) gained prominence.

4.Shift from ritualism:Gradual move away from Vedic ritualism towards more introspective and personal spiritual practices.

5.Influence of sages:Visionary sages like Yajnavalkya, Uddalaka, and Katyayana contributed to the development of Upanishadic thought.

The key Upanishads that emerged during this period were:

1.Brihadaranyaka Upanishad

2.Chandogya Upanishad

3.Taittiriya Upanishad

4.Aitareya Upanishad

5.Kena Upanishad

Impact of the Upanishadic Period:

a)Shaping Hindu philosophy:Upanishadic ideas continue to influence Hindu thought and spirituality.

b)Influence on Buddhism and Jainism: Upanishadic concepts, like karma and rebirth, shaped the development of these religions.

c)Spiritual practices:Upanishadic era saw the emergence of spiritual practices, like meditation and yoga, which remain essential in Hinduism.

The Upanishadic Period marked a significant turning point in ancient Indian thought, laying the groundwork for the development of Hindu philosophy, spirituality, and culture.

(ii)Expansion of Hindu thought and practices to southern India:

During the Upanishadic Period (800 BCE - 400 BCE), Hindu thought and practices expanded from the Indo-Gangetic Plain to southern India, marking a significant geographical and cultural shift. This expansion led to:

1.Spread of Vedic culture:Vedic rituals, philosophy, and practices reached the Dravidian-speaking regions of southern India.

2.Emergence of new centres of learning: Places like Tamil Nadu, Kerala, and Karnataka became hubs for spiritual and philosophical inquiry.

3.Influence on local cultures:Upanishadic ideas blended with existing Dravidian cultures, leading to the development of distinct regional traditions.

4.Growth of Bhakti movement:The seeds of the Bhakti movement, emphasizing devotion and love for a personal deity, were sown in southern India during this period.

5.Development of Tamil Sangam literature: The Upanishadic period saw the emergence of Tamil Sangam literature, which explored themes of love, war, and spirituality.

Key figures from southern India who contributed to the expansion of Hindu thought and practices include:

1.Thiruvalluvar:A Tamil sage and poet who authored the Tirukkural, a classic work on ethics and spirituality.

2.Agastya:A Vedic sage who traveled to southern India and played a significant role in spreading Vedic culture.

3.Tamil sages:Sages like Azhwar and Nayanar contributed to the development of Vaishnavism and Shaivism in southern India.

The expansion of Hindu thought and practices to southern India during the Upanishadic Period:

a) Enriched Hinduism:The blending of Vedic and Dravidian cultures enriched Hinduism, making it more diverse and vibrant.

b) Shaped regional traditions:The unique cultural and philosophical traditions of southern India continue to influence Hindu practices and thought to this day.

c) Paved the way for future movements: The Bhakti movement, Tantrism, and other spiritual movements that emerged in southern India during later periods built upon the foundations laid during the Upanishadic era.

III. Epic Period (400 BCE - 400 CE):

(i) Composition of epics like Ramayana and Mahabharata:

The Epic Period (400 BCE - 400 CE) in ancient India saw the composition of two monumental epics:

1.Ramayana:Attributed to Valmiki, it tells the story of Rama, a legendary prince, and his journey to defeat the demon king Ravana.

2.Mahabharata:Attributed to Vyasa, it narrates the story of the Pandavas and Kauravas, two groups of cousins, and their epic battle at Kurukshetra.

Key aspects of the Epic Period:

1.Oral tradition:These epics were composed and transmitted orally before being written down.

2.Sanskrit literature:The Ramayana and Mahabharata are considered some of the greatest works of Sanskrit literature.

3.Hindu mythology:The epics are rich in mythological stories, characters, and themes that continue to influence Hindu thought and culture.

4.Philosophical and ethical themes:The epics explore complex ideas like dharma (duty), karma (action), and moksha (liberation).

5.Cultural significance:The Ramayana and Mahabharata have shaped Indian art, literature, music, and film for centuries.

Impact of the Epic Period:

1.Shaping Hindu identity:The epics helped create a shared cultural and religious heritage for Hindus.

2.Influence on art and literature:The stories and characters from the epics have inspired countless works of art, literature, and performance.

3.Ethical and philosophical guidance:The epics continue to provide moral and philosophical guidance for millions of people.

4.Cultural exchange:The epics have been translated and adapted into many languages, facilitating cultural exchange between India and other civilizations.

Key figures from the Epic Period:

1.Valmiki:The author of the Ramayana, considered the "Adi Kavi" (first poet) of Sanskrit literature.

2.Vyasa:The author of the Mahabharata, also credited with compiling the Vedas and Puranas.

3.Other poets and sages:Many other poets and sages contributed to the composition and transmission of the epics.

The Epic Period marked a significant milestone in ancient Indian literature and culture, leaving a lasting impact on Hindu thought, art, and identity.

(ii)Spread of Hindu mythology and legends:

During the Epic Period (400 BCE - 400 CE), Hindu mythology and legends spread throughout the Indian subcontinent, shaping the cultural and religious landscape. Key aspects of this spread include:

1.Diffusion of epic stories:The Ramayana and Mahabharata stories travelled to various regions, influencing local cultures and traditions.

2.Emergence of Puranas:The Puranas, a collection of mythological texts, were composed during this period, further enriching Hindu mythology.

3.Development of regional mythologies: Local mythologies and legends emerged, blending with the epic stories and Puranic myths.

4.Growth of temple culture:Temples became centres for mythological storytelling, art, and worship, spreading Hindu mythology and legends.

5.Influence on art and literature:Hindu mythology inspired art, literature, music, and dance, making it an integral part of Indian culture.

The spread of Hindu mythology and legends had the following impacts:

1.Unification of diverse cultures:Hindu mythology helped unify diverse regional cultures and traditions.

2.Shaping of Hindu identity:The spread of mythology and legends contributed to the development of a shared Hindu identity.

3.Influence on daily life: Mythological stories and legends guided daily life, influencing ethics, morals, and values.

4.Inspiration for art and literature:Hindu mythology continues to inspire artistic and literary works.

5.Evolution of Hinduism:The spread of mythology and legends contributed to the evolution of Hinduism, incorporating diverse beliefs and practices.

Key figures who contributed to the spread of Hindu mythology and legends:

1.Sages and seers:Sages like Valmiki, Vyasa, and others composed and transmitted mythological stories.

2.Temple priests and storytellers:Temple priests and storytellers shared mythological stories with the masses.

3.Artists and craftsmen:Artists and craftsmen depicted mythological themes in their work, further popularizing the legends.

4.Traveling bards and performers:Traveling bards and performers shared mythological stories through music, dance, and drama.

The spread of Hindu mythology and legends during the Epic Period had a profound impact on Indian culture, shaping art, literature, and daily life, and continues to influence Hinduism and Indian identity to this day.

IV. Mauryan Empire (322 BCE - 185 BCE):

(i)Spread of Hinduism to eastern and central India-

The Mauryan Empire (322 BCE - 185 BCE) played a significant role in the spread of Hinduism to eastern and central India. Key factors that contributed to this spread include:

1.Imperial patronage:Mauryan emperors, particularly Ashoka, supported Hinduism and encouraged its spread.

2.Trade and commerce:The Mauryan Empire's extensive trade networks facilitated the exchange of ideas, cultures, and religions.

3.Migration and settlement:People from the Indo-Gangetic Plain migrated to eastern and central India, taking their religious beliefs and practices with them.

4.Buddhist-Hindu syncretism:The Mauryan period saw a blending of Buddhist and Hindu ideas, leading to the spread of Hinduism in areas where Buddhism was prevalent.

5.Establishment of temples and shrines: Mauryan rulers built temples and shrines, promoting Hindu worship and pilgrimage.

Consequences of the spread of Hinduism during the Mauryan Empire:

i)Hinduization of eastern and central India: Hinduism became a dominant religion in these regions, shaping local cultures and traditions.

ii)Emergence of new Hindu centres:Cities like Pataliputra, Ujjain, and Taxila became important Hindu centres, rivalling older centres, like Varanasi.

iii)Development of Hindu art and architecture:Mauryan art and architecture, such as the Sanchi Stupa, reflect Hindu influences and themes.

iv)Growth of Hindu scriptures:The Mauryan period saw the composition and compilation of Hindu scriptures, like the Mahabharata and Puranas.

v)Influence on Indian identity:The spread of Hinduism during the Mauryan Empire contributed to the development of a shared Indian identity.

Key figures who contributed to the spread of Hinduism during the Mauryan Empire:

1.Ashoka:The Mauryan emperor who converted to Buddhism but also supported Hinduism and encouraged its spread.

2.Chandragupta Maurya:The founder of the Mauryan Empire, who patronized Hinduism and established Hindu temples.

3.Hindu sages and scholars:Sages like Katyayana and Patanjali contributed to the development of Hindu scriptures and philosophy.

4.Temple priests and officials:Temple priests and officials played a crucial role in promoting Hindu worship and pilgrimage.

The Mauryan Empire's support and patronage of Hinduism facilitated its spread to eastern and central India, shaping the religious and cultural landscape of the region.

(ii)Patronage of Hinduism by Mauryan rulers:

The Mauryan Empire (322 BCE - 185 BCE) saw a significant patronage of Hinduism by its rulers, particularly:

1.Chandragupta Maurya (322-298 BCE):A Hindu himself, Chandragupta supported Hinduism and established Hindu temples.

2.Bindusara (298-273 BCE):Bindusara continued his father's patronage of Hinduism, promoting Hindu rituals and sacrifices.

3.Ashoka (273-232 BCE):Although Ashoka converted to Buddhism, he also supported Hinduism and encouraged its spread. He built Hindu temples and promoted Hindu festivals.

4.Dasharatha Maurya (232-224 BCE): Dasharatha, Ashoka's grandson, was a devout Hindu and patronized Hinduism, building temples and promoting Hindu rituals.

Mauryan patronage of Hinduism:

a)Temple construction:Mauryan rulers built numerous Hindu temples, such as the Mahabodhi Temple in Bodh Gaya.

b)Hindu festivals:Mauryan rulers promoted and participated in Hindu festivals like the Vedic sacrifices and the festival of Indra.

c)Hindu rituals:Mauryan rulers supported Hindu rituals, such as the Ashvamedha (horse sacrifice) and the Rajasuya (royal consecration).

d)Hindu scriptures:Mauryan rulers patronized the composition and compilation of Hindu scriptures, like the Mahabharata and Puranas.

e)Hindu scholars and sages:Mauryan rulers supported Hindu scholars and sages, like Katyayana and Patanjali, who contributed to Hindu philosophy and scriptures.

Impact of Mauryan patronage on Hinduism:

The Mauryan patronage had a profound impact on Hinduism, leading to:

1.Spread of Hinduism:Mauryan patronage helped spread Hinduism to eastern and central India, beyond its traditional stronghold in the Indo-Gangetic Plain.

2.Development of Hindu art and architecture:Mauryan patronage led to the development of Hindu art and architecture, influencing Indian art and culture.

3.Growth of Hindu scriptures:Mauryan patronage contributed to the growth and compilation of Hindu scriptures, such as the Mahabharata and Puranas.

4.Establishment of Hindu centres:Mauryan patronage led to the establishment of Hindu centres, like Pataliputra and Ujjain, which became important Hindu pilgrimage sites.

5.Standardization of Hindu rituals:Mauryan patronage helped standardize Hindu rituals and practices, leading to a more unified Hindu tradition.

6.Emergence of new Hindu sects:Mauryan patronage facilitated the emergence of new Hindu sects, such as the Bhagavata and the Shaiva traditions.

7.Increased emphasis on devotion:Mauryan patronage led to an increased emphasis on devotion (bhakti) in Hinduism, which became a central aspect of Hindu worship.

8.Development of Hindu philosophy: Mauryan patronage contributed to the development of Hindu philosophy, particularly the Nyaya and Vaisheshika schools.

9.Hinduization of local cultures:Mauryan patronage led to the Hinduization of local cultures, as Hinduism became a dominant force in Indian society.

10.Legacy of Mauryan patronage:The Mauryan patronage of Hinduism set a precedent for future Indian rulers, who continued to support and patronize Hinduism.

The Mauryan patronage played a significant role in shaping Hinduism, contributing to its growth, development, and spread, and leaving a lasting impact on Indian religion, art and culture.

V. Gupta Empire (320 CE - 550 CE):

(i)Golden age of Hinduism:

The Gupta Empire (320 CE - 550 CE) is considered the "Golden Age of Hinduism" due to:

1.Revival of Hinduism:A resurgence of Hinduism, marked by a renewed interest in Hindu scriptures, rituals, and philosophy.

2.Cultural achievements:Significant advancements in art, architecture, literature, music, and science.

3.Temple construction:Widespread building of Hindu temples, showcasing architectural innovations and artistic excellence.

4.Sanskrit literature:Flourishing of Sanskrit literature, including works like Kalidasa's plays and the Puranas.

5.Philosophical developments:Emergence of new Hindu philosophical schools, such as Advaita Vedanta and Vaisheshika.

6.Scientific advancements:Notable progress in mathematics, astronomy, and medicine.

7.Hindu iconography:Development of iconic representations of Hindu deities and mythological figures.

8.Pilgrimage and festivals:Increased emphasis on pilgrimage sites and festivals, strengthening Hindu religious practices.

9.Royal patronage:Gupta rulers' patronage of Hinduism, supporting scholars, artists, and religious leaders.

10.Hinduism's spread:Hinduism's expansion beyond India, influencing Southeast Asian cultures and societies.

Key figures from the Gupta period:

a)Chandragupta-I (320-335 CE):Founder of the Gupta Empire.

b)Samudragupta (335-375 CE):Expanded the empire and patronized Hinduism.

c)Chandragupta-II (375-415 CE):Supported Hindu scholars and artists.

d)Kumarajiva (350-410 CE):A Buddhist scholar who translated Sanskrit texts into Chinese.

e)Kalidasa (4th-5th century CE):Renowned Sanskrit poet and playwright.

f)Aryabhata (476 CE):Mathematician and astronomer who developed the decimal system.

The Gupta period's cultural, scientific, and philosophical achievements had a lasting impact on Hinduism, Indian culture, and the world at large.

(ii)Spread of Hinduism to southern and western India:

The Gupta Empire (320-550 CE) played a significant role in the spread of Hinduism to southern and western India, through:

1.Conquests and expansion:Gupta rulers extended their empire to southern and western regions, taking Hinduism with them.

2.Trade and commerce:Trade networks established during the Gupta period facilitated the exchange of ideas, cultures, and religions.

3.Migration and settlement:People from the Indo-Gangetic Plain migrated to southern and western India, taking their religious beliefs and practices with them.

4.Establishment of temples and shrines: Gupta rulers built temples and shrines in newly conquered regions, promoting Hindu worship and pilgrimage.

5.Patronage of Hindu scholars and priests: Gupta rulers supported Hindu scholars and priests, who travelled to southern and western India, spreading Hinduism.

Key regions affected by the spread of Hinduism during the Gupta period:

i)Southern India:Hinduism spread to the Deccan Plateau, Tamil Nadu, and Kerala.

ii)Western India:Hinduism spread to Gujarat, Maharashtra, and Rajasthan.

Consequences of the spread of Hinduism:

a)Hinduization of local cultures:Local cultures and traditions blended with Hinduism, creating new forms of worship and expression.

b)Emergence of new Hindu centres:New Hindu centres emerged, such as the temples of Kanchipuram and Mahabalipuram.

c)Growth of Hindu scriptures:Hindu scriptures, like the Puranas and the Mahabharata, became more widespread.

d)Development of regional Hindu traditions: Regional Hindu traditions, like the Alvar and Nayanar movements, emerged in southern India.

Key figures who contributed to the spread of Hinduism:

1.Gupta rulers:Chandragupta-I, Samudragupta, and Chandragupta-II.

2.Hindu scholars and priests:Traveling scholars and priests who spread Hinduism to new regions.

3.Local rulers:Local rulers who adopted Hinduism and supported its spread.

The Gupta period marked a significant milestone in the spread of Hinduism, extending its reach to southern and western India, and shaping the religious and cultural landscape of the subcontinent.

(iii)Development of Hindu art, architecture, and literature:

The Gupta Empire (320-550 CE) saw a significant development of Hindu art, architecture, and literature, characterized by:

Art:

1.Classical style:Emergence of a classical style, marked by balance, proportion, and harmony.

2.Temple sculptures:Intricate sculptures depicting Hindu deities and mythological scenes.

3.Cave paintings:Cave paintings, such as those at Ajanta, showcasing Hindu mythology and culture.

Architecture:

i)Temple architecture:Development of the Nagara style, characterized by towering spires and intricate carvings.

ii)Monolithic temples:Construction of monolithic temples, like the Mahabalipuram temples.

iii)Cave temples: Excavation of cave temples, such as those at Ellora and Elephanta.

Literature:

a)Sanskrit literature:Flourishing of Sanskrit literature, including works like Kalidasa's plays and the Puranas.

b)Hindu epics:Composition of Hindu epics, like the Mahabharata and Ramayana.

c)Poetry and drama:Development of poetry and drama, with works like the Bhagavata Purana and the Mudrarakshasa.

Key features of Gupta art, architecture, and literature:

1.Symbolism:Extensive use of symbolism, reflecting Hindu mythology and philosophy.

2.Naturalism:Emergence of naturalism, depicting everyday life and human emotions.

3.Regional styles:Development of regional styles, reflecting local traditions and influences.

Notable figures:

a)Kalidasa:Renowned Sanskrit poet and playwriter.

b)Aryabhata:Mathematician and astronomer who wrote the Aryabhatiya.

c)Varahamihira:Astronomer and mathematician who wrote the Pancha Siddhantika.

The Gupta period's cultural achievements had a lasting impact on Hindu art, architecture, and literature, shaping the course of Indian cultural heritage.

Key figures:

1.Vedic seers and sages (e.g., Agastya, Vasistha)

2.Upanishadic philosophers (e.g., Yajnavalkya, Uddalaka)

3.Epic poets (e.g., Valmiki, Vyasa)

4.Mauryan rulers (e.g., Chandragupta Maurya, Ashoka)

5.Gupta rulers (e.g., Chandragupta I, Samudragupta)

Hinduism's expansion during this period was characterized by:

a) Geographic spread:

The Gupta Empire (320-550 CE) had a vast geographic spread, covering much of the Indian subcontinent, including:

1.Northern India:The Ganges-Yamuna valley, including modern-day Uttar Pradesh, Bihar, and Madhya Pradesh.

2.Eastern India:Bengal, including modern-day West Bengal and Bangladesh.

3.Central India:Malwa, including modern-day Madhya Pradesh and parts of Maharashtra.

4.Western India:Gujarat, including modern-day Gujarat and parts of Rajasthan.

5.Southern India:Deccan Plateau, including modern-day Maharashtra, Karnataka, and parts of Tamil Nadu.

6.Northwestern India:Punjab and Kashmir, including modern-day Punjab, Haryana, and Jammu and Kashmir.

Key regions and cities:

i)Pataliputra (modern-day Patna):Capital city of the Gupta Empire.

ii)Ayodhya (modern-day Uttar Pradesh): Important Hindu pilgrimage site.

iii)Varanasi (modern-day Uttar Pradesh): Major centre of Hinduism and learning.

iv)Ujjain (modern-day Madhya Pradesh): Important centre of Hinduism and trade.

v)Nalanda (modern-day Bihar):Renowned Buddhist university and centre of learning.

The Gupta Empire's geographic spread facilitated:

1.Cultural exchange:Exchange of ideas, cultures, and traditions across the subcontinent.

2.Trade and commerce:Extensive trade networks, including the Silk Road.

3.Spread of Hinduism:Hinduism spread to new regions, influencing local cultures and traditions.

4.Imperial administration:Effective administration, with a strong centralized government.

The Gupta Empire's vast geographic spread played a significant role in shaping Indian culture, religion, and politics, leaving a lasting legacy in the subcontinent.

b)Development of philosophical and spiritual thought:

The Gupta Empire (320-550 CE) saw significant developments in philosophical and spiritual thought, including:

1.Advaita Vedanta:Emergence of Advaita Vedanta, a non-dualistic school of thought, by Adi Shankaracharya.

2.Vaisheshika:Development of Vaisheshika, a school of atomistic philosophy, by Kanada and Prashastapada.

3.Nyaya:Growth of Nyaya, a school of logic and epistemology, by Gautama and Vatsyayana.

4.Mimamsa:Development of Mimamsa, a school of ritual and philosophical thought, by Jaimini and Shabara.

5.Buddhist philosophy:Continued development of Buddhist philosophy, including the Yogacara and Madhyamaka schools.

6.Jain philosophy:Growth of Jain philosophy, including the development of the concept of anekantavada (non-absolutism).

7.Tantra:Emergence of Tantric thought, emphasizing the worship of Shakti and the use of rituals and mantras.

8.Bhakti movement:Early beginnings of the Bhakti movement, emphasizing devotion and love for a personal deity.

Key figures:

i)Adi Shankaracharya (788-820 CE): Renowned Advaita Vedantin philosopher and commentator.

ii)Kanada (6th century CE):Founder of the Vaisheshika school.

iii)Gautama (6th century CE):Author of the Nyaya Sutras.

iv)Jaimini (4th century CE):Founder of the Mimamsa school.

v)Nagarjuna (2nd century CE):Buddhist philosopher and founder of the Madhyamaka school.

vi)Mahavira (6th century BCE):Founder of Jainism.

vii)Bhartrihari (5th century CE):Philosopher and poet, known for his works on Tantra and Advaita Vedanta.

These developments in philosophical and spiritual thought had a profound impact on Indian intellectual and cultural heritage, shaping the course of Indian philosophy, religion, and spirituality.

c)Emergence of Hindu mythology and legends:

The Gupta Empire (320-550 CE) saw the emergence and development of Hindu mythology and legends, including:

1.Puranas:Compilation of the Puranas, ancient texts that contain myths, legends, and genealogies of gods and goddesses.

2.Mahabharata and Ramayana:Finalization of the epics Mahabharata and Ramayana, which contain stories of gods, goddesses, and legendary heroes.

3.Devi Mahatmyam:Emergence of the Devi Mahatmyam, a text that celebrates the goddess Durga and her legends.

4.Krishna legends:Development of legends around Krishna, including his childhood stories and exploits.

5.Ganesha and Kartikeya myths:Emergence of myths and legends around Ganesha and Kartikeya, sons of Shiva and Parvati.

6.Shiva and Vishnu mythology:Development of myths and legends around Shiva and Vishnu, two of the principal deities of Hinduism.

7.Local legends and folklore:Emergence of local legends and folklore, often centred around regional deities and sacred sites.

Key figures:

i)Vyasa:Legendary author of the Mahabharata and Puranas.

ii)Valmiki:Author of the Ramayana.

iii)Kalidasa:Playwriter and poet, who wrote works like Abhijnanasakuntalam, which draws on Hindu mythology.

The emergence of Hindu mythology and legends during the Gupta period had a significant impact on:

1.Hinduism:Shaping the religious and cultural landscape of Hinduism.

2.Art and literature:Influencing art, literature, and performance traditions.

3.Regional cultures:Contributing to the development of regional cultures and identities.

4.Folk traditions:Shaping folk traditions and practices.

These mythological stories and legends continue to be an integral part of Hinduism and Indian culture, inspiring art, literature, and worship to this day.

d)Patronage by ruling dynasties:

The Gupta Empire (320-550 CE) received patronage from various ruling dynasties, including:

1.Gupta dynasty (320-550 CE):The ruling dynasty of the Gupta Empire, who patronized Hinduism, art, literature, and science.

2.Vakataka dynasty (250-500 CE):A feudatory dynasty that ruled in central India and patronized Buddhist and Hindu art and literature.

3.Kadamba dynasty (345-525 CE):A dynasty that ruled in western India and patronized Hinduism and Jainism.

4.Pallava dynasty (275-897 CE):A dynasty that ruled in southern India and patronized Hinduism, art, and architecture.

5.Maitraka dynasty (475-767 CE):A dynasty that ruled in western India and patronized Hinduism and Jainism.

These ruling dynasties patronized various aspects of Gupta culture, including:

i)Hinduism:Patronage of Hindu temples, priests, and rituals.

ii)Art and architecture:Patronage of artists, architects, and craftsmen, leading to the development of Gupta art and architecture.

iii)Literature:Patronage of poets, writers, and scholars, leading to the development of Gupta literature.

iv)Science and technology:Patronage of scientists, mathematicians, and astronomers, leading to significant advances in these fields.

v)Education:Patronage of universities, scholars, and students, leading to the spread of knowledge and learning.

The patronage by these ruling dynasties contributed to the:

1.Cultural achievements of the Gupta Empire.

2.Spread of Hinduism and other religions.

3.Development of art, literature, and architecture.

4.Advances in science and technology.

5.Growth of education and learning.

The patronage by ruling dynasties played a significant role in shaping the cultural, religious, and intellectual landscape of the Gupta Empire.

e)Cultural and artistic achievements:

The Gupta Empire (320-550 CE) is renowned for its cultural and artistic achievements, including:

1.Gupta art:Characterized by its elegance, balance, and proportion, Gupta art is considered a golden age of Indian art.

2.Temple architecture:Development of the Nagara style, marked by towering spires and intricate carvings.

3.Sculpture:Intricate sculptures depicting Hindu deities, mythological scenes, and everyday life.

4.Painting:Cave paintings, such as those at Ajanta, showcasing Hindu mythology and culture.

5.Literature:Flourishing of Sanskrit literature, including works like Kalidasa's plays and the Puranas.

6.Music and dance:Development of classical music and dance, like Bharatanatyam and Kathakali.

7.Theatre:Emergence of Sanskrit theatre, with works like Kalidasa's plays.

8.Poetry:Development of Sanskrit poetry, with poets like Kalidasa and Bhartrihari.

9.Astronomy and mathematics:Significant advances in astronomy and mathematics, with scholars like Aryabhata and Varahamihira.

10.Medicine:Development of Ayurveda, with scholars like Charaka and Sushruta.

Key figures:

i)Kalidasa:Renowned Sanskrit poet and playwright.

ii)Aryabhata:Mathematician and astronomer who wrote the Aryabhatiya.

iii)Varahamihira:Astronomer and mathematician who wrote the Pancha Siddhantika.

iv)Charaka: Ayurvedic scholar who wrote the Charaka Samhita.

v)Sushruta: Ayurvedic scholar who wrote the Sushruta Samhita.

These cultural and artistic achievements had a lasting impact on Indian culture, shaping the course of Indian art, literature, music, and science.

This period laid the foundation for Hinduism's future growth and diversification as Hinduism emerged in the Indian subcontinent and it spread to Southeast Asia through trade and migration.

Chapter 2

Medieval Period (500 - 1500 CE)

The Medieval Period in India, spanning from 500 to 1500 CE, was a transformative era marked by significant political, social, cultural, and religious changes. This period saw the rise and fall of various dynasties, empires, and kingdoms, including:

1.Gupta Empire (320-550 CE):A golden age of Hindu culture, art, and literature.

2.Vardhana Empire (550-647 CE):A brief but significant empire that saw the emergence of Buddhism and Jainism.

3.Pala Empire (750-1174 CE):A major Buddhist empire that patronized art, literature, and learning.

4.Rashtrakuta Empire (753-982 CE):A powerful empire that saw the rise of Hinduism and Jainism.

5.Delhi Sultanate (1206-1526 CE):A Muslim empire that introduced Islamic culture, art, and architecture.

6.Vijayanagara Empire (1336-1646 CE):A Hindu empire that resisted Muslim rule and patronized art, literature, and culture.

This period also witnessed:

i)Spread of Islam:Islam arrived in India through trade, conquest, and Sufi mystics.

ii)Bhakti Movement:A devotional movement that emphasized personal devotion to gods and goddesses.

iii)Sufism:A mystical form of Islam that emphasized love and devotion.

iv)Temple architecture:Development of distinctive temple styles, like the Nagara and Dravida.

v)Classical literature:Emergence of classical literature in Sanskrit, Tamil, Telugu, and Kannada.

The Medieval Period laid the foundation for India's rich cultural heritage, shaping its art, literature, religion, and society.

During this period:

(a)Hinduism reached Indonesia, Malaysia, and the Philippines:

During the Medieval Period (500-1500 CE), Hinduism spread to Southeast Asia, specifically to:

1.Indonesia:Hinduism arrived in Indonesia around the 1st century CE, influencing the development of Indonesian culture, art, and architecture.

2.Malaysia:Hinduism reached Malaysia around the 3rd century CE, with the establishment of Hindu kingdoms like the Kadaram and the Majapahit Empire.

3.Philippines:Hinduism arrived in the Philippines around the 10th century CE, influencing the indigenous cultures and the development of Filipino art and architecture.

Key aspects of Hinduism's spread:

i)Trade and commerce:Hindu traders and merchants played a significant role in spreading Hinduism to Southeast Asia.

ii)Buddhist and Hindu kingdoms:Kingdoms like the Srivijaya and the Majapahit Empire patronized Hinduism and Buddhism, facilitating their spread.

iii)Cultural exchange:Cultural exchange between India and Southeast Asia led to the adoption of Hindu customs, rituals, and practices.

iv)Temples and architecture:Hindu temples and architecture were built in Southeast Asia, showcasing Indian influences.

Influence on local cultures:

1.Blending of cultures:Hinduism blended with local cultures, creating unique cultural practices and traditions.

2.Art and architecture:Hinduism influenced the development of art and architecture in Southeast Asia.

3.Literature and language:Hinduism influenced the development of literature and language in Southeast Asia.

4.Philosophy and spirituality:Hinduism shaped the philosophical and spiritual landscape of Southeast Asia.

Key figures:

1.Adityawarman (14th century CE):A Hindu king who ruled over the Majapahit Empire in Indonesia.

2.Rajendra Chola (11th century CE):A Hindu king who ruled over the Chola Empire in southern India and expanded Hinduism to Southeast Asia.

Hinduism's spread to Southeast Asia had a profound impact on the cultural, artistic, and spiritual landscape of the region.

(b)Influence on Southeast Asian cultures and kingdoms:

During the Medieval Period (500-1500 CE), Hinduism and Buddhism from India significantly influenced Southeast Asian cultures and kingdoms, including:

1.Khmer Empire (802-1432 CE):Hinduism shaped Khmer art, architecture, and culture, evident in Angkor Wat.

2.Srivijaya Empire (650-1377 CE):A Buddhist kingdom that flourished in Sumatra, influencing Southeast Asian art and culture.

3.Majapahit Empire (1293-1520 CE):A Hindu kingdom that ruled much of Indonesia, promoting Hindu art, literature, and culture.

4.Ayutthaya Kingdom (1350-1767 CE):A Buddhist kingdom in Siam (Thailand) that adopted Hindu and Buddhist art and architecture.

5.Champa Kingdoms (2nd-19th centuries CE):Hindu kingdoms in central Vietnam that developed a unique culture blending Indian and local influences.

Influence on Southeast Asian cultures:

i)Art and architecture:Hindu and Buddhist art, architecture, and iconography were adopted and adapted in Southeast Asia.

ii)Literature and language:Sanskrit and Pali languages influenced Southeast Asian literature and language.

iii)Philosophy and spirituality:Hindu and Buddhist philosophies shaped Southeast Asian spiritual practices and beliefs.

iv)Politics and governance:Indian political systems and administrative structures were adopted by Southeast Asian kingdoms.

v)Cultural practices:Hindu and Buddhist customs, rituals, and festivals were incorporated into Southeast Asian cultures.

Key figures:

1.Jayavarman-II (9th century CE):A Khmer king who adopted Hinduism and established the Khmer Empire.

2.Rajendra Chola (11th century CE):A Chola king who expanded Hinduism to Southeast Asia.

3.Adityawarman (14th century CE):A Majapahit king who promoted Hinduism in Indonesia.

The influence of Hinduism and Buddhism on Southeast Asian cultures and kingdoms had a lasting impact, shaping the region's art, literature, philosophy, and spirituality.

Chapter 3

Bhakti Movement (500 - 1700 CE)

The Bhakti Movement, spanning from 500 to 1700 CE, was a powerful spiritual and cultural phenomenon that swept across India, transforming the landscape of Hinduism and leaving an indelible mark on Indian society. Characterized by an emphasis on intense personal devotion, emotional connection, and love for a chosen deity, Bhakti Movement sought to democratize spirituality, making it accessible to people from all walks of life, regardless of caste, creed, or social status. Through the passionate expressions of poet-saints, mystics, and devotees, Bhakti Movement gave voice to the longing for a direct, personal experience of the divine, challenging traditional ritualistic practices and ushering in a new era of spiritual fervour that continues to inspire and influence Indian thought and culture to this day. During this period-

(i)Spread of Devotional traditions across India:

The Bhakti Movement's devotional traditions spread across India, encompassing various regions and languages, and giving rise to distinct schools of thought and practice. Some key aspects of this spread include:

-Southern India:The Alvars (6th-9th centuries CE) and Nayanars (6th-10th centuries CE) in Tamil Nadu, and the Haridasas (13th-16th centuries CE) in Karnataka, developed a rich tradition of devotional poetry and music.

-Eastern India:The Mahabhavas (12th-13th centuries CE) in Bengal, and the Odia poets (12th-16th centuries CE) in Odisha, contributed to the growth of Bhakti literature and culture.

-Western India:The Pandharpur tradition (13th-17th centuries CE) in Maharashtra, and the Gujarati poet-saints (14th-16th centuries CE), enriched the Bhakti Movement with their unique expressions.

-Northern India:The Bhakti poets (14th-17th centuries CE) in Hindi, Punjabi, and Rajasthani, such as Kabir, Mirabai, and Surdas, further popularized the movement.

This widespread dissemination of Bhakti ideas and practices helped create a shared cultural heritage, transcending regional and linguistic boundaries, and shaping Indian spirituality and identity.

(ii) Emphasis on personal devotion and love:

The Bhakti Movement emphasized personal devotion and love for a chosen deity, fostering a deep sense of intimacy and connection with the divine. Key aspects of this emphasis include:

-Personal relationship:Devotees sought a direct, personal relationship with their chosen deity, often addressing them as a beloved friend, parent, or lover.

-Emotional intensity:Bhakti poetry and music expressed intense emotions, such as love, longing, and surrender, to convey the depth of devotion.

-Love as a path to liberation:Bhakti Movement teachings emphasized that love and devotion could lead to spiritual liberation, making it accessible to all, regardless of caste or creed.

-Saguna and Nirguna Bhakti:Two approaches emerged - Saguna Bhakti (love for a deity with attributes) and Nirguna Bhakti (love for a deity without attributes), catering to different devotional preferences.

-Role of the guru:The guru-disciple relationship became crucial, with gurus guiding devotees on their spiritual journey and helping them develop a personal connection with the divine.

This emphasis on personal devotion and love transformed the spiritual landscape of India, empowering individuals to experience the divine in a more intimate and personal way.

Chapter 4

Colonial Era (1500 - 1947 CE)

During the colonial era, Hinduism underwent significant transformations and expansions, both within India and globally. Despite facing challenges from colonial powers and Christian missionaries, Hinduism adapted and evolved, leading to its spread and growth. Key aspects of this expansion include:

-Migration and diaspora:Hindu migrants and indentured laborers travelled to various parts of the world, establishing Hindu communities and temples in regions like Southeast Asia, Africa, and the Caribbean.

-Reform movements:Hindu reformers like Ram Mohan Roy, Swami Vivekananda, and Dayananda Saraswati emerged, aiming to modernize and unify Hinduism, and counter colonial and Christian influences.

-Globalization and proselytization:Hindu missionaries and organizations, such as the Ramakrishna Mission and the Hare Krishna Movement, actively spread Hindu teachings and practices worldwide.

-Colonial patronage:British colonial authorities, recognizing Hinduism's significance, provided patronage to Hindu institutions and supported the publication of Hindu texts, contributing to Hinduism's expansion.

-Indigenous resistance and revival:In response to colonialism, indigenous Hindu movements and leaders emerged, emphasizing Hindu identity, culture, and traditions, and resisting colonial and Christian dominance.

The expansion of Hinduism during the colonial era demonstrates its resilience, adaptability, and appeal, shaping the modern Hindu landscape and its global presence.

(i)Hinduism introduced to the West by European colonizers:

The expansion of Hinduism to the West was facilitated by European colonizers and scholars, who encountered Hinduism during their colonization of India. As they learned about Hinduism, they began to share their knowledge with others in Europe and beyond. Key aspects of this introduction include:

-Translation of Hindu texts:European scholars translated Hindu scriptures like the Upanishads, Bhagavad Gita, and Rigveda into European languages, making them accessible to a wider audience.

-Academic study of Hinduism:European scholars began to study Hinduism systematically, leading to a greater understanding and appreciation of its philosophy, practices, and culture.

-Travelogues and accounts:European travellers and colonizers wrote about their experiences with Hinduism, generating interest and curiosity among Westerners.

-Theosophical Society and Eastern spirituality:Organizations like the Theosophical Society, founded by Helena Blavatsky and Henry Steel Olcott, popularized Eastern spirituality, including Hinduism, among Westerners.

-Immigration and diaspora:Hindu immigrants and diaspora communities in the West introduced their traditions and practices to new audiences, further expanding Hinduism's global presence.

These factors contributed to the introduction and growth of Hinduism in the West, fostering greater understanding, appreciation, and adoption of Hindu practices and philosophy.

(ii)Indian diaspora communities established in the Caribbean, Africa, and Asia:

The Indian diaspora played a significant role in the expansion of Hinduism, establishing vibrant communities in the Caribbean, Africa, and Asia. These communities maintained their cultural heritage and religious practices, adapting to new environments while preserving their Hindu traditions. Key aspects of this expansion include:

-Caribbean:Indian indentured laborers arrived in the Caribbean (1830s-1910s), establishing Hindu communities in Trinidad and Tobago, Guyana, Suriname, and Jamaica.

-Africa:Indians migrated to Africa, particularly to South Africa, Kenya, Tanzania, and Uganda, forming Hindu communities and temples.

-Southeast Asia:Indian traders, laborers, and settlers established Hindu communities in Malaysia, Singapore, Indonesia, and Thailand, blending with local cultures.

-Mauritius and Fiji:Indian laborers were brought to these islands (1830s-1920s), forming significant Hindu populations.

These diaspora communities:

-Maintained traditions:Preserved Hindu practices, festivals, and customs in new environments.

-Adapted to local cultures:Incorporated local elements, creating unique Hindu traditions.

-Established temples and organizations: Built temples, ashrams, and cultural organizations to support their communities.

-Contributed to local societies:Played significant roles in the economic, social, and cultural development of their host countries.

The Indian diaspora's expansion of Hinduism demonstrates the religion's adaptability, resilience, and appeal, enriching the cultural diversity of their adopted homelands.

Chapter 5

Modern Era (1947 CE - present)

In the Modern Era (1947-present), Hinduism continued to expand and evolve, both globally and within India. Key aspects of this expansion include:

-Post-Independence India (1947):Hinduism experienced a resurgence in India, with a renewed focus on cultural and spiritual heritage.

-Globalization and migration (1950s-1980s): Hindu migrants and professionals spread Hinduism to new regions, including the United States, United Kingdom, Canada, and Australia.

-Hindu revivalism (1980s-1990s):The Hindu revivalist movement, led by organizations like the Vishva Hindu Parishad (VHP), emphasized Hindu identity, culture, and unity.

-Internet and digital age (1990s-present): The internet and social media have enabled global access to Hindu scriptures, teachings, and communities, facilitating the spread of Hinduism.

-Yoga and Wellness (1990s-present):The global popularity of yoga and wellness has introduced Hindu spiritual practices to new audiences, often outside traditional religious contexts.

-Interfaith dialogue and exchange (1990s-present): Hindu leaders and organizations engage in interfaith dialogue, promoting mutual understanding and cooperation.

-Hindu diaspora communities (present day): Thriving Hindu communities in the Caribbean, Africa, Asia, and the West maintain their cultural heritage and religious practices.

-Innovative expressions and fusion (present day):Hinduism continues to evolve, incorporating local and global influences, and giving rise to new expressions and fusion of traditions.

The expansion of Hinduism in the Modern Era reflects its adaptability, diversity, and appeal, as it continues to shape the lives of millions worldwide as explained hereunder:

(i)Globalization and migration spread Hinduism worldwide:

Globalization and migration have been key factors in the spread of Hinduism worldwide. As Hindus travel, migrate, and connect globally, they share their culture, traditions, and spiritual practices with others. This has led to:

-Establishment of Hindu temples and centres:Hindu migrants have built temples, cultural centres, and organizations in new countries, creating hubs for Hindu practice and community.

-Dissemination of Hindu texts and teachings: Global access to Hindu scriptures, online resources, and social media has made Hindu teachings and philosophy widely available.

-Growth of Hindu communities:Hindu populations have grown in countries like the United States, United Kingdom, Canada, Australia, and Southeast Asia, creating vibrant diaspora communities.

-Fusion of Hindu practices with local cultures: Hinduism has blended with local traditions, resulting in unique expressions of Hinduism, such as Hindu-Caribbean and Hindu-African traditions.

-Increased visibility and recognition: Hinduism has gained recognition as a major world religion, with Hindu festivals, symbols, and practices becoming more mainstream.

-Exchange and dialogue with other faiths: Globalization has facilitated interfaith dialogue, enabling Hindus to engage with other religious traditions and share their perspectives.

Countries with significant Hindu populations due to migration and globalization include:

-United States (3.36 million)

-United Kingdom (1.5 million)

-Canada (828,000)

-Australia (684,000)

-South Africa (652,000)

-Malaysia (2 million)

-Singapore (250,000)

-Indonesia (150,000)

The spread of Hinduism through globalization and migration demonstrates its adaptability, resilience, and appeal, as it continues to shape the lives of millions worldwide.

(ii)Establishment of Hindu temples and organizations in the West:

The establishment of Hindu temples and organizations in the West has played a crucial role in the expansion of Hinduism globally. These institutions serve as:

-Centres of worship and community: Temples provide a space for Hindus to practice their faith, celebrate festivals, and connect with their cultural heritage.

-Hubs for cultural and spiritual activities: Organizations host events, classes, and workshops on Hindu philosophy, yoga, and arts, promoting Hindu culture and values.

-Support networks for Hindus: Temples and organizations offer guidance, resources, and community support for Hindus navigating Western societies.

-Ambassadors of Hinduism:These institutions introduce Hinduism to Western audiences, promoting understanding, tolerance, and acceptance.

Notable Hindu temples and organizations in the West include:

-BAPS Swaminarayan Sanstha (Global)

-ISKCON (International Society for Krishna Consciousness) (Global)

-Hindu Temple Society of North America (USA)

-National Council of Hindu Temples (NCHT)(UK)

-Hindu American Foundation (HAF) (USA)

-Vedanta Society (USA, UK, Canada)

These temples and organizations have:

-Preserved Hindu traditions:Maintained authentic Hindu practices and rituals in new environments.

-Adapted to local contexts:Incorporated local customs and languages, making Hinduism accessible to Western audiences.

-Fostered community engagement: Encouraged interfaith dialogue, cultural exchange, and social service initiatives.

The establishment of Hindu temples and organizations in the West has facilitated the growth of Hinduism, providing a foundation for its continued expansion and evolution.

(iii)Increased interest in Hindu spirituality and philosophy:

In recent decades, there has been a growing interest in Hindu spirituality and philosophy worldwide, contributing to the expansion of Hinduism. This increased interest can be attributed to:

-Seeking spiritual meaning:Many people are looking for deeper spiritual connections and meaning in their lives, finding Hinduism's rich philosophical and spiritual traditions appealing.

-Wellness and self-improvement:Hindu practices like yoga, meditation, and Ayurveda have gained popularity for their physical, mental, and emotional benefits.

-Philosophical curiosity:Hinduism's diverse philosophical schools, such as Advaita Vedanta and Bhakti, offer unique perspectives on existence, consciousness, and the human condition.

-Fusion of Eastern and Western thought: Hindu ideas are being integrated with Western philosophies, creating new spiritual and intellectual frameworks.

-Accessibility of Hindu texts and teachings: Translations of Hindu scriptures, online resources, and social media have made Hindu philosophy and spirituality more accessible globally.

-Influence of Hindu teachers and gurus: Charismatic Hindu teachers and gurus, like Ram Dass, Deepak Chopra, and Sadhguru, have introduced Hindu spirituality to new audiences.

This increased interest has led to:

-Growth of Hindu-inspired spiritual movements: Movements like the Hare Krishna Movement, Transcendental Meditation, and modern yoga styles have emerged, drawing on Hindu spiritual practices.

-Academic and scholarly interest:Hindu studies have become a significant field in academia, with scholars exploring Hindu philosophy, history, and culture.

-Cultural exchange and dialogue:The interest in Hindu spirituality has facilitated interfaith dialogue, cultural exchange, and collaboration between East and West.

The increased interest in Hindu spirituality and philosophy demonstrates Hinduism's timeless appeal and relevance, as it continues to inspire and guide seekers worldwide.

Regions with significant Hindu populations:

1.India

2.Nepal

3.Indonesia (Bali)

4.Sri Lanka

5.Pakistan (minority)

6.Bangladesh (minority)

7.Southeast Asia (Singapore, Malaysia, Thailand)

8.Caribbean (Guyana, Suriname, Trinidad and Tobago)

9.Africa (South Africa, Mauritius)

10.Western countries (USA, UK, Canada, Australia)

Hinduism's expansion has been shaped by trade, migration, colonialism, and globalization, leading to a diverse and widespread presence worldwide.

Chapter 6

Key Factors Contributing to the Expansion of Hinduism

Hinduism, one of the world's oldest and most diverse religions, has undergone significant expansion throughout its history. From its ancient roots in the Indian subcontinent to its current global presence, Hinduism has evolved and adapted, influenced by various factors. Several key factors have contributed to the expansion of Hinduism, including:

1.Indianization of Southeast Asia:Hinduism spread to Southeast Asia through trade, migration, and cultural exchange, influencing the region's art, architecture, and literature.
2.Buddhist and Jain influences:The spread of Buddhism and Jainism helped Hinduism expand, as these religions shared common roots and ideas.
3.Trade and commerce:Hindu merchants and traders travelled extensively, sharing their beliefs and practices with others.
4.Conquests and migrations:Indian rulers and empires, like the Gupta and Vijayanagara empires, expanded Hinduism through military campaigns and migrations.
5.Cultural and religious exchange:Hinduism influenced and was influenced by other cultures, such as the Persians, Greeks, and Chinese.
6.Missionary work:Hindu saints, sages, and reformers like Adi Shankara and Vivekananda spread Hindu teachings and values.

7.Colonialism and diaspora:Hinduism spread globally through the migration of Indians during colonial times and the modern diaspora.
8.Philosophical and literary works:The dissemination of Hindu scriptures, epics, and philosophical texts helped spread Hindu ideas and values.
9.Royal patronage:Support from Indian rulers and monarchs helped establish and spread Hinduism.
10.Syncretism and adaptation:Hinduism's ability to absorb and adapt local beliefs and practices facilitated its expansion.
11.Reform and revival movements:Hindu reformers and revivalists sought to revitalize and modernize Hinduism, making it more appealing to new audiences.
12.Increased interest in Hindu spirituality and philosophy:Growing global interest in Hindu thought, yoga, and spirituality has attracted new followers and enthusiasts.
13.Establishment of Hindu temples and organizations:The construction of temples and formation of organizations have provided hubs for Hindu practice, community, and outreach.
14.Internet and digital age:The internet and social media have enabled global access to Hindu teachings, resources, and communities, facilitating the spread of Hinduism.

These factors have collectively contributed to the expansion of Hinduism, transforming it into a global religion with a diverse and dynamic presence.

By conquests of Kings:

Here are some key examples of Hinduism's expansion through the conquests and patronage of Indian kings and empires:

1.Gupta Empire (320-550 CE):Spread Hinduism throughout India, reviving Vedic traditions and patronizing Hindu scholars and artists.
2.Vijayanagara Empire (1336-1646 CE): Expanded Hinduism in South India, building temples and promoting Hindu culture.
3.Pallava Dynasty (275-897 CE):Spread Hinduism in South India, particularly in the Tamil region, through temple construction and religious patronage.
4.Chola Empire (300-1279 CE):Expanded Hinduism in South India and Southeast Asia, building temples and promoting Hindu art and literature.
5.Rashtrakuta Dynasty (753-982 CE):Spread Hinduism in the Deccan region, patronizing Hindu scholars and building temples.
6.Pandya Dynasty (550-1350 CE):Expanded Hinduism in South India, particularly in the Tamil region, through temple construction and religious patronage.
7.Kushan Empire (60-375 CE):Spread Hinduism in North India and Central Asia, patronizing Hindu and Buddhist scholars and artists.
8.Chalukya Dynasty (543-757 CE):Expanded Hinduism in the Deccan region, building temples and promoting Hindu culture.
9.Hoysala Empire (1026-1343 CE):Spread Hinduism in South India, building temples and promoting Hindu art and literature.

10.Maratha Empire (1674-1818 CE): Expanded Hinduism in India, patronizing Hindu scholars and building temples.

These kingdoms and empires played a significant role in spreading Hinduism through military conquests, religious patronage, and cultural exchange.

Part – III

Decline

Of

Hinduism

Introduction

Despite its widespread expansion and adaptability, Hinduism has faced periods of decline and challenges throughout its history. The decline of Hinduism has been a complex and multifaceted phenomenon, influenced by various factors that have impacted its practice, popularity, and influence. Part-III explores the key factors that have contributed to the decline of Hinduism, including:

Foreign invasions and conquests: Repeated invasions and conquests by foreign powers, such as the Muslim conquests of India and European colonialism, disrupted Hindu traditions and institutions.

Conversions and proselytization: Efforts by Christian, Muslim, and Buddhist missionaries to convert Hindus have led to a decline in Hindu populations in certain regions.

Social and economic changes: Modernization, urbanization, and economic development have led to changes in values, lifestyles, and beliefs, causing some Hindus to drift away from traditional practices.

Internal challenges and divisions: Hinduism's inherent diversity and internal divisions have sometimes hindered its ability to respond effectively to external challenges and maintain a unified presence.

Persecution and discrimination: Hindus have faced persecution and discrimination in certain regions, leading to a decline in their numbers and influence.

Lack of effective leadership and reform: In some periods, Hinduism has lacked effective leadership and reform, failing to adapt to changing circumstances and address internal weaknesses.

This part examines these factors and their impact on Hinduism's decline, providing a nuanced understanding of the complex historical and contemporary contexts that have shaped the religion's trajectory.

Chapter 1

Emergence and Spread of Islam

Islam came into being in the 7th century CE, specifically in the year 610 CE, when Prophet Muhammad received his first revelation from Allah (God) through the angel Gabriel in the cave of Hira, near Mecca, Arabia. This event marks the beginning of Islam as a religion.

Here's a brief timeline:

-570 CE:Birth of Prophet Muhammad in Mecca, Arabia

-610 CE:First revelation received by Prophet Muhammad, marking the beginning of Islam

-613 CE:Prophet Muhammad begins preaching publicly in Mecca

-622 CE:Hijra (migration) of Prophet Muhammad and his followers from Mecca to Medina, marking the beginning of the Islamic calendar

-632 CE:Death of Prophet Muhammad, succeeded by Abu Bakr as the first Caliph

-634-644 CE:Spread of Islam beyond Arabia, into the Middle East and North Africa

Note that Islam did not emerge suddenly, but rather built upon the existing Abrahamic traditions and the cultural context of Arabia at the time. The Quran, the holy book of

Islam, was revealed to Prophet Muhammad over a period of 23 years, until his death in 632 CE.

Muhammad and his followers engaged in military campaigns against the polytheistic tribes of Arabia, known as the mushrikun, from 622 to 632 CE. These campaigns were aimed at unifying Arabia under Islamic rule and ending the persecution of Muslims by the polytheistic tribes. While some conversions were indeed forced, many Arabs converted to Islam voluntarily, attracted by the message of monotheism and the social and economic benefits of joining the Muslim community.

The Kaaba, a cube-shaped building in Mecca, which was a pagan shrine before Islam, housed various idols and was a center of polytheistic worship. In 630 CE, Muhammad conquered Mecca and cleansed the Kaaba of its idols, rededicating it to the worship of one God, Allah.

The spread of Islam in Arabia was a complex process involving both military campaigns and voluntary conversions. And, in a short span of 10-12 years, all idol worshippers of Arabia got converted to Islam.

The conversion of Parsis (Zoroastrians) to Islam also started in 633 CE but it was a gradual process that occurred over several centuries as explained hereunder:

-The Arab conquest of Persia (modern-day Iran) began in 633 CE and lasted until 651 CE, when the Sassanid Empire was defeated.

-Following the conquest, many Zoroastrians were forced to convert to Islam, but this process was not uniform or instantaneous.

-Some Zoroastrians resisted conversion and maintained their faith, while others converted to Islam to avoid persecution, taxation, or social exclusion.

-The process of conversion continued over the next few centuries, with many Zoroastrians converting to Islam during the Abbasid Caliphate (750-1258 CE).

-However, a significant number of Zoroastrians continued to practice their faith, and their communities survived in certain regions, such as Yazd and Kerman in modern-day Iran.

Islam arrived in Egypt in 641 CE, when the Arab army conquered the country. The initial conquest was followed by a period of tolerance, during which Christians and Jews were allowed to practice their faiths. Over time, many Egyptians converted to Islam, but this process was not uniform or instantaneous. By the end of the 7th century CE, Islam had become the dominant religion in Egypt, but significant Christian and Jewish communities also remained there. It wasn't until the 10th century CE that Islam became the majority religion in Egypt, with the Christian population declining significantly. Even then, a small but significant Christian minority remained in Egypt, and they continue to exist to this day.

The conversion of Egyptians to Islam was influenced by various factors, including:

-Economic incentives

-Social and political advantages

-Islamic missionary work

-Interfaith marriages

-Gradual cultural shift

Moreover, the Arab conquest of North Africa began in 647 CE and lasted until 709 CE, when the region came fully under Islamic rule. The conquest was followed by a process of Islamization, which occurred over several centuries. While some Berbers (indigenous North Africans) were forced to convert to Islam, many others converted voluntarily, attracted by the message of Islam and the social and economic benefits of joining the Muslim community. The process of conversion was gradual, with many Berbers maintaining their traditional practices and beliefs alongside Islamic ones.

By the 10th century CE, Islam had become the dominant religion in North Africa, but significant Christian and Jewish communities remained, particularly in urban areas.

The spread of Islam in North Africa was also influenced by trade, cultural exchange, and missionary work.

It's to be noted that the conversion of North Africans to Islam was a complex and multifaceted process that cannot be reduced to a single time frame or method. While force played a role, it was not the sole factor, and many North Africans embraced Islam voluntarily.

To understand the situation realistically, the Arab conquests were a series of military campaigns that lasted for several centuries. The conquests were driven by a combination of political, economic, and religious factors, including the expansion of the Islamic empire and the spread of Islam. While force was used in the conquests, it was not the only factor. Many local populations, including Christians and Jews, were allowed to maintain their faiths and practices under Islamic rule.

The conquests also brought significant cultural, scientific, and economic exchanges between the Islamic world and the conquered regions.

The impact of the conquests on local populations was varied, with some experiencing displacement, violence, and loss, while others benefited from the stability and prosperity brought by Islamic rule.

As regards Spain and Portugal, the Umayyad conquest of Hispania (modern-day Spain and Portugal) began in 711 CE, when a small force of Arabs and Berbers landed in Gibraltar. By 719 CE, the Muslims had conquered most of the Iberian Peninsula, but the process of conquest and consolidation took several decades. The conversion of the local population to Islam was a gradual process that occurred over several centuries. Estimates suggest that by the mid-9th century CE (around 850 CE), around 50-60% of the population of Al-Andalus (Muslim Spain) was Muslim. Here also, the conversion process was influenced by various factors, including Islamic missionary work, economic incentives, social and political advantages, and interfaith marriages.

It's essential to note that the demographic changes in medieval Spain were complex and occurred over an extended period. While the initial conquest was rapid, the conversion of the population to Islam took several centuries.

Coming to Turks, the Arab conquest of Central Asia, where the Turks lived, began in the 7th century CE, and it was a gradual process that took several centuries. The Arabs faced fierce resistance from the Turks and other local tribes, and the conquest was not a straightforward or rapid process. Many Turks converted to Islam over time, but it was not a uniform or forced conversion. Some Turks maintained their traditional beliefs and practices, while others adopted Islam voluntarily. This conversion process was also influenced by various factors, including Islamic missionary work, trade, cultural exchange, and political alliances and by 10th century CE, many Turks had adopted Islam.

It's essential to note that the history of the Turks and their conversion to Islam was also complex and multifaceted. While the Arabs did conquer Central Asia, the conversion of the Turks to Islam was a gradual process that occurred over several centuries.

Islam arrived in Indonesia through trade and cultural exchange in the 13th century CE. The conversion of Indonesians to Islam was a gradual process that occurred over several centuries. The spread of Islam in Indonesia was facilitated by Muslim traders, missionaries, and Sufi mystics, who emphasized peaceful conversion and cultural exchange. While there were instances of violence and conflict, such as the conquest of the Hindu-Buddhist kingdom of Majapahit by the Muslim kingdom of Demak in the 15th century CE, these were not representative of the entire conversion process. Many Indonesians voluntarily adopted Islam, attracted by its message, social and economic benefits, and cultural exchange. By 16th century CE, Islam had become a dominant religion in Indonesia, but significant Hindu, Buddhist, and animist communities remained, particularly in Bali and other islands. Thus, the conversion of Indonesians to Islam was a complex and multifaceted process.

The Arab conquest of the Levant (Palestine, Syria, Lebanon, and Jordan) began in 634 CE and lasted until 638 CE, when the region came fully under Islamic rule. While some local populations were forced to convert to Islam, many others converted voluntarily, attracted by the message of Islam, social and economic benefits, and cultural exchange. The conversion process was gradual, occurring over several centuries. The Umayyad Caliphate, which ruled the region from 661 to 750 CE, implemented policies that encouraged conversion, such as taxing non-Muslims and offering incentives for conversion. However, significant Christian, Jewish, and other minority communities remained in the region, and many maintained their faiths despite Islamic rule.

It may be noted that the conversion of the Levant's population to Islam was also a complex and multifaceted process. While force played a role in conversions, it was not the sole factor, and many locals embraced Islam voluntarily.

The conversion of Syria to Islam was a gradual process that occurred over several centuries. Here's a brief overview:

-Arab conquest of Syria (634-638 CE):The Rashidun Caliphate, led by Khalid ibn al-Walid, conquered Syria from the Byzantine Empire.

-Initial tolerance (638-661 CE):The Muslim rulers allowed Christians, Jews, and other minorities to maintain their faiths and practices, with some restrictions.

-Gradual conversion (661-750 CE):During the Umayyad Caliphate, Islam spread through Syria, particularly among the urban population, through missionary work, trade, and cultural exchange.

-Increased Islamic influence (750-1258 CE): The Abbasid Caliphate and subsequent Islamic dynasties further solidified Islam's presence in Syria, with many Syrians adopting Islam.

-Majority Muslim population (13th century CE): By the 13th century, Syria had become a majority Muslim population, with significant Christian and minority communities remaining.

Key factors contributing to the conversion of Syria to Islam include:

-Trade and cultural exchange

-Missionary work and Islamic scholarship

-Social and economic benefits of adopting Islam

-Interfaith marriages and cultural assimilation

-Gradual replacement of Byzantine and Persian influences with Islamic ones

This was a complex, centuries-long process, and the conversion of Syria to Islam was not uniform or sudden.

Chapter 2

Muslim Invasions of India

Within a century of the Prophet Muhammad's death in 632 CE, Islam had spread to many countries and regions beyond the Arabian Peninsula, including:

1.Middle East: Syria, Jordan, Palestine, Lebanon, Iraq, and parts of Turkey

2.North Africa: Egypt, Libya, Tunisia, Algeria, and Morocco

3.Horn of Africa: Ethiopia, Eritrea, and parts of Somalia

4.Central Asia: Uzbekistan, Kazakhstan, Tajikistan, and parts of Afghanistan

5.South Asia: Sindh region (present-day Pakistan) and parts of India

6.Iberian Peninsula (Spain and Portugal)

7.Parts of France and Italy

This rapid expansion was due to various factors, including:

1.Military conquests

2.Trade and cultural exchange

3.Missionary work and conversion

4.Migration and settlement of Arab tribes

By the end of the 8th century CE, Islam had become a dominant religion in many regions, and its influence continued to spread in subsequent centuries.

At that time, i.e. during the 7th-8th centuries CE, the western border-land of India was dominated by several powerful Hindu kingdoms. The kingdom of Kapisa was a kingdom located in the north-western part of the Indian subcontinent, in present-day Afghanistan and Pakistan. The kingdom of Sindhu or Sind (also known as Sindh) was a real kingdom located in the southern part of the region, in present-day Pakistan.

It's worth noting that the region was also home to other kingdoms and tribes, and the political landscape was complex and fluid.

As mentioned in the beginning, around 700 CE, Muslim armies had already expanded Islam's reach from Arabia to the Middle East, North Africa, and Central Asia. The Arab invaders had conquered Persia (modern-day Iran) in the 7th century CE and had established a vast empire. The Umayyad Caliphate, which ruled the Islamic empire at that time, set its sights on the Indian subcontinent. There, they attempted to invade India, particularly the Sindh region, as early as the 8th century CE.

Prior to that, the first Arab invasion of India occurred in 636 CE, during the reign of Caliph Umar, but it was not a full-scale attack. Arab general Uthman ibn Abi al-As led a small expedition to the Sindh region (modern-day Pakistan and north-western India). The expedition was not a decisive victory, and the Arabs withdrew after a brief encounter with local forces.

The first major Arab invasion of India occurred in 711 CE, led by Muhammad bin Qasim, who conquered the Sindh region and Multan.

Some notable Indian rulers who fought against Muslim invaders from 700 CE onwards were:

1.King Dahir of Sindh (663-712 CE):Fought against the Arab invader Muhammad bin Qasim.

2.Nagabhata I of Gurjara-Pratihara (730-760 CE):Defeated the Arab invaders and protected his kingdom.

3.Bappa Rawal of Mewar (8th century CE): Fought against the Arab invaders and established the Mewar kingdom.

4.Mihir Bhoj of Gurjara-Pratihara (836-885 CE):Fought against the Muslim invaders and expanded his kingdom.

5.Mahipala I of Gurjara-Pratihara (913-943 CE):Defeated the Muslim invaders and protected his kingdom.

6.Paramara Bhoja of Malwa (1010-1055 CE): Fought against the Muslim invaders and expanded his kingdom.

7.Vijayaditya of Chalukya (696-733 CE): Defeated the Arab invaders and protected his kingdom.

8.Raja Durgalal of Sindh (10th century CE): Fought against the Muslim invaders and protected his kingdom.

9.Prithviraj Chauhan of Ajmer (1166-1192 CE):Fought against Muhammad Ghori and lost, leading to Muslim rule in Delhi.

10.Rana Hammir of Mewar (1326-1364 CE): Fought against the Muslim invaders and expanded his kingdom.

11.Maharana Pratap of Mewar (1540-1597 CE) fought against the Mughal Empire.

Since the Rajput empire, which comprised various kingdoms and dynasties, existed in India during that period, there were battles and skirmishes between Arab armies and Rajput kingdoms, such as the Battle of Rajasthan in 738 CE, where the Rajputs repelled an Arab invasion.

The Rajput empire, which comprised various kingdoms and dynasties, played a significant role in resisting Arab invasions and expansions into India. The Battle of Rajasthan in 738 CE is a notable example of Rajput bravery and military prowess.

Some key battles fought by the Rajputs to resist Arab invasions were:

-A battle took place in 738 CE, when the Arab armies, led by Junaid ibn Abd al-Rahman al-Murri, invaded Rajasthan.

-The Rajput kingdoms, led by the Chauhan dynasty, united to repel the Arab invasion.

-The battle was fierce, but the Rajputs emerged victorious, forcing the Arabs to retreat.

-This battle marked a significant turning point in Indian history, as it halted Arab expansion into India and secured Rajput dominance in the region.

Other notable battles and skirmishes between Arab armies and Rajput kingdoms include:

-The Battle of Kayatha (730 CE):Rajputs defeated the Arabs, led by Al-Hajjaj ibn Yusuf.

-The Battle of Navsari (739 CE):Rajputs repelled an Arab invasion, led by Amr ibn al-As.

-The Battle of Bahraich (761 CE):Rajputs defeated the Arabs, led by Al-Mansur.

These battles demonstrate the Rajputs' determination to protect their territories and culture from foreign invasions, and their military prowess in resisting Arab expansions into India.

Nonetheless, the Arab invaders did not succeed in establishing a lasting presence in India beyond the Sindh region until much later, when the Delhi Sultanate was established in the 13th century CE.

Emperor Mihir Bhoj Pratihara (836-885 CE) was a powerful ruler of the Gurjara-Pratihara dynasty, which dominated northern India, encompassing present-day Uttar Pradesh, Madhya Pradesh, Rajasthan, and parts of Punjab and Haryana. During his reign, Mihir Bhoj implemented notable military campaigns, administrative reforms, and cultural achievements. He expanded the empire, established trade and cultural relations with neighbouring kingdoms, and patronized art, literature, and architecture. Under his leadership, the Gurjara-Pratihara kingdom reached its zenith, and Mihir Bhoj is regarded as one of the most important rulers of the dynasty.

Mihir Bhoj's reign coincided with the early stages of Islamic expansion into India, particularly during the Abbasid Caliphate (750-1258 CE). While his military campaigns and political strategies focused on maintaining territorial integrity and defending against external threats, they also had the effect of limiting Islamic expansion in his kingdom. He fought against Islamic forces, including the Abbasid Caliphate's governors in Sindh and Arab armies in Gujarat, to consolidate his power and protect his kingdom.

Overall, Mihir Bhoj's efforts were geared towards strengthening his kingdom, rather than specifically targeting the spread of Islam. Nevertheless, his military campaigns played a significant role in shaping the regional political landscape and influencing the trajectory of Islamic expansion in India.

Despite repeated attempts, the Arab invaders were unable to establish a lasting presence in India beyond the Sindh region until the 13th century CE, when the Delhi Sultanate was established.

The Arab conquest of Sindh in 712 CE, led by Muhammad bin Qasim, marked the beginning of Muslim rule in India. However, their expansion beyond Sindh was limited, and they faced fierce resistance from Indian kingdoms, including the Rajputs.

For several centuries, the Arab presence in India was largely confined to the Sindh region, which became a province of the Abbasid Caliphate. It wasn't until the 13th century CE, with the establishment of the Delhi Sultanate by Qutb-ud-din Aibak, that Muslim rule expanded beyond Sindh and into the Indo-Gangetic Plain.

The Delhi Sultanate marked the beginning of a new era of Muslim rule in India, which would eventually lead to the establishment of the Mughal Empire in the 16th century CE. However, it's important to note that the Arab invaders' initial attempts to expand into India were met with significant resistance, and their early conquests were limited to the Sindh region.

In 711 CE, Arab general Muhammad bin Qasim invaded modern-day Pakistan and north-western India, conquering the Sindh region and Multan. However, this initial invasion was not followed by a full-scale conquest of India.

For the next several centuries, Muslim rulers and invaders, such as Mahmud of Ghazni (971-1030 CE) and Muhammad of Ghor (1140-1206 CE), launched periodic raids and campaigns into Indian territories. These invasions were motivated by a mix of political, economic, and religious factors, including:

1.Expansion of Islamic rule and influence

2.Wealth and resources, such as India's rich textiles, spices, and precious stones

3.Strategic trade routes and access to the Indian Ocean

However, it wasn't until the 13th century CE, with the establishment of the Delhi Sultanate (1206-1526 CE), that Muslim rule became more firmly established in India. The Delhi Sultanate and later the Mughal Empire (1526-1858 CE) went on to shape Indian history, culture, and society for centuries to come.

Chapter 3

Impact on Hinduism of Islamic Conquests

Hinduism has a long and complex history that spans thousands of years, and its influence and popularity have waxed and waned over time.

When Islam emerged in the 7th century CE, Hinduism was still a dominant religion in the Indian subcontinent. Here's a brief overview:

-Hinduism's golden age is often considered to be the Gupta period (320-550 CE), which saw significant cultural, scientific, and philosophical advancements.

-By the 7th century CE, Hinduism had already faced challenges from other religions like Buddhism and Jainism, and its influence had declined somewhat.

-However, Hinduism was still widely practiced, and its traditions, temples, and scriptures continued to thrive.

-The arrival of Islam in India, particularly with the Arab conquest of Sindh in 711 CE, marked the beginning of a new era of cultural and religious exchange.

-Over time, Islam spread throughout the Indian subcontinent, and Hinduism faced new challenges, including conversions, temple destructions, and theological debates.

Arab conquest of Sindh

The Arab conquest of Sindh, a region in modern-day Pakistan, occurred in the early 8th century CE. Here's a brief overview:

-711 CE:Arab general Muhammad bin Qasim, aged 17, leads an army from Basra, Iraq, to Sindh, with the aim of spreading Islam and expanding the Umayyad Caliphate.

-712 CE:Bin Qasim defeats the Hindu ruler of Sindh, Raja Dahir, in the Battle of Debal, near modern-day Karachi.

-713 CE:Bin Qasim captures the strategic city of Nerun (modern-day Hyderabad, Sindh) and makes it his capital.

-714 CE:Bin Qasim conquers the city of Brahmanabad (modern-day Mansura, Sindh) and incorporates Sindh into the Umayyad Caliphate.

-715 CE:Bin Qasim is recalled to Iraq and later executed, but his legacy establishes Islam in Sindh.

The Arab conquest of Sindh had significant consequences:

-Introduction of Islam to the Indian subcontinent

-Establishment of the first Muslim dynasty in India, the Umayyad Caliphate

-Cultural exchange and blending of Arab, Persian, and local traditions

-Shift in the regional balance of power, influencing the course of Indian history

The Arab conquest of Sindh was not a single event, but rather a process of expansion and consolidation that occurred over several decades.

After 715 CE, several Muslim invasions and conquests took place in the Indian subcontinent, including:

-736-740 CE:Umayyad Caliphate's campaigns in Kashmir and Punjab

-775-785 CE:Abbasid Caliphate's campaigns in Sindh and Punjab

-1000-1027 CE:Mahmud of Ghazni's invasions of North India, including Delhi, Punjab, and Uttar Pradesh

-1173-1206 CE:Muhammad of Ghor's conquests of North India, including Delhi, Ajmer, and Bengal

-1206-1290 CE:Delhi Sultanate's expansion across North India

-1325-1351 CE:Muhammad bin Tughlaq's campaigns in South India

These invasions and conquests led to:

-Expansion of Muslim rule across the Indian subcontinent

-Establishment of Muslim dynasties, such as the Delhi Sultanate and the Mughal Empire

-Conversion of some Indians to Islam

-Cultural exchange and blending of Muslim, Persian, and local traditions

-Impact on Hindu and Buddhist communities, including temple destruction and forced conversions

Key figures involved in these invasions and conquests include:

-Mahmud of Ghazni

-Muhammad of Ghor

-Qutb-ud-din Aibak

-Iltutmish

-Muhammad bin Tughlaq

-Babur (founder of the Mughal Empire)

It is to be noted that these invasions and conquests were not uniform and had varying impacts on different regions and communities.

Hindus who helped Muslims in their conquests on Indian Territories

Unfortunately, there were instances where some Hindus collaborated with or assisted Muslim conquerors in their campaigns against other Hindu kingdoms and territories. Here are a few examples:

1.Raja Dahir's own brother, Jaisimha, defected to the Arab side during the conquest of Sindh in 711 CE.

2.In the 10th century, the Hindu king of Kannauj, Jaipal, formed an alliance with the Muslim ruler of Ghazni, Mahmud, against other Hindu kingdoms.

3.In the 12th century, the Hindu king of Bengal, Lakshman Sen, collaborated with the Muslim ruler of Delhi, Qutb-ud-din Aibak, against other Hindu kingdoms.

4.In the 13th century, the Hindu king of Kashi, Jaichand Rathor, formed an alliance with the Muslim ruler of Delhi, Muhammad bin Tughlaq, against other Hindu kingdoms.

5.Some Hindu rulers, like the Tomara rulers of Delhi, even converted to Islam and became vassals of the Muslim rulers.

Notable Hindu collaborators include:

1.Jaisimha (Raja Dahir's brother)

2.Jaipal (Hindu king of Kannauj)

3.Lakshman Sen (Hindu king of Bengal)

4.Jaichand Rathor (Hindu king of Kashi)

5.Man Singh Tomar (Hindu ruler who converted to Islam and became a vassal of the Delhi Sultanate)

Please note that these instances of collaboration were often driven by political expediency, self-preservation, or personal gain, rather than a desire to aid Muslim conquests. Additionally, many Hindus resisted Muslim invasions and conquests, and some even formed alliances to counter them.

Chapter 4

Conversions in Muslim Rule

The Muslim invasions of India were a complex phenomenon with multiple motivations. While the spread of Islam was one of the factors, it was not the only reason. Here are some additional reasons:

1.Territorial expansion and conquest: Muslim rulers sought to expand their dominions and control the lucrative trade routes of India.

2.Wealth and resources:India was known for its wealth, including gold, jewels, silk, and spices. Muslim invaders sought to capture these resources.

3.Power and prestige:Conquering India gave Muslim rulers power, prestige, and legitimacy in their own region.

4.Diffusion of Islamic culture:Along with religion, the Muslim invasion brought Islamic culture, architecture, literature, and art, which blended with existing Indian culture.

5.Weakening Hindu kingdoms:Some Muslim rulers sought to weaken or destroy Hindu kingdoms to prevent future threats to their rule.

The spread of Islam was a significant factor, especially during the initial invasions. However, over time, conversion to Islam occurred more for social, economic, and political reasons than direct coercion. Many Hindus converted to Islam to:

1.Avoid taxes and restrictions:Muslims were exempt from certain taxes and restrictions.

2.Improve social status:Conversion to Islam could offer greater social mobility and opportunities.

3.Join the ruling class:Some Hindus converted to join the Muslim ruling class and participate in power.

Chronology

It's essential to note that the Muslim invasion of India was a complex process with multiple motivations and consequences.

After the Muslim invasion of India in 711 CE, conversions to Islam occurred in various forms and phases. Here are some key aspects:

1.Initial conversions (711-1000 CE):During the initial Arab conquests, some Hindus converted to Islam, particularly in the Sindh region. These conversions were often voluntary, with some Hindus attracted to Islam's message and the political and economic benefits of being part of the ruling class.

2.Forced conversions (1000-1300 CE):As Muslim rule expanded, forced conversions became more common. Hindus were coerced into converting to Islam, especially during the Ghaznavid and Ghurid invasions. Many temples were destroyed, and Hindus were forced to choose between conversion or death.

3.Mass conversions (1300-1500 CE):During the Delhi Sultanate period, mass conversions occurred, particularly in the Punjab and Bengal regions. Many Hindus converted to Islam to escape the jizya tax, avoid social discrimination, or gain political and economic advantages.

4.Sufi influence (1500-1700 CE):Sufi mystics played a significant role in converting Hindus to Islam, especially in the rural areas. Sufis emphasized the universal message of love and equality, attracting many Hindus to Islam.

5.Mughal era (1526-1756 CE):During the Mughal period, conversions continued, with some emperors like Aurangzeb actively promoting Islam. However, other emperors like Akbar and Jahangir adopted more tolerant policies, allowing Hindus to practice their faith freely.

Notable examples of conversions to Islam include:

1.Malik Kafur:A Hindu convert who became a powerful general in the Delhi Sultanate army.

2.Ziauddin Barani:A Hindu convert who became a renowned historian and political advisor to the Delhi Sultans.

3.Salim Chishti:A Hindu convert who became a revered Sufi saint and spiritual advisor to the Mughal emperor Akbar.

Keep in mind that conversions to Islam during this period were complex and multifaceted, driven by various factors, including political, social, economic, and spiritual motivations.

Forced conversions

During the Mughal rule period (1526-1756 CE), there were instances of forced conversions to Islam, particularly during the reign of certain emperors. Here are some examples:

1.Aurangzeb (1658-1707 CE):Aurangzeb, a devout Muslim, implemented policies aimed at converting Hindus to Islam. He:

-Imposed the jizya tax on non-Muslims, which led to forced conversions.

-Destroyed Hindu temples and built mosques in their place.

-Forced Hindu nobles and officials to convert to Islam.

2.Shah Jahan (1627-1658 CE):Shah Jahan, Aurangzeb's father, also promoted conversions to Islam. He:

-Offered incentives, such as land grants and tax exemptions, to Hindus who converted.

-Encouraged interfaith marriages between Muslims and Hindus.

3.Akbar (1556-1605 CE):Although Akbar is known for his religious tolerance, there were instances of forced conversions during his reign also. He:

-Encouraged conversions to Islam, especially among the nobility.

-Imposed the jizya tax on non-Muslims, leading to some forced conversions.

Forced conversions were often carried out through:

i)Coercion and violence:Non-Muslims were threatened, attacked, or killed if they refused to convert.

ii)Economic incentives:Converts were offered land, money, or tax exemptions.

iii)Social pressure:Converts were given higher social status, and non-Muslims faced discrimination.

Notable examples of forced conversions include:

a)Kashmiri Pandits:Many Kashmiri Pandits were forced to convert to Islam during the Mughal period.

b)Rajput nobles:Some Rajput nobles were forced to convert to Islam to maintain their positions and privileges.

c)Hindu artisans:Hindu artisans, such as weavers and craftsmen, were forced to convert to Islam to continue their work.

It's essential to note that not all Mughal emperors engaged in forced conversions, and some, like Akbar, promoted religious tolerance. However, forced conversions did occur during the Mughal period, and their impact is still felt in Indian society today.

Chapter 5

Destruction of Temples

Though temples are stated to have been destroyed in India before Muslim invasions also but the intensity of destruction during Muslim rule was much higher than in earlier periods as the temples are not believed to have been destroyed owing to religious persecution but owing to enmity resulting in clashes amongst other reasons, such as:

1.Religious conflicts:

-Buddhist-Hindu conflicts:Differences in beliefs and practices led to destruction of temples.

-Jain-Hindu conflicts:Competing religious ideologies resulted in temple destruction.

2.Political rivalries:

-Dynastic conflicts:Rival Hindu kingdoms and dynasties clashed, leading to temple destruction.

-Regional power struggles:Local chieftains and rulers destroyed temples to assert dominance.

3.Economic motivations:

-Plunder and loot:Temples were destroyed for their wealth, treasures, and valuable resources.

-Land appropriation:Temples were destroyed to acquire land for agriculture, settlements, or other purposes.

4.Tribal raids:

-Tribal groups like Hunas, Shakas, and Pahlavas raided temples for resources and strategic advantages.

5.Iconoclasm:

-Some rulers and sects rejected idol worship, leading to destruction of temples and icons.

6.Natural disasters:

-Earthquakes, floods, and other natural disasters damaged or destroyed temples.

7.Neglect and abandonment:

-Temples were left to decay or were abandoned due to changing religious practices or shifting population centres.

These reasons are not exhaustive, and the motivations behind temple destruction were often complex and multifaceted. Additionally, many temples were rebuilt, restored, or renovated over time, reflecting the resilience of Indian religious traditions.

Some examples of destruction of temples before Muslim invasions are:

1.Buddhist-Hindu conflicts (3rd century BCE - 7th century CE):

-Buddhist rulers like Pushyamitra Shunga (185-151 BCE) and Vasishtha (1st century CE) destroyed Hindu temples.

-Hindu rulers like Samudragupta (335-375 CE) and Chandragupta II (375-415 CE) destroyed Buddhist monasteries and temples.

2.Jain-Hindu conflicts (5th century BCE - 12th century CE):

-Jain rulers like Kharavela (193-161 BCE) destroyed Hindu temples in Odisha.

-Hindu rulers like the Pallavas (275-897 CE) destroyed Jain temples in Tamil Nadu.

3.Tribal conflicts and raids (pre-10th century CE):

-Tribal groups like the Hunas, Shakas, and Pahlavas raided and destroyed temples in various regions.

4.Hindu dynastic conflicts (pre-10th century CE):

-Rival Hindu kingdoms and dynasties clashed, leading to temple destruction, such as the Chalukyas vs. Pallavas (6th-8th century CE).

However, it's essential to note that:

-The scale and frequency of temple destruction increased significantly during the Muslim invasions and rule.

-The motivations behind temple destruction varied, including religious, political, and economic factors.

-Many temples were rebuilt, restored, or renovated over time, reflecting the resilience and adaptability of Indian religious traditions.

However, the scale of destruction of Hindu temples due to Muslim invasions and in Muslim reigns was manifold as compared to the period before Muslims came to India. A brief overview of the destruction of temples in India as a result of Muslim invasions is as under:

i)Early Islamic invasions (700-1200 CE):

-711-715 CE:Muhammad bin Qasim's destruction of temples in Sindh

-1000-1027 CE:Mahmud of Ghazni's raids on Somnath, Mathura, and other temples

ii)Delhi Sultanate (1206-1526 CE):

-1192-1210 CE:Qutb-ud-din Aibak's destruction of temples in Delhi and Ajmer

-1297-1316 CE:Alauddin Khalji's destruction of temples in Chidambaram and Madurai

-1330-1340 CE:Muhammad bin Tughlaq's destruction of temples in Gujarat and Maharashtra

iii)Mughal Empire (1526-1858 CE):

-1526-1530 CE:Babur's destruction of temples in Ayodhya and Varanasi

-1658-1707 CE:Aurangzeb's widespread destruction of temples, including the Kashi Vishwanath Temple

iv)Regional Islamic kingdoms (1200-1800 CE):

-1204 CE:Bakhtiyar Khalji's destruction of temples in Bengal

-1411-1442 CE:Ahmad Shah I's destruction of temples in Gujarat

-1565 CE:Bahmani Sultanate's destruction of temples in Vijayanagara

v)Late Islamic rule and British colonial era (1700-1857 CE):

-1750-1800 CE:Maratha-Muslim conflicts and temple destruction

-1800-1857 CE:British colonial era, during which some temples were destroyed or desecrated

It is to be noted that these periods are approximate and overlapping, and the destruction of temples was a recurring phenomenon throughout Indian history.

Chapter 6

British Rule

During British rule in India (1757-1947), Hinduism faced significant challenges and decline in various aspects:

1.Christian missionary activities:

Conversion efforts and criticism of Hinduism led to a decline in Hindu population.

Christian missionary activities during British rule in India (1757-1947) played a significant role in the decline of Hinduism, particularly through:

1.Conversion efforts:

-Missionaries actively converted Hindus to Christianity, especially among lower castes and tribal communities.

-Converts were often attracted by promises of education, employment, and social mobility.

2.Criticism of Hinduism:

-Missionaries and British colonialists criticized Hinduism as "heathen," "idolatrous," and "backward."

-They portrayed Hinduism as inferior to Christianity, leading to a decline in Hindu self-esteem and cultural confidence.

3.Education and literature:

-Missionaries established schools and colleges, teaching Western values and Christianity.

-They published literature criticizing Hinduism and promoting Christianity, influencing Hindu intellectuals and youth.

4.Social and economic incentives:

- Converts received preferential treatment in education, employment, and government jobs.

-Missionaries provided economic aid, healthcare, and social services, attracting Hindus to convert.

5.Targeting vulnerable groups:

Missionaries focused on converting lower castes, tribals, and outcastes, exploiting their social and economic vulnerabilities.

These activities led to a decline in Hindu population, particularly among:

1.Lower castes and tribals

2.Urban educated classes

3.Regions with significant missionary presence (e.g., South India, Northeast India)

However, it's essential to note that:

i)Many Hindus resisted conversion efforts and maintained their faith.

ii)Hindu reform movements emerged to counter missionary activities and revitalize Hinduism.

iii)The Indian independence movement and nationalist leaders like Swami Vivekananda and Mahatma Gandhi challenged missionary activities and promoted Hinduism.

2.British education system:

The British education system, introduced in India during colonial rule (1757-1947), had a profound impact on traditional Hindu learning and practices, leading to erosion in several ways:

i)Western curriculum:

-Emphasis on Western subjects like English, mathematics, science, and history replaced traditional Hindu subjects like Sanskrit, philosophy, and scriptures.

-Western values and world view were embedded in the curriculum, influencing Hindu students' perspectives.

ii)Displacement of traditional institutions:

-British schools and colleges replaced traditional Hindu institutions like gurukuls, pathshalas, and madrasas.

-Traditional Hindu teachers and scholars were marginalized or replaced by Western-educated teachers.

iii)Decline of Sanskrit and classical languages:

-Sanskrit, the language of Hindu scriptures and classical texts, was gradually replaced by English as the language of education.

-Other classical languages like Tamil, Telugu, and Kannada also declined in importance.

iv)Loss of traditional knowledge and practices:

-Traditional Hindu knowledge systems like Ayurveda, Jyotish, and Yoga were marginalized or replaced by Western sciences.

-Traditional practices like pujas, rituals, and festivals were seen as "superstitious" or "backward."

v)Cultural alienation:

-Western education created a cultural disconnect between Hindus and their heritage.

-Hindus were encouraged to adopt Western values, customs, and practices, leading to a decline in traditional Hindu practices.

vi)Brain drain and cultural assimilation:

-Talented Hindu students were drawn to Western education and values, leading to a brain drain from traditional Hindu institutions.

-Many Hindus assimilated into Western culture, adopting Western customs, practices, and values.

vii)Impact on Hindu identity:

-The British education system contributed to a decline in Hindu identity and cultural confidence.

-Hindus began to question their own traditions and values, leading to a sense of cultural inferiority.

However, this is to be noted that:

a)Many Hindus resisted the erosion of traditional learning and practices.

b)Hindu reform movements emerged to revitalize traditional Hindu education and practices.

c)India's independence movement and nationalist leaders like Swami Vivekananda and Mahatma Gandhi promoted Hinduism and traditional learning.

The colonization of India by European powers had a profound impact on the country's cultural and educational landscape. The imposition of Western education and values led to a decline in traditional Hindu learning and practices, resulting in a sense of cultural inferiority among some Hindus. However, it's crucial to acknowledge the following:

i)Resistance and resilience:Many Hindus continued to practice and preserve their traditional learning and customs, despite the colonial efforts to suppress them.

ii)Reform movements:Hindu reform movements emerged, aiming to revitalize and modernize traditional Hindu education and practices, making them relevant to the changing times.

iii)Nationalist revival:India's independence movement and leaders like Swami Vivekananda and Mahatma Gandhi played a significant role in promoting Hinduism and traditional learning, helping to restore national pride and cultural identity.

These factors helped counterbalance the erosion of traditional Hindu culture and learning, ensuring its continued relevance and significance in modern India.

Some notable Hindu reform movements include:

-Arya Samaj (1875)

-Brahmo Samaj (1828)

-Ramakrishna Mission (1897)

-Hindu Mahasabha (1915)

These movements aimed to reform and revitalize Hinduism, promoting education, social reform, and cultural revival.

3.Social reforms:

Britishers initiated reforms, such as the abolition of Sati and child marriage, challenging traditional Hindu customs.

British-initiated social reforms in India, particularly during the 19th century, aimed to modernize and Westernize Hindu society. While these reforms addressed certain social evils, they also challenged traditional Hindu customs and practices, leading to a decline in Hinduism's influence:

i)Abolition of Sati (1829):

Sati, the practice of widow immolation, was banned, but this also led to the criminalization of Hindu priests and the erosion of traditional Hindu rituals.

ii)Child Marriage Restraint Act (1929):

Child marriage was restricted, but this also led to the interference in traditional Hindu family and social structures.

iii)Widow Remarriage Act (1856):

Hindu widows were allowed to remarry, but this challenged traditional Hindu norms and customs surrounding widowhood.

iv)Caste Disabilities Removal Act (1850):

This Act aimed to remove legal disabilities faced by lower castes, but it also undermined the traditional Hindu caste system.

v)Hindu Women's Right to Property Act (1937):

Hindu women were granted property rights, but this challenged traditional Hindu laws and customs governing inheritance and property.

These reforms, although well-intentioned, had unintended consequences:

a)Erosion of traditional Hindu authority:

British reforms undermined the authority of Hindu priests, scholars, and community leaders.

b)Cultural imperialism:

British values and practices were imposed upon Hindu society, leading to cultural homogenization.

c)Loss of traditional practices:

Reforms led to the decline of traditional Hindu practices, rituals, and customs.

d)Hindu-Muslim divide:

Reforms created divisions between Hindus and Muslims, as Muslims were exempt from some reforms, leading to a sense of separate identities.

e)Backlash and resistance:

Some Hindus resisted reforms, leading to a backlash against British rule and Western influences.

These social reforms, while addressing certain social evils, also contributed to the decline of Hinduism's influence and the erosion of traditional Hindu customs and practices.

4.Economic changes:

British economic policies led to poverty, landlessness, and migration, affecting Hindu religious practices.

British economic policies in India, particularly during the 18th and 19th centuries, had far-reaching consequences for Hindu society, leading to:

i)Deindustrialization:

-British policies led to the decline of traditional Indian industries, such as textiles and handicrafts.

-Hindu artisans and craftsmen lost their livelihoods, leading to poverty and urban migration.

ii)Land reforms:

British land reforms, such as the Permanent Settlement of 1793, led to:

-Land grabbing by British officials and zamindars (landlords).

-Displacement of Hindu peasants and small landholders.

-Increased landlessness and poverty.

iii)Agricultural exploitation:

-British policies focused on cash crops for export, rather than food crops for local consumption.

-Hindu peasants were forced to grow crops like indigo, tea, and cotton, leading to:

-Soil degradation.

-Decreased food security.

-Increased debt and poverty.

iv)Migration and urbanization:

-Poverty and landlessness led to mass migration to cities, disrupting traditional Hindu social structures.

-Urbanization eroded traditional Hindu practices, as people adapted to new environments and cultures.

v)Economic dependence:

-British policies created economic dependence on British goods and industries.

-Hindu entrepreneurs and traders were marginalized, leading to a decline in traditional Hindu commercial activities.

These economic changes affected Hindu religious practices in several ways:

a)Decline of traditional rituals and ceremonies.

b)Reduced patronage for Hindu temples and institutions.

c)Decreased observance of traditional festivals and customs.

d)Increased conversion to Christianity, as missionaries offered economic aid and education.

e)Erosion of traditional Hindu values and social structures.

The economic impact of British policies on Hindu society was devastating, leading to widespread poverty, landlessness, and cultural disruption.

5.Caste system:

British colonial policies and Christian missionary activities contributed to the decline of the traditional caste system in several ways:

i)Critique of caste:

-British colonialists and Christian missionaries criticized the caste system as "oppressive" and "backward".

-They portrayed caste as a major obstacle to Indian progress and modernization.

ii)Legal reforms:

-British laws, such as the Caste Disabilities Removal Act (1850), aimed to remove legal disabilities faced by lower castes.

-However, these reforms also undermined the traditional caste system's social and economic structures.

iii)Education and conversion:

Christian missionaries provided education and conversion opportunities to lower castes, leading to:

-Social mobility and escape from traditional caste roles.

-Erosion of traditional caste identities and practices.

iv)Colonial administration:

British colonial administration:

-Disrupted traditional caste-based governance and leadership.

-Imposed Western-style administration, further eroding caste structures.

v)Economic changes:

British economic policies:

-Created new economic opportunities, leading to social mobility and changes in traditional caste occupations.

-Disrupted traditional caste-based economic structures and relationships.

vi)Social reform movements:

-Indian social reformers, influenced by Western ideas, campaigned against caste and promoted social reform.

-Movements like the Brahmo Samaj and Arya Samaj aimed to modernize and rationalize Hindu society, further eroding traditional caste structures.

These factors contributed to the decline of the traditional caste system, leading to:

a)Erosion of traditional caste identities and practices.

b)Changes in social and economic structures.

c)Increased social mobility and modernization.

d)Decline of traditional caste-based governance and leadership.

e)Increased conversion to Christianity and other religions.

However, it's essential to note that the caste system remains a complex and persistent aspect of Indian society, with ongoing debates and efforts towards reform and social justice.

6.Urbanization and modernization:

Rapid urbanization and modernization in India during the British colonial era and post-independence period led to a decline in traditional Hindu practices and values in several ways:

i)Cultural displacement:

-Urbanization led to the displacement of traditional Hindu cultural practices and values.

-Modernization introduced Western cultural influences, eroding traditional Hindu customs.

ii)Changing lifestyles:

-Urbanization brought changes in lifestyle, occupation, and social interactions.

-Traditional Hindu practices, such as daily puja (worship) and festivals, became less relevant.

iii)Education and secularization:

-Modern education emphasized secularism and Western values.

-Traditional Hindu knowledge and practices were marginalized.

iv)Media and globalization:

-Globalization and media exposure introduced Western values and cultural practices.

-Traditional Hindu values and practices were challenged by modern ideas and lifestyles.

v)Changing family structures:

-Urbanization led to nuclear families, replacing traditional joint families.

-Traditional Hindu family values and practices, such as respect for elders, declined.

vi)Increased individualism:

-Modernization emphasized individualism, leading to a decline in community-oriented traditional Hindu practices.

vii)Decline of traditional occupations:

-Urbanization led to the decline of traditional Hindu occupations, such as artisans and craftsmen.

-Traditional skills and knowledge were lost.

viii)Changing attitudes towards rituals:

-Modernization led to a decline in the importance of traditional Hindu rituals and ceremonies.

-Rituals were seen as outdated or superstitious.

These factors contributed to a decline in traditional Hindu practices and values, leading to:

a)Erosion of traditional Hindu identity.

b)Changes in social and cultural structures.

c)Increased adoption of Western values and practices.

d)Decline of traditional Hindu knowledge and skills.

e)Changes in family structures and values.

However, it's essential to note that traditional Hindu practices and values continue to evolve and adapt to modernization and urbanization, with many Hindus finding ways to balance tradition and modernity.

7.Hindu-Muslim divide:

British policies and historical events, such as the Partition of India, exacerbated Hindu-Muslim tensions, affecting Hinduism's social and political influence.

The Hindu-Muslim divide was exacerbated by British policies and historical events, leading to a decline in Hinduism's social and political influence:

i)Divide and Rule:

-British colonialists exploited existing Hindu-Muslim tensions to maintain control.

-They created separate electorates, reserved seats, and encouraged communal politics.

ii)Partition of India (1947):

-The violent partition led to massive displacement, bloodshed, and trauma.

-It created a permanent sense of mistrust and hostility between Hindus and Muslims.

iii)British policies and legislation:

-The British introduced laws like the Muslim Personal Law (Shariat) Application Act (1937).

-This created separate legal frameworks for Hindus and Muslims, reinforcing communal divisions.

iv)Historical events:

-The Moplah Rebellion (1921), the Direct Action Day (1946), and other incidents fuelled Hindu-Muslim tensions.

-These events were often exploited by British colonialists to justify their rule.

v)Communal politics:

-The British encouraged communal politics, allowing Muslim leaders to demand separate rights and representation.

-This led to the rise of Muslim nationalism and the eventual creation of Pakistan.

vi)Post-independence tensions:

-The Indo-Pakistani Wars (1947, 1965, 1971) and the Kashmir dispute maintained tensions.

-Hindu-Muslim riots and violence continued, affecting social cohesion.

These factors contributed to:

a)Erosion of Hindu-Muslim unity.

b)Decline of Hinduism's social and political influence.

c)Rise of Hindu nationalism and communalism.

d)Increased polarization and violence.

e)Challenges to India's secular fabric.

However, in spite of this many Hindus and Muslims continued to coexist peacefully, and efforts towards reconciliation and communal harmony have been ongoing.

8.Lack of patronage:

British rule ended traditional royal patronage for Hindu temples and institutions, leading to a decline in their maintenance and upkeep.

The lack of patronage during British rule had a significant impact on Hindu temples and institutions:

i)End of royal patronage:

-British colonialism abolished the traditional system of royal patronage for Hindu temples and institutions.

-This meant that temples no longer received funding, protection, and support from local rulers.

ii)Decline of temple maintenance:

-Without patronage, temples suffered from neglect, disrepair, and abandonment.

-Many temples were left to decay, and their upkeep became a challenge.

iii)Loss of traditional revenue streams:

-British rule disrupted traditional revenue streams, such as land grants and donations.

-Temples struggled to maintain their financial stability.

iv)Shift to British administration:

-British authorities took control of temple administration, imposing Western-style management.

-This led to a disconnect between temples and their traditional communities.

v)Decline of priestly classes:

-The loss of patronage and revenue affected the livelihoods of priests and other temple staff.

-Many priests had to seek alternative employment, leading to a decline in temple rituals and practices.

vi)Impact on Hindu festivals and traditions:

-The decline of temples and institutions affected the observance of Hindu festivals and traditions.

-Many festivals and rituals were simplified, modified, or discontinued.

vii)Cultural heritage neglect:

-The lack of patronage and maintenance led to the neglect of Hindu cultural heritage sites.

-Many historical temples and monuments were left to ruin.

These factors contributed to a decline in Hinduism's cultural and religious heritage, leading to:

a)Erosion of traditional practices and rituals.

b)Decline of temple-based education and learning.

c)Loss of cultural identity and community cohesion.

d)Neglect of historical and cultural heritage sites.

e)Challenges in preserving Hindu traditions and customs.

However, post-independence efforts have been made to revive and restore Hindu temples and institutions, and many organizations and individuals continue to work towards preserving Hindu cultural heritage.

9.Cultural suppression:

British colonialism suppressed Hindu cultural practices, festivals, and traditions, in several ways leading to a decline in their observance as explained hereunder:

i)Disapproval of "heathen" practices:

-British colonialists viewed Hindu practices as "heathen" or "superstitious".

-They discouraged or banned practices deemed "backward" or "uncivilized".

ii)Promotion of Western culture:

-British colonialism promoted Western culture, values, and practices.

-Hindu cultural practices were marginalized or replaced by Western-style education, art, and literature.

iii)Restriction of festivals and traditions:

-British authorities restricted or banned Hindu festivals and traditions deemed "too noisy", "too colourful", or "too superstitious".

-For example, the British banned the Hindu festival of Holi, citing it as a "public nuisance".

iv)Suppression of traditional art and music:

-British colonialism suppressed traditional Hindu art, music, and dance forms.

-Western art and music were promoted as more "refined" and "civilized".

v)Erasure of Hindu history and heritage:

-British colonialism erased or distorted Hindu history and heritage.

-Hindu historical figures and events were marginalized or misrepresented in British-written history books.

vi)Imposition of Western values:

-British colonialism imposed Western values, such as individualism and rationalism.

-Hindu values, such as collectivism and spirituality, were marginalized or suppressed.

vii)Education system:

-The British education system taught Western values, history, and culture.

-Hindu cultural practices, traditions, and history were ignored or marginalized.

These factors contributed to a decline in the observance of Hindu cultural practices, festivals, and traditions, leading to:

a)Erosion of cultural identity.

b)Loss of traditional knowledge and practices.

c)Marginalization of Hindu cultural heritage.

d)Suppression of Hindu creativity and expression.

e)Disconnection from Hindu roots and traditions.

However, India's independence and subsequent cultural revival efforts have helped to revive and reclaim Hindu cultural practices, festivals, and traditions.

It's essential to note that Hinduism also showed resilience and adaptability during this period, with various reform movements and revivals emerging to address these challenges.

Chapter 7

The Bhakti Movement: A Response to Islamic Dominance

The Bhakti movement, which emerged in India between the 6th and 16th centuries, was a response to Islamic dominance in several ways:

1.Counter to Islamic orthodoxy:

Bhakti emphasized personal devotion and love for a deity, contrasting with Islamic emphasis on submission to Allah.

2.Inclusive and tolerant:

Bhakti movement accepted people from all castes and backgrounds, unlike Islamic conversion practices.

3.Revival of Hinduism:

Bhakti helped revive Hinduism during a period of Islamic dominance, promoting Hindu values and practices.

4.Emphasis on emotional connection:

Bhakti focused on emotional connection with the divine, differing from Islamic emphasis on ritual and law.

5.Vernacular languages:

Bhakti literature used vernacular languages, making it accessible to common people, unlike Islamic scriptures in Arabic.

6.Social reform:

Bhakti movement challenged social hierarchies and promoted equality, contrasting with Islamic practices.

7.Spiritual freedom:

Bhakti emphasized individual spiritual experience and freedom, differing from Islamic authoritarianism.

Key figures like Kabir, Mirabai, and Guru Nanak emerged during this period, promoting Bhakti ideals and contributing to India's rich spiritual and cultural heritage.

The Bhakti movement played a significant role in:

i)Preserving Hindu identity

ii)Promoting social reform

iii)Fostering spiritual growth

iv)Encouraging inclusivity and tolerance

v)Countering Islamic dominance

However, it is to be noted that the Bhakti movement was not solely a response to Islamic dominance but also a natural evolution of Hinduism, influenced by various social, cultural, and spiritual factors.

<u>Role of Bhakti saints and their teachings</u>

Bhakti saints played a vital role in shaping the Bhakti movement, emphasizing devotion, love, and surrender to the divine. Their teachings:

i)Emphasized personal devotion:

Saints like Kabir, Mirabai, and Tukaram stressed intense personal devotion to a deity.

ii)Focused on love and surrender:

Teachings emphasized surrendering to the divine, cultivating love, and devotion.

iii)Challenged social hierarchies:

Saints like Ravidas and Kabir criticized caste systems and social inequalities.

iv)Promoted inclusivity:

Bhakti saints welcomed people from all backgrounds, castes, and religions.

v)Used vernacular languages:

Saints composed poetry and songs in local languages, making their teachings accessible.

vi)Encouraged spiritual growth:

Emphasis on personal spiritual experience and growth through devotion.

vii)Critiqued ritualism:

Saints like Kabir and Nanak criticized empty rituals, emphasizing genuine devotion.

Some of the notable Bhakti saints and their teachings:

1. Kabir (1440-1518):

   -Emphasized devotion, love, and surrender.

   -Critiqued social hierarchies and ritualism.

2. Mirabai (1498-1557):

   -Focused on love and devotion to Krishna.

   -Defied social conventions, embracing devotion above all.

3.Guru Nanak (1469-1539):

   -Founded Sikhism, emphasizing devotion, love, and service.

   -Critiqued social inequalities and ritualism.

4.Tukaram (1608-1649):

   -Emphasized devotion, love, and surrender to Vitthala (Krishna).

   -Composed poetry in Marathi, making teachings accessible.

5.Ravidas (1450-1520):

   -Critiqued caste systems and social inequalities.

-Emphasized devotion and love for the divine.

These Bhakti saints and their teachings:

a)Revolutionized Hinduism

b)Promoted social reform

c)Fostered spiritual growth

d)Encouraged inclusivity and tolerance

e)Shaped Indian culture and literature

Their legacy continues to inspire devotion, love, and spiritual growth in millions of people worldwide.

However, while the Bhakti movement did help to revitalize Hinduism and challenge Islamic rule, its impact was limited in many ways as mentioned hereunder:

1.Continued Islamic expansion:Despite the Bhakti movement, Islamic rule continued to expand in India, and many Hindu kingdoms fell to Muslim conquerors.

2.Conversion and Islamization:Many Hindus converted to Islam, either voluntarily or forcibly, leading to a decline in Hindu populations and influence.

3.Limited geographical impact:The Bhakti movement was mainly confined to certain regions, such as the Deccan Plateau and North India, while Islamic rule prevailed in other areas.

4.Internal divisions:Hindu society was fragmented, with internal divisions and caste hierarchies, which hindered a unified response to Islamic rule.

5.Lack of political power:The Bhakti movement was primarily a religious and social movement, lacking the political power to challenge Islamic rule effectively.

But, it's important to note that the Bhakti movement had significant cultural and religious impact, helping to:

i)Preserve Hindu traditions and scriptures

ii)Promote devotional practices and spiritual growth

iii)Inspire resistance against Islamic rule

iv)Foster a sense of Hindu identity and unity

The complex dynamics between the Bhakti movement and Islamic rule in India cannot, therefore, be reduced to a simple narrative of success or failure. Both perspectives have validity, and a nuanced understanding acknowledges the multifaceted nature of this period in Indian history.

Chapter 8

The Decline of Hindu Kingdoms: Political Fragmentation

The decline of Hindu kingdoms and political fragmentation in India occurred due to various factors:

1.External invasions:

-Muslim invasions (11th-16th centuries) led to the decline of Hindu kingdoms like the Gurjara-Pratihara, Vijaynagara, and others.

-Mughal Empire's expansion (16th-18th centuries) further weakened Hindu kingdoms.

2.Internal conflicts:

-Inter-kingdom wars and rivalries weakened Hindu kingdoms, making them vulnerable to external attacks.

-Succession disputes and palace intrigues led to instability.

3.Economic factors:

-Decline of trade and commerce due to external invasions and internal conflicts.

-Economic strain due to excessive taxation and military expenses.

4.Social and cultural factors:

-Caste system rigidity and social hierarchies led to internal divisions.

-Decline of traditional Hindu values and practices.

5.Political fragmentation:

-Breakup of large empires into smaller kingdoms and principalities.

-Regionalism and localism led to political fragmentation.

Key events and dates:

-11th century:Muslim invasions begin, weakening Hindu kingdoms.

-12th century:Delhi Sultanate establishes Muslim rule in North India.

-14th century:Vijaynagara Empire rises in South India, but eventually declines.

-16th century:Mughal Empire expands, conquering most of India.

-17th-18th centuries:Maratha Empire and other regional powers emerge, but eventually decline.

-19th century:British colonial rule establishes itself in India.

Consequences:

-Loss of political power and autonomy for Hindu kingdoms.

-Decline of Hindu culture, art, and architecture.

-Rise of Muslim and British influence in India.

-Eventual colonization of India by the British.

However, Hinduism continued to thrive, and Hindu kingdoms like the Marathas, Sikhs, and others resisted external forces, preserving Hindu culture and traditions.

Role of regional kingdoms and their inability to resist Islamic invasions

Regional kingdoms in India played a significant role in the country's history, but their inability to resist Islamic invasions was due to various factors:

i)Fragmentation:

-Regional kingdoms were fragmented, with each kingdom focused on its own interests.

-This led to a lack of unity and coordination against external threats.

ii)Weak military:

-Regional kingdoms had weak militaries, making them vulnerable to invasions.

-They relied on feudal levies, which were often disorganized and poorly trained.

iii)Internal conflicts:

-Regional kingdoms were often engaged in internal conflicts, weakening their ability to resist external threats.

-Succession disputes, palace intrigues, and regional rivalries distracted from the external threat.

iv)Economic strain:

-Regional kingdoms faced economic strain due to excessive taxation, military expenses, and trade disruptions.

-This limited their ability to invest in military modernization and defence.

v)Lack of strategic alliances:

-Regional kingdoms failed to form strategic alliances to counter the Islamic invasions.

-They often fought individually, allowing the invaders to pick them off one by one.

vi)Technological disparities:

-Islamic invaders had access to superior military technology, such as cavalry and archery.

-Regional kingdoms were often unable to match this technological advantage.

vii)Leadership weaknesses:

-Regional kingdoms often had weak or ineffective leadership.

-This led to poor decision-making and a lack of strategic vision.

Examples of regional kingdoms that failed to resist Islamic invasions include:

a)The Rajput kingdoms of North India (e.g., Delhi, Ajmer, Kanauj)

b)The Deccan kingdoms of South India (e.g., Vijaynagara, Bahmani)

c)The Eastern Indian kingdoms (e.g., Bengal, Bihar)

However, some regional kingdoms did offer significant resistance, such as:

i)The Vijaynagara Empire, which resisted Islamic invasions for over two centuries

ii)The Maratha Empire, which successfully resisted Mughal rule and expanded its territories

iii)The Sikh Kingdom, which resisted Mughal and Afghan invasions and established a powerful empire

These examples demonstrate that while regional kingdoms faced significant challenges, some were able to resist Islamic invasions and even thrive.

Thus, decline of Hindu kingdoms in India led to a decline in Hinduism's influence and practice in several ways:

1.Loss of patronage:

-Hindu kingdoms were traditional patrons of Hindu temples, priests, and scholars.

-Without royal patronage, Hindu institutions struggled to survive.

2.Reduced temple construction and maintenance:

-Hindu kingdoms built and maintained temples, which were centers of Hindu worship and culture.

-With fewer kingdoms, temple construction and maintenance declined.

3.Decreased support for Hindu scholars and priests:

-Hindu kingdoms supported scholars and priests who preserved and transmitted Hindu scriptures and traditions.

-Without royal support, Hindu scholarship and priestly classes declined.

4.Suppression of Hindu festivals and traditions:

-Hindu kingdoms celebrated Hindu festivals and traditions, which were an integral part of Hindu culture.

-With Islamic and British rule, many Hindu festivals and traditions were suppressed or modified.

5.Conversion and proselytization:

-With Hindu kingdoms weakened, Muslim and Christian missionaries gained opportunities to convert Hindus.

-Many Hindus converted to Islam or Christianity, leading to a decline in Hinduism's adherents.

6.Loss of Hindu cultural and artistic heritage:

-Hindu kingdoms patronized Hindu art, architecture, music, and literature.

-With their decline, Hindu cultural and artistic heritage suffered.

7.Disruption of Hindu education and social systems:

-Hindu kingdoms supported traditional Hindu education and social systems.

-With their decline, these systems were disrupted, leading to a decline in Hindu values and practices.

8.Weakening of Hindu identity and community:

-Hindu kingdoms helped maintain Hindu identity and community.

-With their decline, Hindu identity and community were weakened.

Whereas Muslims continued to spread their religion through wars and atrocities and forced conversion on the basis of sword, Christians kept on spreading Christianity through various means, including:

1.Missionary work:Christians traveled to different parts of the world to share the Gospel and establish churches.

2.Evangelism:They shared their faith with others through personal testimonies and preaching.

3.Bible translation:They translated the Bible into various languages to make it accessible to more people.

4.Education:They established schools and universities to teach people about Christianity and other subjects.

5.Charity and social work:They demonstrated their faith through acts of love and service, such as building hospitals, orphanages, and caring for the poor.

6.Apologetics:They defended their faith through reasoning and argumentation, helping to establish Christianity as a credible and rational belief system.

7.Martyrdom:Many Christians willingness to suffer persecution and even death for their faith inspired others and demonstrated the depth of their conviction.

8.Church planting:They established new churches and congregations, creating communities of believers who could support and encourage one another.

9.Print media:They used books, tracts, and other written materials to spread Christian teachings and ideas.

10.Modern technologies:They leveraged technologies like radio, television, internet, and social media to reach a wider audience.

These methods, used over centuries, helped spread Christianity from its origins in the Middle East to become a global religion with millions of followers

All these factors contributed to a decline in Hinduism's influence and practice, making it vulnerable to external influences and challenges. However, Hinduism continued to evolve and adapt, and efforts to revive and preserve Hindu traditions and culture are ongoing.

Chapter 9

Socio-Economic Factors: Caste Rigidity and Economic Decline

Socio-economic factors that contributed to the decline of Hinduism:

1.Poverty and economic instability:

-Limited access to education, healthcare, and economic opportunities.

-Increased vulnerability to conversion and proselytization.

2.Caste system and social hierarchy:

-Rigidity and discrimination led to social and economic exclusion.

-Lower castes and marginalized groups sought alternative religions.

3.Urbanization and modernization:

-Migration to cities led to disconnection from traditional Hindu practices.

-Adoption of Western values and lifestyles eroded Hindu traditions.

4.Education and cultural influence:

-Western-style education emphasized secularism and modernity.

-Cultural influence of British colonialism and Christian missionaries.

5.Demographic changes:

-Decline of Hindu population due to conversion, urbanization, and low birth rates.

-Increased population of other religions, particularly Islam and Christianity.

6.Lack of effective leadership and reform:

-Hindu institutions and leaders failed to adapt to changing times.

-Inability to address social and economic issues.

7.Corruption and mismanagement:

-Misuse of temple funds, corruption, and mismanagement.

-Erosion of trust in Hindu institutions.

8.Globalization and cultural homogenization:

-Increased exposure to global cultures and values.

-Homogenization of cultures, leading to loss of traditional practices.

9.Government policies and laws:

-Post-independence Indian government's secular policies.

-Laws and regulations affecting Hindu temples, education, and practices.

10.Conversion and proselytization:

-Active conversion efforts by Christian and Islamic missionaries.

-Use of economic incentives, education, and healthcare to attract converts.

These socio-economic factors contributed to the decline of Hinduism, but Hinduism has also undergone revival and reform movements, and efforts to preserve and promote Hindu culture and traditions continue.

Caste rigidity, economic decline, and the impact on Hindu society

Caste Rigidity:

1.Social hierarchy: Caste system created a rigid social hierarchy, limiting social mobility.

2.Occupational restrictions:Castes were tied to specific occupations, restricting economic opportunities.

3.Endogamy:Marriage within castes reinforced social boundaries, limiting social interaction.

4.Discrimination:Lower castes faced discrimination, exclusion, and marginalization.

Economic Decline:

i)Agricultural decline:Decline of agriculture led to economic instability for rural communities.

ii)Industrialization:Slow industrialization and lack of job opportunities exacerbated economic struggles.

iii)Urbanization:Migration to cities led to overcrowding, poverty, and social dislocation.

iv)Globalization:Economic liberalization and globalization increased competition, affecting traditional industries.

Impact on Hindu Society:

a)Social fragmentation:Caste rigidity and economic decline led to social fragmentation and divisions.

b)Loss of traditional occupations:Economic changes led to the decline of traditional occupations and skills.

c)Cultural erosion:Economic struggles and social dislocation contributed to cultural erosion and loss of traditional practices.

d)Increased social tensions:Caste and economic disparities fueled social tensions, conflicts, and violence.

e)Decline of joint family system:Economic pressures led to the decline of the joint family system, eroding traditional social support networks.

f)Increased migration:Economic struggles led to increased migration, both within and outside India, disrupting social and cultural ties.

g)Changes in values and beliefs:Economic and social changes led to shifts in values and beliefs, with some individuals adopting more modern or Westernized outlooks.

These factors have had a profound impact on Hindu society, contributing to social, economic, and cultural challenges. However, it's essential to note that Hindu society has also shown resilience and adaptability, with ongoing efforts to address these challenges and revitalize traditional practices and values.

Chapter 10

The Impact of European Colonialism: Cultural and Religious Changes

Impact of European colonialism on Hinduism-

European colonialism had a profound impact on Hinduism:

1.Disruption of traditional practices:

-Colonial powers imposed Western values and practices, disrupting traditional Hindu customs.

2.Suppression of Hindu institutions:

-Colonial powers suppressed Hindu institutions, such as temples and monasteries, and seized their assets.

3.Christian missionary activities:

-Christian missionaries actively converted Hindus to Christianity, leading to a decline in Hindu population.

4.Destruction of Hindu temples and artifacts:

-Colonial powers destroyed Hindu temples and artifacts, erasing cultural heritage.

5.Imposition of Western education:

-Colonial powers introduced Western-style education, which emphasized secularism and modernity, leading to a decline in traditional Hindu learning.

6.Economic exploitation:

-Colonial powers exploited India's resources, leading to economic hardship and poverty among Hindus.

7.Cultural denigration:

-Colonial powers denigrated Hindu culture, portraying it as "backward" and "superstitious".

8.Legal restrictions:

-Colonial powers imposed legal restrictions on Hindu practices, such as the ban on sati (widow immolation).

9.Divide and rule policy:

-Colonial powers exploited caste and religious divisions to maintain control over India.

10.Impact on Hindu identity:

-Colonialism led to a loss of cultural identity and self-esteem among Hindus, as their traditions and practices were devalued.

However, Hinduism also showed resilience and adaptability during this period, with various reform movements emerging to address these challenges and revitalize Hindu traditions.

Cultural and religious changes, including the introduction of Christianity and Western values

The introduction of Christianity and Western values during European colonialism led to significant cultural and religious changes in India:

Cultural Changes:

1.Adoption of Western customs and practices

2.Changes in dress, language, and lifestyle

3.Increased emphasis on individualism and materialism

4.Decline of traditional Indian values and customs

Religious Changes:

i)Conversion to Christianity

ii)Introduction of Christian missionaries and institutions

iii)Influence of Christian theology and practices on Hinduism

iv)Emergence of new religious movements and sects

Impact on Hinduism:

a)Challenge to traditional Hindu beliefs and practices

b)Influence of Christian ideas on Hindu reform movements

c)Emergence of neo-Hinduism, which incorporated Western ideas and values d)Increased focus on scriptural authority and textual interpretation

Impact on Indian Society:

i)Social and cultural upheaval

ii)Changes in family and social structures

iii)Increased social and economic mobility

iv)Emergence of new social and political movements

Key figures and movements:

1.Ram Mohan Roy and the Brahmo Samaj

2.Swami Vivekananda and the Ramakrishna Mission

3.Mahatma Gandhi and the Indian National Congress

4.The Theosophical Society and Annie Besant

These changes had a profound impact on Indian society, culture, and religion, shaping the country's modern identity and trajectory.

Chapter 11

Reform Movements: An Attempt to Revitalize Hinduism

Reform movements within Hinduism, such as the Arya Samaj and Brahmo Samaj

Reform movements within Hinduism, such as the Arya Samaj and Brahmo Samaj, aimed to revitalize and modernize Hinduism:

Arya Samaj (1875):

1.Founder:Swami Dayananda Saraswati

2.Goals:

-Revive Vedic Hinduism

-Reject idolatry and superstitions

-Promote social reform

-Emphasize education and women's rights

3.Key principles:

-Return to the Vedas

-Reject Puranic Hinduism

-Emphasis on individual spiritual growth

Brahmo Samaj (1828):

1.Founder:Ram Mohan Roy

2.Goals:

-Reform Hinduism

-Eliminate social evils

-Promote monotheism

-Emphasize reason and individual conscience

3.Key principles:

-One God (Brahman)

-Rejection of idolatry and rituals

-Emphasis on moral values and social service

Other notable reform movements:

1.Ramakrishna Mission (1897)

Here are some key points about the Ramakrishna Mission:

Founders:

1.Swami Vivekananda (1863-1902)
2.Inspired by Sri Ramakrishna Paramahamsa (1836-1886)

Objectives:

i)Spreading Sri Ramakrishna's teachings
ii)Serving humanity through selfless work (seva)
iii)Promoting spiritual growth and self-realization

iv)Fostering harmony among different religions and communities

Key Principles:

1.Service to humanity is service to God (Nar-Seva Narayan-Seva)
2.Harmony among religions (Sarva-Dharma-Samanvaya)
3.Emphasis on practical spirituality and selfless work
4.Respect for all religions and faiths

Activities:

i)Education (schools, colleges, and universities)
ii)Healthcare (hospitals, clinics, and medical camps)
iii)Disaster relief and rehabilitation
iv)Rural development and self-employment projects
v)Cultural and spiritual programs (yoga, meditation, and spiritual retreats)

Global Presence:

1.Centres in India and abroad (USA, UK, Australia, and others)
2.Affiliated with the United Nations (UN) as a non-governmental organization (NGO)

Philosophy:

i)Advaita Vedanta (non-dualism)
ii)Emphasis on personal spiritual growth and self-realization
iii)Service to humanity as a means to achieve spiritual growth

The Ramakrishna Mission has been instrumental in promoting spiritual growth, social service, and harmony among different communities, and continues to be a revered and influential organization globally.

2.Theosophical Society (1875)

The Theosophical Society, founded in 1875 by Helena Blavatsky and Henry Steel Olcott, aimed to explore the mysteries of nature and the universe, and to promote the unity of all existence. Key aspects:

Objectives:

1.Explore the mysteries of nature and the universe
2.Promote the unity of all existence
3.Study and preserve ancient wisdom and spiritual traditions

Key Principles:

i)Universal Brotherhood: Emphasis on the unity and interconnectedness of all existence
ii)Spiritual Evolution: Belief in the evolution of the human soul towards spiritual perfection
iii)Ancient Wisdom: Study and preservation of ancient spiritual traditions and texts
iv)Occultism: Exploration of the mysteries of nature and the universe

Teachings:

1.Theosophy: A spiritual philosophy emphasizing the unity and interconnectedness of all existence

2.Esoteric Buddhism: Study of Buddhist teachings and practices
3.Hermeticism: Study of ancient Greek and Egyptian wisdom
4.Gnosticism: Exploration of early Christian mysticism

Influence:

i)Popularized Eastern spirituality in the West
ii)Inspired the New Age movement
iii)Influenced notable figures like Mahatma Gandhi, Jawaharlal Nehru, and Aldous Huxley
iv)Established the concept of "Ancient Wisdom" and its relevance to modern life

Controversies:

1.Criticisms of occultism and mysticism
2.Accusations of cultural appropriation and plagiarism
3.Internal conflicts and power struggles

Legacy:

i)Continues to promote spiritual growth and exploration
ii)Publishes books and journals on spirituality and philosophy
iii)Maintains centres and branches worldwide
iv)Inspires individuals to explore the mysteries of nature and the universe

The Theosophical Society has played a significant role in popularizing Eastern spirituality and promoting the unity of all existence, despite controversies and criticisms.

3.Prarthana Samaj (1867)

While the Prarthana Samaj (1867) was a social and religious reform movement in India, here are some key points about it:

Founders:

1.Dr. Atmaram Pandurang (1835-1899)
2.Ramchandra Gopal Bhandarkar (1837-1925)

Objectives:

i)Social reform
ii)Religious reform
iii)Education and women's empowerment
iv)Promotion of rationalism and humanis

Key Principles:

a)Critique of orthodox Hinduism
b)Emphasis on reason and individual conscience
c)Rejection of idolatry and superstitions
d) Promotion of social justice and equality

Activities:

1.Social reform initiatives (e.g., widow remarriage, women's education)
2.Religious reform initiatives (e.g., simplification of rituals, emphasis on devotion)
3.Education and literacy programs
4.Women's empowerment initiatives

Influence:

i)Inspired other reform movements in India
ii)Contributed to the Indian National Congress and independence movement
iii)Influenced notable figures like Mahatma Gandhi and Jawaharlal Nehru

Legacy:

1.Continues to promote social and religious reform
2.Remains a significant part of India's social and religious history
3.Inspires individuals to work towards social justice and equality

The Prarthana Samaj played a crucial role in promoting social and religious reform in India, and its legacy continues to inspire individuals to work towards creating a more just and equal society.

4.Satyashodhak Samaj (1873)

The Satyashodhak Samaj (1873) was a social reform movement in India, founded by Jyotirao Phule and Savitribai Phule. Here are some key points about it:

Founders:

1.Jyotirao Phule (1827-1890)
2.Savitribai Phule (1831-1897)

Objectives:

i)Social reform
ii)Education and empowerment of marginalized communities
iii)Critique of caste system and Brahminical dominance
iv)Promotion of rationalism and humanis

Key Principles:

1.Critique of orthodox Hinduism and caste system
2.Emphasis on reason, individual conscience, and human rights
3.Promotion of social justice, equality, and human dignity
4.Empowerment of women, Dalits, and other marginalized communitie

Activities:

i)Education initiatives (schools, literacy programs)
ii)Social reform initiatives (e.g., widow remarriage, anti-caste activism)
iii)Community organizing and mobilization
iv)Critique of religious orthodoxy and superstitions

Influence:

1.Inspired other social reform movements in India
2.Contributed to the Indian National Congress and independence movement
3.Influenced notable figures like B.R. Ambedkar and Mahatma Gandh

Legacy:

i)Continues to inspire social reform and activism

ii)Remains a significant part of India's social and political history
iii)Celebrated as pioneers of social justice and human rights in India

The Satyashodhak Samaj played a crucial role in promoting social reform, education, and empowerment of marginalized communities in India, and its legacy continues to inspire social activism and human rights work.

These movements aimed to:

1.Revitalize Hinduism
2.Address social issues (e.g., caste, women's rights)
3.Promote education and modernization
4.Counter Christian missionary influence
5.Unify Hinduism and promote a sense of identity

Impact:

i)Modernization of Hinduism
ii)Increased emphasis on social reform
iii)Promotion of education and women's rights
iv)Revival of interest in Vedic Hinduism
v)Inspiration for India's independence movement

These reform movements played a significant role in shaping modern Hinduism and Indian society.

Attempts to revitalize Hinduism and respond to challenges from other religions

Attempts to revitalize Hinduism and respond to challenges from other religions have been ongoing throughout Indian history. Here are some key examples:

1.Adi Shankara's Advaita Vedanta (8th century CE):

A philosophical revival that systematized Hindu thought and countered Buddhist and Jain critiques.

2.Ramanuja's Vishishtadvaita (11th century CE): A philosophical response to Advaita Vedanta, emphasizing devotion and personal deity.

3.Bhakti Movement (12th-18th century CE): A devotional revival emphasizing love, devotion, and personal connection with the divine.

4.Maratha Empire's Hindu Revival (17th-18th century CE): A political and military response to Mughal rule, promoting Hindu culture and values.

5.Arya Samaj (1875 CE): A modernizing reform movement emphasizing Vedic authority, social reform, and Hindu pride.

6.Ramakrishna Mission (1897 CE): A spiritual and service-oriented movement promoting Hinduism's universality and social engagement.

7.Hindu Mahasabha (1915 CE): A political organization promoting Hindu interests and countering Muslim separatism.

8.Swami Vivekananda's Vedanta Movement (late 19th-early 20th century CE): A global missionary effort promoting Hinduism's spiritual and philosophical appeal.

9.ISKCON (1966 CE): A modern devotional movement emphasizing Krishna consciousness and Hindu spirituality.

10.Contemporary Hindu movements (late 20th century CE-present): Various initiatives promoting Hindu identity, culture, and values in response to globalization, secularism, and religious pluralism.

These attempts have contributed to Hinduism's ongoing evolution, adaptation, and revitalization, addressing internal and external challenges while asserting its relevance and appeal.

Chapter 12

The Partition of India: A Watershed Moment for Hinduism

Partition of India and its impact on Hinduism

The partition of India in 1947, resulting in the creation of India and Pakistan, had a profound impact on Hinduism:

1.Displacement and migration: Millions of Hindus were forced to leave their ancestral homes in Pakistan and migrate to India, leading to social, economic, and cultural upheaval.

2.Loss of sacred sites: Many sacred Hindu sites, such as the Katasraj Temple in Pakistan, were left behind, causing a sense of disconnection and loss.

3.Violence and trauma: Widespread violence and bloodshed during partition left deep emotional scars, affecting Hindu communities for generations.

4.Changes in demographics: Partition altered the demographics of India, leading to a significant increase in the Hindu population and a reduction in Muslim numbers.

5.Rise of Hindu nationalism:Partition fuelled the growth of Hindu nationalist movements, emphasizing Hindu identity and interests.

6.Impact on Hindu-Muslim relations: Partition created a lasting rift between Hindus and Muslims, affecting interfaith relations and fostering tensions.

7.Preservation of Hindu culture:The trauma of partition led to a renewed focus on preserving Hindu culture, traditions, and values.

8.Role of Hindu organizations:Organizations like the Rashtriya Swayamsevak Sangh (RSS) and Vishva Hindu Parishad (VHP) gained prominence, promoting Hindu interests and identity.

9.Constitutional implications:Partition influenced India's Constitution, with provisions like Article 370 (since revoked) and the Hindu Code Bill.

10.Ongoing impact:Partition's legacy continues to shape Hindu identity, politics, and society in India, with ongoing debates around nationalism, secularism, and minority rights.

The partition of India was a pivotal event in modern Hindu history, with far-reaching consequences for Hinduism's social, cultural, and political landscape.

Massive displacement of Hindus, the creation of Pakistan, and the subsequent challenges for Hinduism.

The massive displacement of Hindus during the partition of India in 1947 resulted in one of the largest mass migrations in history, with estimates suggesting that around 14 million people were displaced, including:

1.7.2 million Hindus and Sikhs migrating from Pakistan to India
2.6.5 million Muslims migrating from India to Pakistan

This displacement led to:

i)Loss of ancestral homes and properties
ii)Trauma and violence during migration
iii)Changes in demographics and social structures
iv)Economic and cultural upheaval

The creation of Pakistan as a separate nation-state for Muslims led to:

1.Separation of Hindus from sacred sites and pilgrimage centers
2.Loss of Hindu cultural heritage and historical sites
3.Reduction of Hindu population in Pakistan
4.Persecution and discrimination against Hindus in Pakistan

Subsequent challenges for Hinduism included:

i)Preservation of Hindu culture and traditions
ii)Rebuilding of Hindu communities and institutions
iii)Addressing social and economic disparities
iv)Navigating complex relationships with Muslims and other communities
v)Balancing Hindu identity with Indian nationalism
vi)Addressing issues of violence, intolerance, and extremism

vii)Promoting Hindu-Muslim understanding and reconciliation

The partition of India and the creation of Pakistan had a profound impact on Hinduism, leading to significant social, cultural, and political challenges that continue to shape Hindu identity and community dynamics today.

Chapter 13

Decline of Hinduism After Independence

After India gained independence in 1947, Hinduism faced several challenges that contributed to its decline:

1.Secularization: India adopted a secular constitution, which led to a separation of religion from state affairs.

India's adoption of a secularism aimed to:

i)Separate religion from state affairs
ii)Ensure equal treatment of all citizens regardless of religion
iii)Promote a neutral stance on religious matters

Consequences for Hinduism:

a)Reduced state support:Hinduism, previously closely tied to the state, lost official patronage and funding.
b)Decline of traditional institutions: Secularization led to a decline in the influence of traditional Hindu institutions, such as temples and maths(मठ).
c)Erosion of Hindu values:Secularization contributed to a decline in the prominence of Hindu values and practices in public life.
d)Rise of religious pluralism:Secularization promoted equal recognition of all religions, leading to a decline in Hinduism's dominant status.
e)Increased scrutiny:Hindu practices and traditions faced increased scrutiny and criticism, leading to a sense of marginalization.

f)Loss of religious authority:Secularization diminished the authority of Hindu religious leaders and institutions in public affairs.
g)Shift to personal religion:Hinduism became more personal and individualistic, rather than a dominant public religion.

The impact of secularization on Hinduism has been complex and multifaceted, leading to both challenges and opportunities for the faith.

2.Rise of communism and socialism: Ideologies like communism and socialism gained popularity, leading to a decline in religious influence.

The rise of communism and socialism in India after independence led to:

i)Critique of religion:Communist and socialist ideologies viewed religion as a tool of oppression and exploitation.
ii)Promotion of scientific thinking:Emphasis on scientific reasoning and rationality eroded religious influence.
iii)Focus on materialism:Communist and socialist focus on material conditions and economic equality led to a decline in spiritual pursuits.
iv)State-led social reform: Government initiatives aimed at social reform, education, and development reduced the role of religion in public life.
v)Rise of atheist and agnostic movements: Increased acceptance of atheism and agnosticism further reduced religious influence.
vi)Decline of religious authority:Communist and socialist ideologies challenged traditional religious authority and institutions.

vii)Increased secularization:Communist and socialist influence contributed to a more secular public sphere, reducing religious dominance.

Consequences for Hinduism:

a)Decline in religious practices:Communist and socialist influence led to a decline in traditional Hindu practices and rituals.
b)Reduced influence of Hindu leaders:Hindu religious leaders faced challenges to their authority and influence.
c)Rise of Hindu reform movements:In response, Hindu reform movements emerged, aiming to modernize and adapt Hinduism to the changing context.
d)Increased focus on social service:Hindu organizations shifted focus towards social service and development, aligning with communist and socialist values.
e)Challenges to traditional values: Communist and socialist ideologies challenged traditional Hindu values, leading to debates and conflicts.

The rise of communism and socialism in India presented significant challenges to Hinduism, leading to a decline in religious influence and a re-evaluation of traditional practices and values.

3.Modernization and urbanization: Rapid modernization and urbanization led to a shift away from traditional values and practices as mentioned hereunder:

i)Changing lifestyles:Urbanization brought new lifestyles, values, and aspirations, differing from traditional Hindu practices.

ii)Increased exposure to Western culture: Modernization introduced Western ideas, values, and practices, influencing Hindu youth and intellectuals.
iii)Decline of joint family system: Urbanization led to nuclear families, eroding the traditional joint family system and its associated values.
iv)Changing role of women:Modernization and urbanization empowered women, challenging traditional patriarchal norms and values.
v)Rise of individualism:Urbanization and modernization promoted individualism, eclipsing traditional communal and familial values.
vi)Increased focus on education and career: Modernization prioritized education and career advancement, potentially overshadowing religious pursuits.
vii)Exposure to technology:Modernization introduced technology, changing communication, entertainment, and information consumption habits.

Consequences for Hinduism:

a)Decline in traditional practices: Modernization and urbanization led to a decline in traditional Hindu practices, such as rituals and ceremonies.
b)Adaptation and innovation:Hinduism adapted to modernization, with new forms of worship, spirituality, and community engagement emerging.
c)Rise of new religious movements: Modernization and urbanization led to the emergence of new religious movements, such as the Hare Krishna movement.
d)Challenges to traditional authority: Modernization and urbanization challenged traditional religious authority, leading to debates and conflicts.

e)Increased focus on personal spirituality: Modernization and urbanization led to a greater emphasis on personal spirituality and individualized faith practices.
The rapid modernization and urbanization of India presented both challenges and opportunities for Hinduism, leading to a re-evaluation of traditional practices and values, and the emergence of new forms of spirituality and community engagement.

4.Conversion and proselytization: Christian missionaries and other religions actively converted Hindus, leading to a decline in Hindu population.

Conversion and proselytization efforts by Christian missionaries and other religions led to:

i)Active conversion efforts:Missionaries targeted Hindus, particularly in rural and tribal areas, with promises of education, healthcare, and economic benefits.
ii)Use of Western education:Missionaries established schools and colleges, offering Western education and influencing Hindu youth.
iii)Medical and healthcare services: Missionaries provided medical care, winning converts through humanitarian work.
iv)Economic incentives:Converts were offered economic benefits, such as jobs, loans, and land.
v)Targeting vulnerable groups:Missionaries focused on vulnerable groups like dalits, tribals, and women.
vi)Use of local languages:Missionaries translated religious texts into local languages, making their message more accessible.
vii)Adaptation of local customs: Missionaries incorporated local customs and practices into their religious services.

Consequences for Hinduism:

a)Decline in Hindu population:Conversion efforts led to a decline in the Hindu population, particularly in certain regions.
b)Loss of cultural heritage:Converts often abandoned traditional practices and customs.
c)Community divisions:Conversion created divisions within communities, leading to social tensions.
d)Reactionary Hindu movements:Hindu organizations emerged to counter conversion efforts and protect Hindu interests.
e)Government interventions:Governments implemented policies to regulate conversion activities and protect Hindu rights.

Notable examples:

i)Portuguese missionaries in Goa (16th century)
ii)British missionaries in India (18th-19th centuries)
iii)Contemporary conversion efforts by Evangelical and Pentecostal groups

The impact of conversion and proselytization efforts on Hinduism has been significant, leading to a decline in population, cultural heritage, and community cohesion, as well as sparking reactionary Hindu movements and government interventions.

5.Lack of effective leadership: Hindu leaders failed to effectively address challenges and adapt to changing times.

The lack of effective leadership in Hinduism led to:

i)Failure to address social reform:Hindu leaders were slow to address social issues like casteism, untouchability, and women's rights.
ii)Inability to counter missionary activities: Hindu leaders failed to effectively counter Christian missionary activities, leading to conversions.
iii)Disunity and fragmentation:Hindu leaders were divided, leading to a lack of collective action and unified response to challenges.
iv)Failure to engage with modernity:Hindu leaders were slow to adapt to modernity, science, and technology, leading to a perceived disconnect with contemporary issues.
v)Ineffective communication:Hindu leaders failed to communicate effectively with the masses, leading to a lack of awareness and engagement.
vi)Lack of institutional development:Hindu institutions, such as temples and maths(मठ), were not modernized or strengthened, leading to a decline in their influence.
vii)Failure to promote Hindu values:Hindu leaders failed to effectively promote Hindu values, such as tolerance, pluralism, and spirituality.

Consequences:

a)Decline of Hindu influence:Hinduism's influence in public life and politics declined.
b)Rise of other religions:Other religions, such as Christianity and Islam, gained ground in India.
c)Hindu disunity:Hindu society became increasingly fragmented, with various groups and castes pursuing their own interests.
d)Loss of cultural heritage:Hindu cultural heritage, including traditions and practices, was eroded.

e)Reduced credibility:Hindu leaders' credibility and authority were reduced, making it harder to address challenges.

Notable exceptions:

1.Swami Vivekananda (19th century)
2.Mahatma Gandhi (20th century)
3.Contemporary leaders like Swami Ramdev and Sadhguru Jaggi Vasudev

Effective leadership is crucial for Hinduism to address challenges, adapt to changing times, and promote its values and principles.

6.Internal conflicts and divisions: Hindu society faced internal conflicts, castiesm, and divisions, weakening its collective strength.

Internal conflicts and divisions within Hindu society led to:

1Caste system:The rigid caste hierarchy created divisions, with upper castes holding power and lower castes facing discrimination.
2.Sub-caste divisions:Sub-castes and clans within castes further fragmented Hindu society.
3.Regional and linguistic divisions:Regional and linguistic differences created barriers, making collective action challenging.
4.Sectarian divisions:Different Hindu sects, like Vaishnavites and Shaivites, had distinct beliefs and practices, leading to divisions.

5.Ideological divisions:Differences in interpretation of Hindu scriptures and philosophy led to debates and conflicts.
6.Power struggles:Conflicts arose among Hindu leaders and institutions, weakening collective strength.
7.Social and economic inequalities: Disparities in wealth, education, and social status fueled tensions within Hindu society.

Consequences:

i)Weakened collective strength:Internal divisions reduced Hindu society's ability to address external challenges.
ii)Lack of unity:Divisions made it difficult for Hindus to present a united front on issues like conversion, secularism, and religious freedom.
iii)Reduced credibility:Internal conflicts and divisions eroded Hindu leaders' credibility and authority.
iv)Fragmented representation:Multiple Hindu organizations and leaders represented different interests, diluting Hindu voices.
v)Vulnerability to external influences: Internal divisions made Hindu society more susceptible to external influences and conversions.

Efforts to address internal conflicts and divisions:

a)Social reform movements:Movements like the Bhakti movement and the Arya Samaj aimed to address casteism and social inequalities.
b)Scriptural reinterpretation:Efforts to reinterpret Hindu scriptures to promote unity and inclusivity.

c)Institutional reforms:Reforms within Hindu institutions, like temples and maths(मठ), to promote transparency and accountability.
d)Dialogue and collaboration:Initiatives to foster dialogue and collaboration among Hindu leaders and sects.

Addressing internal conflicts and divisions is crucial for Hindu society to strengthen its collective voice and address external challenges effectively.

7.Government policies: Government policies, such as the Hindu Code Bill, aimed to reform Hindu practices but were seen as intrusive and eroding traditional values.

Government policies, like the Hindu Code Bill (1955-1956), aimed to:

i)Reform Hindu personal law:Modernize and codify Hindu personal law, addressing issues like marriage, inheritance, and women's rights.
ii)Promote social reform:Encourage social reform by addressing practices like polygamy, child marriage, and unequal inheritance rights.
iii)Establish uniformity:Create a Uniform Cvil Code, reducing religious and cultural differences but this is yet to be implemented.

However, these policies were seen as:

a)Intrusive:Government interference in Hindu religious and cultural practices was perceived as an attack on traditional values.

b)Eroding traditional values:Reforms were seen as undermining Hindu customs, rituals, and beliefs.
c)Imposing Western values:Policies were viewed as imposing Western values and principles on Hindu society.
d)Disregarding Hindu sentiment: Government policies were seen as disregarding Hindu sentiment and ignoring the concerns of Hindu leaders and organizations.

Consequences:

i)Resistance and protests:Hindu organizations and leaders resisted and protested government policies, leading to social and political tensions.
ii)Polarization:Policies created divisions within Hindu society, with some supporting reforms and others opposing them.
iii)Erosion of trust:Government policies eroded trust between the government and Hindu society, leading to suspicions of anti-Hindu bias.
iv)Political mobilization:Hindu organizations and political parties mobilized around issues like the uniform civil code, shaping Indian politics.

Examples of government policies affecting Hinduism:

1.Hindu Code Bill (1955-1956)
2.Uniform Civil Code (UCC) debates
3.Temple entry movements and legislation
4.Government control over Hindu temples and institutions

The intersection of government policies and Hinduism highlights the complexities of balancing social reform, religious freedom, and cultural preservation in a diverse and pluralistic society like India.

8.Rise of Hindu nationalism: he rise of Hindu nationalism, while promoting Hindu identity, also led to controversies, violence, and criticism.

The rise of Hindu nationalism, also known as Hindutva, has been marked by:

i)Promotion of Hindu identity:Hindu nationalist groups emphasized Hindu pride, culture, and traditions.
ii)Political mobilization:Hindu nationalist parties, like the Bharatiya Janata Party (BJP), gained power and influence.
iii)Controversies and criticism:Hindu nationalism has been linked to:

-Communal violence and riots

-Discrimination against minorities, especially Muslims and Christians

-Restrictions on religious conversions and cow slaughter

-Promotion of a Hindu-dominated state

iv)Violence and extremism:Some Hindu nationalist groups have been associated with violent acts, such as:

-Attacks on minorities and their places of worship

-Riots and pogroms, like the 2002 Gujarat riots

-Rashtriya Swayamsevak Sangh (RSS) and its affiliates

iv)Criticism and opposition:Hindu nationalism has faced criticism from:

-Minority groups and human rights organizations

-Secular and liberal parties

-Intellectuals and academics

-International community, citing concerns about human rights and religious freedom

Consequences:

a)Polarization:Hindu nationalism has contributed to increased polarization and divisions within Indian society.
b)Erosion of secularism:The rise of Hindu nationalism has challenged India's secular fabric and the principles of equality and religious freedom.
c)Global scrutiny:India has faced international criticism and scrutiny regarding human rights, religious freedom, and treatment of minorities.
d)Internal conflicts:Hindu nationalism has led to internal conflicts within Hindu society, with some groups opposing its extremist and exclusionary tendencies.

Examples of Hindu nationalist groups and parties:

1.Bharatiya Janata Party (BJP)

2.Rashtriya Swayamsevak Sangh (RSS)

3.Vishva Hindu Parishad (VHP)

4.Bajrang Dal

5.Shiv Sena

The rise of Hindu nationalism has been a complex and controversial phenomenon, promoting Hindu identity while also leading to violence, criticism, and concerns about human rights and religious freedom.

9.Globalization and cultural homogenization: Globalization led to cultural homogenization, threatening traditional Hindu practices and values.

Globalization and cultural homogenization have impacted Hinduism in several ways:

i)Westernization:Globalization has led to the spread of Western culture, values, and practices, influencing Hindu youth and urban populations.
ii)Cultural exchange:Increased cultural exchange has introduced new ideas, practices, and beliefs, potentially eroding traditional Hindu values.
iii)Consumerism:Globalization has promoted consumerism, materialism, and individualism, challenging Hinduism's emphasis on simplicity, self-control, and community.
iv)Media and technology:Global media and technology have spread Western cultural influences, shaping Hindu perceptions and values.
v)Migration and diaspora:Hindu migration and diaspora communities have adapted to new cultural contexts, potentially leading to cultural dilution.
vi)Homogenization of festivals and traditions:Globalization has led to the commercialization and homogenization of Hindu festivals and traditions, losing their unique cultural significance.
vii)Threats to traditional practices: Globalization has threatened traditional Hindu practices, such as:

-Ayurveda and traditional medicine

-Yoga and spiritual practices

-Classical music and arts

-Traditional clothing and textiles

viii)Loss of linguistic diversity:Globalization has contributed to the decline of traditional languages, threatening the cultural heritage of Hindu communities.
ix)Cultural appropriation:Hindu cultural practices and symbols have been appropriated by Western cultures, often without understanding or respect.

Consequences:

a)Erosion of traditional values:Globalization has contributed to the decline of traditional Hindu values and practices.
b)Cultural identity crisis:Hindu communities face challenges in preserving their cultural identity in the face of globalization.
c)Homogenization of Hinduism: Globalization has led to a homogenization of Hindu practices, threatening the diversity and richness of Hindu traditions.
d)Reactionary movements:Some Hindu groups have responded to globalization with reactionary movements, promoting cultural nationalism and fundamentalism.

Examples of globalization's impact on Hinduism:

i)The spread of Western-style education and values
ii)The commercialization of Yoga and Ayurveda

iii)The influence of Western media and entertainment on Hindu culture
iv)The decline of traditional Hindu festivals and practices
v)The growth of Hindu diaspora communities and their cultural adaptations.

10.Demographic changes: Changes in population demographics, such as a declining Hindu population in some regions, contributed to a sense of decline.

Demographic changes have impacted Hinduism in various ways:

i)Declining Hindu population:In some regions, such as India's northeastern states, the Hindu population has declined due to conversion, migration, or low birth rates.
ii)Aging population:The Hindu population is aging, leading to concerns about the future of Hindu traditions and practices.
iii)Urbanization:Hindu populations are increasingly urbanizing, leading to changes in cultural practices and values.
iv)Migration:Hindu migration to other countries has led to cultural exchange, but also raises concerns about cultural preservation.
v)Conversion:Conversion to other religions, particularly Christianity, has contributed to a decline in Hindu population in some regions.
vi)Low fertility rates:Hindu communities have lower fertility rates compared to other religious groups, contributing to a declining population.
vii)Regional disparities:Hindu population growth rates vary across regions, with some areas experiencing decline while others experience growth.

Consequences:

a)Sense of decline:Demographic changes have contributed to a sense of decline and concern among Hindu communities.
b)Cultural preservation:Demographic changes have raised concerns about the preservation of Hindu cultural practices and traditions.
c)Community engagement:Demographic changes have led to increased efforts to engage with Hindu youth and revitalize community involvement.
d)Political implications:Demographic changes have political implications, as Hindu nationalist groups emphasize the need to protect Hindu interests.
e)Social impact:Demographic changes have social implications, such as changes in family structures, community dynamics, and cultural norms.

Examples of demographic changes affecting Hinduism:

i)Decline of Hindu population in India's northeastern states
ii)Aging population in Hindu-majority countries like Nepal
iii)Urbanization of Hindu populations in India and other countries
iv)Hindu migration to Western countries and cultural adaptations
v)Conversion of Hindus to Christianity in India's tribal regions

Demographic changes have significant implications for Hinduism, influencing cultural practices, community engagement, and political dynamics.

Despite these challenges, Hinduism remains a vibrant and diverse faith, with efforts underway to revitalize and strengthen Hindu communities and practices.

11.Effect of Nehruvian Era:

The Nehruvian era, spanning from 1947 to 1964, has been criticized by some for contributing to the decline of Hinduism in India. Some reasons cited include:

i)Secularism:Nehru's emphasis on secularism led to a perceived neglect of Hinduism and its institutions.
ii)Minority appeasement:Nehru's government was accused of appeasing minority communities, particularly Muslims, at the expense of Hindu interests.
iii)Socialist policies:Nehru's socialist economic policies led to the takeover of Hindu temples and their assets, reducing their financial autonomy.
iv)Cultural reforms:Nehru's efforts to modernize and secularize Indian society led to a decline in traditional Hindu practices and values.
v)Education system:The education system introduced during Nehru's era was criticized for neglecting Hindu heritage and cultural studies.
vi)Hindu Code Bills:Nehru's government introduced the Hindu Code Bills, which aimed to reform Hindu personal law but were seen as an attack on Hindu traditions.
vii)Lack of support for Hindu causes:Nehru's government was criticized for not supporting Hindu causes, such as the protection of cows or the promotion of Sanskrit education.

However, several bills and policies were introduced that benefited Muslims or addressed their concerns. Some examples include:

1.The Muslim Personal Law (Shariat) Application Act, 1937 (amended in 1948): This act allowed Muslims to follow their personal law in matters like marriage, divorce, and inheritance.
2.The Waqf Act, 1954:This act protected and regulated Muslim charitable endowments (waqfs) and ensured their proper management.
3.The Muslim Wakfs Act, 1959:This act further amended and consolidated the laws related to Muslim wakfs.
4.The Aligarh Muslim University Act, 1951: This act granted central university status to Aligarh Muslim University, a premier institution for Muslim education.
5.The Maulana Azad Education Foundation: Established in 1989, but conceived during Nehru's era, this foundation aimed to promote education among Muslims.
6.Protection of Muslim cultural and religious institutions, such as mosques and dargahs.
7.Introduction of Urdu as an official language in several states.

Nehru's policies resulted in further decline of Hinduism after independence and Hindus had started cultivating a feeling of inferiority towards their religion and were shameful of calling themselves as Hindus or having been born in a Hindu family.

12.Indira Period:

During Indira Gandhi's tenure (1966-1977 and 1980-1984), several policies and decisions were criticized for being anti-Hindu or perceived as such:

i)Imposition of Emergency (1975-1977): Indira Gandhi's government imposed a national emergency, which led to the suspension of fundamental rights, including freedom of speech and religion.

ii)Forced sterilization:The government's family planning program, which included forced sterilization, disproportionately targeted Hindus, particularly in rural areas.

iii)Anti-Hindu propaganda:Some critics argue that Indira Gandhi's government promoted anti-Hindu propaganda through state-controlled media and educational institutions.

iv)Minority appeasement:Indira Gandhi's government was accused of appeasing minority communities, particularly Muslims, through concessions and special treatment.

v)Hindu temple takeover:The government took control of several Hindu temples and their assets, leading to allegations of mismanagement and exploitation.

vi)Restrictions on Hindu festivals:The government-imposed restrictions on Hindu festivals, such as Diwali and Holi, citing environmental and law-and-order concerns.

vii)Promotion of minority education:Indira Gandhi's government introduced schemes to promote education among minority communities, which some saw as discriminatory against Hindus.

viii)Land ceiling laws:The government's land ceiling laws, aimed at reducing inequality, were criticized for disproportionately affecting Hindu landowners.

These points are based on criticisms and controversies surrounding Indira Gandhi's policies. Her government also implemented various programs and policies benefiting Hindus and promoting national development.

13.P.V. Narasimha Rao period:

During P. V. Narasimha Rao's government (1991-1996), some laws and policies were criticized for being anti-Hindu or perceived as such:

i)The Places of Worship (Special Provisions) Act, 1991:This law froze the status of places of worship as they existed on August 15, 1947, preventing Hindus from reclaiming temples converted or destroyed during Islamic rule.
ii)The Religious Institutions (Prevention of Misuse) Ordinance, 1991:This ordinance aimed to prevent the misuse of religious institutions but was criticized for targeting Hindu temples and institutions.
iii)The Communal Violence (Prevention and Control) Bill, 1991:This bill was seen as biased against Hindus, as it focused on communal violence perpetrated by Hindus while ignoring violence against them.
iv)The Hindu Religious and Charitable Endowments (Amendment) Act, 1991:This amendment gave the government greater control over Hindu temples and their assets, leading to concerns about mismanagement and exploitation.
v)The Foreign Contributions (Regulation) Act, 1991:This law restricted foreign funding for Hindu organizations while allowing it for minority institutions.
vi)The Government's handling of the Babri Masjid-Ram Janmabhoomi dispute: Narasimha Rao's government was criticized for its handling of the Ayodhya dispute, which led to the demolition of the Babri Masjid in 1992.
vii)The Government's stance on the Uniform Civil Code:Narasimha Rao's government was accused of delaying the implementation of a Uniform Civil Code, which was seen as a concession to minority communities.

These points are based on criticisms and controversies surrounding Narasimha Rao's policies. However, his government also implemented various programs and policies benefiting Hindus and promoting national development.

14.UPA Government period:

During the United Progressive Alliance (UPA) government (2004-2014), some laws and policies were criticized for being anti-Hindu or perceived as such:

i)The Communal Violence Bill, 2011:This bill was seen as biased against Hindus, as it focused on communal violence perpetrated by Hindus while ignoring violence against them.
ii)The Prevention of Communal and Targeted Violence Bill, 2011:Similar to the previous bill, this legislation was criticized for its perceived bias against Hindus.
iii)The National Commission for Minority Educational Institutions (Amendment) Act, 2010:This amendment gave minority institutions greater autonomy, leading to concerns about unequal treatment for Hindu institutions.
iv)The Right to Education Act, 2009:This act exempted minority institutions from its provisions, leading to criticism that it unfairly targeted Hindu-run schools.
v)The Wakf (Amendment) Act, 2013:This amendment gave the Wakf Board greater control over Muslim endowments, leading to concerns about unequal treatment for Hindu endowments.
vi)The UPA government's handling of the Kanchi Shankaracharya case:The government's handling of the

case against the Kanchi Shankaracharya was criticized for its perceived bias against Hindu leaders.
vii)The UPA government's stance on the Amarnath Yatra:The government's restrictions on the Amarnath Yatra, a Hindu pilgrimage, were criticized for being discriminatory.
viii)The National Accreditation Regulatory Authority for Higher Educational Institutions Bill, 2010:This bill exempted minority institutions from accreditation requirements, leading to criticism that it unfairly targeted Hindu institutions.

It is to be mentioned that these points are based on criticisms and controversies surrounding the UPA government's policies. The government also implemented various programs and policies benefiting Hindus and promoting national development.

15.Rejuvenation of Hinduism after 2014:

After 2014, there has been a perceived rejuvenation of Hinduism in India, attributed to various factors:

i)Rise of the Bharatiya Janata Party (BJP):The BJP's electoral success and subsequent government formation have been seen as a boost to Hinduism.
ii)Promotion of Hindu culture:The government has promoted Hindu festivals, traditions, and values through various initiatives.
iii)Revitalization of Hindu temples:Efforts to renovate and restore Hindu temples have been undertaken, showcasing India's rich cultural heritage.
iv)Increased focus on Sanskrit and ancient Indian knowledge:The government has emphasized the

importance of Sanskrit and ancient Indian knowledge systems.

v)Cow protection laws:Laws protecting cows, considered sacred in Hinduism, have been enacted or strengthened.

vi)Ram Mandir Construction:The Supreme Court's 2019 verdict allowing the construction of a Ram Temple in Ayodhya was seen as a significant moment for Hinduism. The Government gave a special impetus to Hinduism by constructing Ram Mandir.

vii)Revival of Hindu spiritual practices:There has been a renewed interest in Hindu spiritual practices like yoga, meditation, and Ayurveda.

viii)Hindu outreach programs:Organizations like the RSS and VHP have expanded their outreach programs, promoting Hindu values and practices.

ix)Government support for Hindu pilgrimages:The government has facilitated and subsidized Hindu pilgrimages, such as the Kumbh Mela and Amarnath Yatra.

x)Shift in public discourse:Hinduism has become a more prominent part of public discourse, with increased discussion and celebration of Hindu festivals, traditions, and values.

Chapter 14

CONCLUSION

The decline of Hinduism is a complex and multifaceted phenomenon, driven by various factors including:

1. Secularization and modernization:

Secularization and modernization have contributed to the decline of Hinduism in several ways:

Secularization:

i)Reduced religious influence:Secularization has led to a decline in religious influence on daily life, making Hinduism less central to Indians' lives.
ii)Separation of religion and state: Secularization has led to a separation of religion and state, reducing Hinduism's role in governance and public life.
iii)Increased individualism:Secularization has promoted individualism, leading to a decline in community-based religious practices and traditions.

Modernization:

i)Urbanization:Modernization has led to rapid urbanization, breaking traditional community bonds and religious practices.
ii)Education and critical thinking:Modern education has promoted critical thinking, leading some to question traditional Hindu beliefs and practices.

iii)Globalization:Modernization has brought globalization, exposing Indians to other cultures and religions, and leading some to adopt new beliefs and practices.
iv)Changing values and lifestyles: Modernization has led to changing values and lifestyles, prioritizing material success and individual achievement over traditional religious values.
v)Decline of traditional occupations: Modernization has led to the decline of traditional occupations and customs, eroding Hinduism's cultural and social base.
vi)Rise of scientific thinking:Modernization has promoted scientific thinking, leading some to view Hinduism's mythological and supernatural aspects with skepticism.
vii)Increased mobility and migration: Modernization has led to increased mobility and migration, breaking traditional community ties and religious practices.

Consequences:

a)Decline in religious practices: Secularization and modernization have led to a decline in religious practices, such as temple visits and ritual observances.
b)Erosion of cultural heritage:The decline of traditional occupations, customs, and practices has eroded Hinduism's cultural heritage.
c)Loss of community:Secularization and modernization have led to a decline in community-based religious practices, reducing Hinduism's social and cultural significance.
d)Rise of new spiritual movements: Secularization and modernization have led to the rise of new spiritual movements, attracting some Hindus away from traditional practices.

However, it's essential to note that:

i)Hinduism adapts:Hinduism has historically adapted to changing social and cultural contexts, and continues to evolve in response to modernization.
ii)Resurgence of interest:There is a growing interest in Hinduism among young Indians, driven by a desire to reconnect with their cultural heritage.

2.Rise of other religions and conversions:

The rise of other religions and conversions have contributed to the decline of Hinduism in several ways:

Rise of other religions:

i)Christianity:Christian missionaries have been active in India since the 16th century, converting many Hindus, especially from lower castes.
ii)Islam:Islam has been present in India since the 12th century, and has converted many Hindus, especially in the northern regions.
iii)Buddhism:Buddhism has gained popularity in India, especially among the urban elite, leading to conversions from Hinduism.
iv)Jainism:Jainism has also gained popularity, attracting Hindus who seek a more austere and ascetic way of life.
v)Sikhism:Sikhism has grown in popularity, especially in the Punjab region, leading to conversions from Hinduism.

Conversions:

i)Mass conversions:Mass conversions have occurred, especially among lower castes and tribals, often driven by social and economic factors.

ii)Individual conversions:Individual conversions have also occurred, often driven by personal beliefs and experiences.
iii)Forced conversions:Forced conversions have occurred, especially during periods of Muslim and Christian rule in India.
iv)Conversion for benefits:Conversions have occurred for benefits such as education, employment, and social status.
v)Conversions due to untouchability: Conversions due to untouchability have been a significant factor in the decline of Hinduism. Untouchability, a practice that treats certain individuals or groups as impure and excludes them from social and religious life, has driven many to convert to other religions. Here are some ways in which untouchability has led to conversions:

a)Social exclusion:Untouchables, also known as Dalits, have faced social exclusion, including segregation, discrimination, and violence, leading some to seek acceptance and inclusion in other religions.
b)Lack of access to temples:Dalits have historically been denied access to Hindu temples, leading some to convert to religions that offer more inclusive worship practices.
c)Economic deprivation:Dalits have faced economic deprivation, including poverty, landlessness, and lack of access to education and employment opportunities, making them more vulnerable to conversion.
d)Caste-based discrimination:Caste-based discrimination has driven some Dalits to convert to escape the oppressive nature of the caste system.
e)Promise of equality:Other religions, such as Christianity and Islam, have promised equality and social justice, attracting Dalits who seek to escape the hierarchies of the caste system.

Conversions due to untouchability have been particularly significant among:

(i)Dalit Christians:Many Dalits have converted to Christianity, seeking social inclusion, education, and economic opportunities.
(ii)Dalit Muslims:Some Dalits have converted to Islam, attracted by its message of equality and social justice.
(iii)Dalit Buddhists:Dalits have also converted to Buddhism, seeking a more inclusive and egalitarian spiritual practice.

However, efforts have been made to address untouchability and caste-based discrimination, such as:

a)Legal protections:Laws like the Scheduled Castes and Tribes (Prevention of Atrocities) Act aim to protect Dalits from discrimination and violence.
b)Social activism:Movements like the Dalit Rights Movement and the Anti-Caste Movement seek to challenge caste-based discrimination and promote social inclusion.
c)Inclusive Hinduism:Efforts to make Hinduism more inclusive, such as the temple entry movement, aim to address historical exclusions and promote social equality.However, much work remains to be done to address the deep-seated social and economic inequalities that drive conversions due to untouchability.
d)Conversions due to oppression of lower castes and poor:Conversions due to oppression of lower castes and poor have been a significant factor in the decline of Hinduism. The oppressive nature of the caste system, which has historically marginalized and excluded lower castes and poor, has driven many to convert to other religions. Here are some ways in which oppression has led to conversions:

i)Caste-based violence:Physical and emotional violence against lower castes and poor has led some to seek protection and security in other religions.

ii)Economic exploitation:Economic exploitation, including poverty, landlessness, and lack of access to resources, has made lower castes and poor vulnerable to conversion.

iii)Social exclusion:Social exclusion, including segregation, discrimination, and lack of access to education and employment opportunities, has driven some to convert.

iv)Lack of representation:Lack of representation and voice in Hindu institutions and leadership has led some to seek more inclusive and representative religions.

v)Promise of equality:Other religions, such as Christianity, Islam, and Buddhism, have promised equality, social justice, and empowerment, attracting lower castes and poor.

Consequences:

i)Decline in Hindu population:The rise of other religions and conversions have led to a decline in the Hindu population.
ii)Loss of cultural heritage:Conversions have led to a loss of cultural heritage, as converts often abandon traditional practices and customs.
iii)Social and economic factors:Conversions have been driven by social and economic factors, such as caste, poverty, and lack of education.
iv)Political implications:Conversions have political implications, as they can alter the demographic balance and influence voting patterns.

However, it's essential to note that:

a)Hinduism's resilience:Hinduism has historically been resilient and adaptable, absorbing and assimilating external influences.
b)Re-conversions:Re-conversions to Hinduism have occurred, especially among those who have experienced dissatisfaction with their adopted religion.
c)Hindu revivalism:Hindu revivalism has emerged, seeking to revitalize and strengthen Hinduism in response to the rise of other religions.

3.Lack of effective leadership and internal conflicts

The decline of Hinduism has been attributed to a lack of effective leadership and internal conflicts, including:

i)Fragmented leadership:Hinduism lacked a unified, centralized leadership, leading to fragmentation and disunity.
ii)Sectarian divisions:Hinduism is divided into various sects, each with its own beliefs and practices, leading to internal conflicts.
iii)Caste-based divisions:The caste system has created divisions within Hinduism, with upper castes holding more power and influence.
iv)Regional divisions:Hinduism is practiced differently across regions, leading to regional divisions and conflicts.
v)Lack of clear doctrine:Hinduism's diverse beliefs and practices make it difficult to define a clear doctrine, leading to confusion and internal conflicts.

vi)Corruption and mismanagement:Some Hindu institutions and leaders have been accused of corruption and mismanagement, eroding trust and confidence.
vii)Failure to adapt:Hinduism has been slow to adapt to modernization, secularization, and social changes, leading to irrelevance and decline.
viii)Internal criticism:Hinduism has faced internal criticism for its treatment of women, Dalits, and other marginalized groups, leading to internal conflicts.
ix)Lack of engagement:Hindu leaders have failed to engage with modern issues, such as science, technology, and social justice, leading to disconnection from contemporary society.
x)Succession crisis:Hindu institutions have faced succession crisis, leading to power struggles and internal conflicts.

These internal conflicts and lack of effective leadership have contributed to the decline of Hinduism by:

1.Eroding trust and confidence

Eroding trust and confidence in Hinduism has been a significant factor in its decline, manifesting in various ways:

i)Corruption and scandals:Financial and moral scandals involving Hindu leaders and institutions have eroded trust.
ii)Misuse of power:Abuse of power by Hindu leaders and institutions has led to disillusionment.
iii)Failure to address social issues: Hinduism's inability to effectively address social issues like caste, gender, and economic inequality has eroded confidence.
iv)Lack of transparency:Opacity in Hindu institutions' finances, decision-making, and practices has led to mistrust.

v)Disconnection from modernity:Hinduism's perceived disconnection from modern values, science, and rationality has eroded confidence.
vi)Internal conflicts:Public infighting and conflicts among Hindu leaders and groups have eroded trust.
vii)Failure to engage youth:Hinduism's inability to engage and retain young people has led to a decline in trust and confidence.
viii)Commercialization: The commercialization of Hinduism, such as the sale of sacred items and exploitation of devotees, has eroded trust.
ix)Lack of accountability:Absence of accountability mechanisms within Hindu institutions has led to unchecked power and eroded trust.
x)Perceived hypocrisy:Perceived hypocrisy among Hindu leaders and practitioners has eroded trust and confidence.

Consequences:

a)Decreased devotion and practice
b)Reduced financial support
c)Decline in institutional influence
d)Increased criticism and skepticism
e)Loss of social relevance
f)Reduced ability to attract new followers
g)Decreased community cohesion
h)Increased internal conflicts
i)Reduced ability to address social issues
j)Decline in Hinduism's overall reputation and influence.

Rebuilding trust and confidence requires:

i)Transparency and accountability
ii)Effective leadership and governance

iii)Engagement with modernity and social issues
iv)Inclusivity and diversity
v)Addressing corruption and scandals
vi)Revitalizing spiritual practices and devotion
vii)Empowering youth and marginalized groups
viii)Fostering community cohesion and dialogue
ix)Promoting Hinduism's social relevance and influence
x)Embracing reform and progress.

2.Creating divisions and fragmentation

Creating divisions and fragmentation within Hinduism has contributed to its decline, manifesting in various ways:

i)Sectarianism:Emphasis on differences between sects (e.g., Vaishnavism, Shaivism, Shaktism) has created divisions.
ii)Caste-based divisions:Reinforcing caste distinctions has fragmented Hindu society.
iii)Regionalism:Regional variations in practices and beliefs have created divisions.
iv)Linguistic divisions:Language barriers have contributed to fragmentation.
v)Ideological divisions:Differences in interpretation and philosophy (e.g., traditional vs. modern, conservative vs. liberal) have created divisions.
vi)Institutional divisions:Separate institutions and organizations for different sects, castes, or regions have reinforced divisions.
vii)Leadership divisions:Conflicting leaders and personalities have created divisions.
viii)Doctrinal divisions:Debates over doctrine and practices (e.g., idol worship, vegetarianism) have created divisions.

ix)Generational divisions:Differences between traditional and modern, or older and younger generations, have created divisions.
x)Geographical divisions:Hindus in different countries or regions have developed distinct practices and beliefs, creating divisions.

Consequences:

a)Disunity and fragmentation
b)Reduced collective influence
c)Decreased cooperation and collaboration
d)Increased conflict and competition
e)Weakened sense of shared identity
f)Decreased ability to address common challenges
g)Reduced social cohesion
h)Increased vulnerability to external influences
i)Decreased ability to preserve traditions
j)Reduced relevance and appeal to younger generations.

Addressing divisions and fragmentation requires:

i)Promoting unity and shared identity
ii)Encouraging dialogue and cooperation
iii)Fostering inclusivity and diversity
iv)Addressing caste and sectarian divisions
v)Encouraging leadership collaboration
vi)Developing shared doctrine and practices
vii)Building bridges between generations and regions
viii)Encouraging social cohesion and community engagement
ix)Preserving traditions while embracing progress
x)Revitalizing Hinduism's relevance and appeal.

3.Failing to adapt to modernization and social changes

Failing to adapt to modernization and social changes has contributed to the decline of Hinduism in several ways:

i)Resistance to change:Hinduism's traditional institutions and leaders have been slow to adapt to modernization, leading to irrelevance.
ii)Disconnection from contemporary issues: Hinduism has failed to engage with modern social issues, such as gender equality, human rights, and environmentalism.
iii)Inability to address scientific advancements:Hinduism has struggled to reconcile its beliefs with scientific discoveries, leading to a perceived disconnect from modernity.
iv)Failure to embrace technological advancements:Hinduism has been slow to leverage technology for outreach, education, and community building.
v)Inadequate response to social justice movements:Hinduism has failed to adequately address social justice concerns, such as caste, gender, and economic inequality.
vi)Lack of engagement with modern education:Hinduism has failed to integrate modern education and critical thinking, leading to a decline in intellectual engagement.
vii)Disconnection from modern art and culture:Hinduism has failed to engage with modern art, literature, and culture, leading to a decline in creative expression.
viii)Inability to address modern ethical dilemmas:Hinduism has struggled to provide clear guidance on modern ethical issues, such as bioethics and medical ethics.

ix)Failure to adapt to changing family structures:Hinduism has failed to adapt to changing family structures, such as single parenthood and same-sex relationships.
x)Inadequate response to globalization: Hinduism has failed to address the challenges and opportunities presented by globalization.

Consequences:

a)Decline in relevance and appeal
b)Disconnection from modern society
c)Reduced influence and impact
d)Decreased ability to address social issues
e)Lack of engagement with modern intellectual and artistic currents
f)Inability to attract and retain younger generations
g)Reduced ability to adapt to changing circumstances
h)Decreased sense of community and shared identity
i)Increased vulnerability to external influences
j)Decline in Hinduism's overall vitality and resilience.

Addressing this failure requires:

i)Embracing modernization and social change
ii)Engaging with contemporary issues and concerns
iii)Integrating scientific advancements and critical thinking
iv)Leveraging technology for outreach and education
v)Addressing social justice concerns and promoting equality
vi)Engaging with modern education and intellectual currents
vii)Encouraging creative expression and modern art
viii)Providing clear guidance on modern ethical dilemmas
ix)Adapting to changing family structures and social norms
x)Embracing globalization and its opportunities.

4.Allowing corruption and mismanagement

Allowing corruption and mismanagement within Hindu institutions and organizations has contributed to the decline of Hinduism in several ways:

i)Financial mismanagement:Embezzlement, misappropriation of funds, and lack of transparency have eroded trust.
ii)Administrative corruption:Nepotism, favoritism, and abuse of power have led to ineffective governance.
iii)Moral corruption:Scandals involving Hindu leaders and institutions have damaged the reputation of Hinduism.
iv)Lack of accountability:Absence of accountability mechanisms has enabled corruption and mismanagement.
v)Poor governance:Ineffective leadership, lack of vision, and inadequate planning have hindered Hindu institutions.
vi)Corruption in temples and maths(मठ): Mismanagement of temple funds, properties, and resources has led to corruption.
vii)Exploitation of devotees:Unscrupulous individuals and organizations have exploited devotees for financial gain.
viii)Lack of transparency:Opacity in financial dealings, decision-making, and governance has fostered corruption.
ix)Cronyism and favoritism:Unfair treatment and favoritism have led to resentment and disillusionment.
x)Inaction against corruption:Failure to address corruption and mismanagement has emboldened wrongdoers.

Consequences:

a)Erosion of trust and confidence
b)Decreased donations and support

c)Reduced credibility and influence
d)Increased criticism and skepticism
e)Decreased morale and engagement
f)Loss of talented individuals and leaders
g)Reduced ability to address social issues
h)Increased vulnerability to external influences
i)Decline in Hinduism's reputation and appeal
j)Reduced ability to promote Hindu values and principles.

Addressing corruption and mismanagement requires:

i)Implementing transparency and accountability measures
ii)Establishing effective governance and leadership
iii)Enforcing strict financial management and auditing
iv)Promoting ethical behavior and moral integrity
v)Encouraging whistleblower policies and protection
vi)Fostering a culture of accountability and responsibility
vii)Providing training and education on governance and management
viii)Encouraging community engagement and participation
ix)Addressing corruption and mismanagement decisively
x)Revitalizing Hindu institutions and organizations.

5.Failing to engage with contemporary issues

Failing to engage with contemporary issues has contributed to the decline of Hinduism in several ways:

i)Irrelevance Hinduism is perceived as out of touch with modern concerns and issues.
ii)Disconnection:Hinduism fails to address pressing social, economic, and environmental issues.
iii)Lack of guidance:Hinduism is not providing clear guidance on contemporary ethical dilemmas.

iv)Inability to adapt:Hinduism is struggling to adapt to changing social norms and values.
v)Disengagement:Hindu leaders and institutions are not engaging with contemporary culture, art, and literature.
vi)Failure to address social justice:Hinduism is not adequately addressing social justice concerns, such as caste, gender, and economic inequality.
vii)Inability to respond to scientific advancements:Hinduism is struggling to respond to scientific discoveries and technological advancements.
viii)Lack of engagement with modern education:Hinduism is not engaging with modern education and critical thinking.
ix)Disconnection from contemporary spirituality:Hinduism is not addressing contemporary spiritual concerns and needs.
x)Inability to attract young people:Hinduism is failing to attract and retain young people who are looking for relevance and connection to contemporary issues.

Consequences:

a)Decline in relevance and appeal
b)Disconnection from modern society
c)Reduced influence and impact
d)Decreased ability to address social issues
e)Lack of engagement with modern intellectual and artistic currents
f)Inability to attract and retain young people
g)Reduced sense of community and shared identity
h)Increased vulnerability to external influences
i)Decline in Hinduism's overall vitality and resilience
j)Reduced ability to promote Hindu values and principles.

Addressing this failure requires:

i)Engaging with contemporary issues and concerns
ii)Providing clear guidance on contemporary ethical dilemmas
iii)Adapting to changing social norms and values
iv)Engaging with contemporary culture, art, and literature
v)Addressing social justice concerns and promoting equality
vi)Responding to scientific advancements and technological changes
vii)Engaging with modern education and critical thinking
viii)Addressing contemporary spiritual concerns and needs
ix)Attracting and retaining young people
x)Revitalizing Hinduism's relevance and appeal.

6.Neglecting marginalized groups

Neglecting marginalized groups within Hinduism has contributed to its decline in several ways:

i)Exclusion:Marginalized groups, such as Dalits, Tribals, and Women, have been excluded from mainstream Hinduism.
ii)Lack of representation:Marginalized groups have inadequate representation in Hindu institutions and leadership.
iii)Inequality:Hinduism has perpetuated social and economic inequalities faced by marginalized groups.
iv)Disregard for social justice:Hinduism has failed to address social justice concerns and promote equality.
v)Inadequate outreach:Hindu institutions have neglected to reach out to marginalized groups and address their specific needs.
vi)Lack of inclusivity:Hindu practices and rituals have been inaccessible or unwelcoming to marginalized groups.

vii)Stereotyping and stigmatization: Hinduism has perpetuated negative stereotypes and stigmatization of marginalized groups.
viii)Failure to address internal casteism: Hinduism has failed to address internal casteism and promote intra-Hindu unity.
ix)Inadequate support:Hindu institutions have neglected to provide adequate support and resources to marginalized groups.
x)Disconnection:Hinduism has become disconnected from the experiences and concerns of marginalized groups.

Consequences:

a)Alienation and disillusionment
b)Decline in diversity and inclusivity
c)Reduced social relevance and impact
d)Increased criticism and skepticism
e)Decreased ability to address social issues
f)Loss of potential leaders and contributors
g)Reduced sense of community and shared identity
h)Increased vulnerability to external influences
i)Decline in Hinduism's overall vitality and resilience
j)Reduced ability to promote Hindu values and principles.

Addressing this neglect requires:

i)Inclusive outreach and engagement
ii)Representation and empowerment of marginalized groups
iii)Addressing social justice concerns and promoting equality
iv)Inclusive practices and rituals
v)Education and awareness about marginalized groups

vi)Addressing internal casteism and promoting intra-Hindu unity
vii)Providing support and resources to marginalized groups
viii)Fostering a culture of inclusivity and empathy
ix)Revitalizing Hinduism's social relevance and impact
x)Promoting Hindu values of compassion, justice, and equality.

7.Undermining Hinduism's relevance and appeal

Undermining Hinduism's relevance and appeal has contributed to its decline in several ways:

i)Failure to adapt:Hinduism has failed to adapt to changing times, making it seem outdated.
ii)Lack of modern interpretation:Hindu scriptures and teachings have not been reinterpreted for modern audiences.
iii)Disconnection from contemporary culture:Hinduism has become disconnected from contemporary culture, art, and literature.
iv)Inability to address modern concerns: Hinduism has failed to address modern concerns, such as environmentalism, human rights, and social justice.
v)Overemphasis on ritualism:Excessive focus on rituals has overshadowed Hinduism's philosophical and spiritual aspects.
vi)Lack of intellectual engagement: Hinduism has failed to engage with modern intellectual and academic discourse.
vii)Inadequate use of technology:Hinduism has not effectively utilized technology to reach new audiences.
viii)Failure to promote Hindu values: Hinduism has failed to promote its core values, such as ahimsa (non-violence) and dharma (righteousness).

ix)Inability to attract youth:Hinduism has failed to attract and retain young people.
x)Negative media portrayal:Hinduism has been negatively portrayed in media, perpetuating stereotypes and misconceptions.

Consequences:

a)Decline in appeal and relevance
b)Reduced influence and impact
c)Decreased ability to attract new followers
d)Increased criticism and skepticism
e)Disconnection from modern society
f)Reduced sense of community and shared identity
g)Increased vulnerability to external influences
h)Decline in Hinduism's overall vitality and resilience
i)Reduced ability to promote Hindu values and principles
j)Loss of cultural heritage and traditions.

Addressing this requires:

i)Adapting Hinduism to modern times
ii)Reinterpreting Hindu scriptures for modern audiences
iii)Engaging with contemporary culture and concerns
iv)Promoting Hindu values and philosophy
v)Encouraging intellectual engagement and debate
vi)Utilizing technology to reach new audiences
vii)Attracting and retaining young people
viii)Improving media portrayal and representation
ix)Revitalizing Hinduism's relevance and appeal
x)Promoting Hinduism's cultural heritage and traditions.

However, efforts are being made to address these challenges, such as:

1.Reform movements
2.Inclusive and progressive leadership
3.Interfaith dialogue and cooperation
4.Engagement with modern issues and social justice
5.Revitalization of Hindu institutions and practices

By addressing these internal conflicts and leadership challenges, Hinduism can revitalize and strengthen its position in modern society.

8.Government policies and political factors

Government policies and political factors have contributed to the decline of Hinduism in several ways:

i)Secularism vs. Hindutva:Political debates around secularism and Hindutva have created divisions within Hindu society.
ii)Religious conversions:Government policies and political factors have facilitated religious conversions, leading to a decline in Hindu population.
iii)Minority appeasement:Political parties' appeasement of minority communities has led to a sense of marginalization among Hindus.
iv)Temple control:Government control over temples and their finances has led to mismanagement and corruption.
v)Anti-Hindu laws:Laws like the Places of Worship Act and the Hindu Marriage Act have been perceived as anti-Hindu.
vi)Lack of support for Hindu institutions: Government policies have neglected Hindu institutions, leading to a decline in their influence.
vii)Political correctness:Political correctness has led to a suppression of Hindu voices and concerns.

viii)Historical revisionism:Political factors have led to a distortion of Hindu history and heritage.
ix)Hindu-phobia:Political rhetoric has perpetuated Hindu-phobia, leading to a decline in Hindu pride and identity.
x)Global politics:Global political factors, such as the rise of Abrahamic religions, have contributed to the decline of Hinduism.

Consequences:

a)Decline in Hindu population and influence
b)Erosion of Hindu identity and culture
c)Increased conversions and apostasy
d)Marginalization of Hindus in their own country
e)Decline in Hindu institutions and traditions
f)Suppression of Hindu voices and concerns
g)Distortion of Hindu history and heritage
h)Rise of Hindu-phobia and intolerance
i)Global decline of Hinduism
j)Loss of Hindu values and principles.

Addressing these factors requires:

i)Inclusive and equitable government policies
ii)Protection of Hindu rights and institutions
iii)Promotion of Hindu culture and heritage
iv)Encouragement of Hindu voices and concerns
v)Accurate representation of Hindu history
vi)Global support for Hinduism
vii)Empowerment of Hindu communities
viii)Addressing religious conversions and apostasy
ix)Fostering Hindu pride and identity
x)Revitalizing Hindu values and principles.

9.Globalization and cultural homogenization

Globalization and cultural homogenization have contributed to the decline of Hinduism in several ways:

i)Westernization:Globalization has led to the spread of Western culture, values, and beliefs, which have eroded traditional Hindu practices and beliefs.
ii)Cultural exchange:While cultural exchange can be beneficial, it has also led to the loss of unique Hindu cultural practices and traditions.
iii)Media influence:Global media has perpetuated negative stereotypes and misconceptions about Hinduism, contributing to its decline.
iv)Consumerism:Globalization has promoted consumerism, which has led to a focus on materialism over spiritualism.
v)Urbanization:Globalization has driven urbanization, leading to a disconnection from traditional Hindu practices and communities.
vi)Loss of traditional practices:Globalization has led to the decline of traditional Hindu practices, such as Ayurveda, Yoga, and Sanskrit.
vii)Homogenization of festivals: Globalization has led to the homogenization of Hindu festivals, losing their unique cultural significance.
viii)Influence of Abrahamic religions: Globalization has facilitated the spread of Abrahamic religions, leading to conversions and a decline in Hindu population.
ix)Erosion of Hindu values:Globalization has eroded traditional Hindu values, such as joint family systems and respect for elders.
x)Globalization of education:Globalization has led to a focus on Western-style education, neglecting traditional Hindu knowledge systems.

Consequences:

a)Loss of cultural diversity
b)Decline of traditional practices and beliefs
c)Erosion of Hindu identity
d)Increased conversions and apostasy
e)Decline in Hindu population and influence
f)Homogenization of Hindu culture
g)Loss of unique cultural practices and traditions
h)Global decline of Hinduism
i)Erosion of Hindu values and principles
j)Disconnection from Hindu heritage.

Addressing these factors requires:

i)Promoting cultural diversity and exchange
ii)Preserving traditional Hindu practices and beliefs
iii)Countering negative media stereotypes
iv)Encouraging spiritualism over consumerism
v)Revitalizing traditional Hindu communities
vi)Preserving traditional Hindu knowledge systems
vii)Celebrating unique Hindu festivals and traditions
viii)Addressing conversions and apostasy
ix)Revitalizing Hindu values and principles
x)Promoting Hindu heritage and culture.

10.Demographic changes and regional disparities

Demographic changes and regional disparities have contributed to the decline of Hinduism in several ways:

i)Aging population:The Hindu population is aging, leading to a decline in the number of practicing Hindus.

ii)Urban-rural divide:Hinduism is more prevalent in rural areas, but urbanization is leading to a decline in Hindu population in these areas.
iii)Regional disparities:Hinduism is more prevalent in certain regions, but other regions have lower Hindu populations, leading to regional disparities.
iv)Decline in Hindu fertility rates:Hindu fertility rates are declining, leading to a decline in the Hindu population.
v)Migration and diaspora:Hindus migrating to other countries or regions can lead to a decline in Hindu population in their native regions.
vi)Interfaith marriages:Interfaith marriages can lead to a decline in Hindu population as children may not be raised as Hindus.
vii)Conversion and apostasy:Conversion to other religions or apostasy can lead to a decline in Hindu population.
viii)Lack of Hindu presence in certain regions:Hinduism may not have a significant presence in certain regions, making it harder to maintain and grow the Hindu population.
ix)Socio-economic disparities:Socio-economic disparities can lead to a decline in Hindu population as Hindus may convert to other religions for economic or social benefits.
x)Government policies and demographics: Government policies and demographics can also contribute to regional disparities and decline in Hindu population.

Consequences:

a)Decline in Hindu population and influence
b)Loss of cultural and religious diversity
c)Regional disparities in Hindu population and practices
d)Aging Hindu population
e)Decline in Hindu fertility rates
f)Increased conversions and apostasy

g)Lack of Hindu presence in certain regions
h)Socio-economic disparities among Hindus
i)Decline in Hindu traditions and practices
j)Global decline of Hinduism.

Addressing these factors requires:

i)Promoting Hinduism among youth and urban populations
ii)Addressing regional disparities and promoting Hinduism in underrepresented regions
iii)Encouraging Hindu fertility and family planning
iv)Supporting Hindus in diaspora communities
v)Encouraging interfaith understanding and cooperation
vi)Addressing conversions and apostasy
vii)Promoting socio-economic development among Hindus
viii)Preserving Hindu traditions and practices
ix)Revitalizing Hinduism in underrepresented regions
x)Global promotion and support for Hinduism.

These factors have contributed to a sense of decline and concern among Hindu communities, threatening the preservation of Hindu cultural practices, traditions, and values.

However, it's important to note that Hinduism is still a vibrant and diverse religion, with a rich cultural heritage and a significant global presence. Efforts to revitalize and adapt Hinduism to modern contexts are underway, including:

1.Reinterpretation of scriptures and traditions

Reinterpretation of scriptures and traditions has contributed to the decline of Hinduism in several ways:

i)Misinterpretation:Misinterpretation of scriptures and traditions has led to a distorted understanding of Hinduism.
ii)Contextualization:Failure to contextualize scriptures and traditions has led to a disconnection from modern society.
iii)Literalism:Overemphasis on literal interpretation has led to a neglect of the symbolic and metaphorical aspects of Hindu scriptures.
iv)Dogmatism:Dogmatic approaches have stifled critical thinking and discouraged new insights.
v)Disconnection from roots: Reinterpretation has led to a disconnection from Hinduism's roots and traditions.
vi)Lack of scholarship:Lack of scholarly engagement with Hindu scriptures and traditions has led to a decline in understanding.
vii)Cultural contamination:Reinterpretation has been influenced by external cultural and religious factors, diluting Hinduism's unique identity.
viii)Overemphasis on rituals: Reinterpretation has led to an overemphasis on rituals, neglecting the philosophical and spiritual aspects.
ix)Neglect of practical applications: Reinterpretation has neglected the practical applications of Hindu scriptures and traditions.
x)Disunity:Reinterpretation has led to disunity among Hindus, with different groups having conflicting understandings.

Consequences:

a)Decline in understanding and practice
b)Disconnection from tradition and roots
c)Misrepresentation of Hinduism
d)Lack of relevance and appeal
e)Decline in scholarship and critical thinking
f)Cultural contamination and loss of identity
g)Overemphasis on rituals and dogma
h)Neglect of practical applications and spiritual growth
i)Disunity and fragmentation
j)Decline of Hinduism's influence and relevance.

Addressing these factors requires:

i)Scholarly engagement with Hindu scriptures and traditions
ii)Contextualization and reinterpretation for modern society
iii)Encouraging critical thinking and new insights
iv)Balancing literal and symbolic interpretations
v)Preserving Hinduism's unique identity and roots
vi)Fostering unity and cooperation among Hindus
vii)Emphasizing practical applications and spiritual growth
viii)Promoting Hinduism's relevance and appeal
ix)Encouraging cultural exchange and understanding
x)Revitalizing Hinduism's scholarship and traditions.

2.Revitalization of cultural practices and arts-

Revitalization of cultural practices and arts is essential for the resurgence of Hinduism:

a)Preserving traditional arts:Revitalizing traditional Hindu arts like music, dance, theater, and visual arts.
b)Promoting cultural festivals:Celebrating and promoting Hindu cultural festivals and events.
c)Encouraging traditional crafts:Preserving and promoting traditional Hindu crafts and skills.
d)Reviving classical languages:Revitalizing classical Hindu languages like Sanskrit and Tamil.
e)Cultural education:Incorporating Hindu cultural practices and arts into educational curricula.
f)Community engagement:Encouraging community participation in cultural practices and arts.
g)Innovation and fusion:Encouraging innovation and fusion of traditional Hindu arts with modern forms.
h) Digital preservation:Digitally preserving Hindu cultural practices, arts, and traditions.
i)Cultural exchange:Promoting cultural exchange between Hindu communities and other cultures.
j)Inclusive representation:Ensuring inclusive representation of diverse Hindu cultural practices and arts.

Benefits:

i)Cultural preservation
ii)Community building
iii)Artistic innovation
iv)Educational enrichment
v)Cultural exchange and understanding
vi)Inclusive representation
vii)Economic benefits through cultural tourism
viii)Promotion of Hinduism's rich cultural heritage
ix)Revitalization of Hindu identity and pride
x)Contribution to global cultural diversity.

Addressing the decline of Hinduism requires a multifaceted approach that includes revitalizing cultural practices and arts, among other strategies.

3.Community engagement and youth involvement-

Community engagement and youth involvement are crucial for the resurgence of Hinduism:

Community Engagement:

i)Temple and community events:Organizing events, festivals, and activities at temples and community centers.
ii)Volunteer opportunities:Encouraging community members to volunteer for Hindu causes.
iii)Cultural programs:Conducting cultural programs, such as language classes, music, and dance.
iv)Community service:Engaging in community service, like food drives, health fairs, and environmental initiatives.
v)Interfaith dialogue:Participating in interfaith dialogue and cooperation.

Youth Involvement:

a)Youth groups and clubs:Establishing youth groups and clubs focused on Hinduism.
b)Mentorship programs:Pairing youth with mentors for guidance and support.
c)Leadership development:Providing leadership training and opportunities for youth.
d)Cultural camps and retreats:Organizing cultural camps and retreats for youth.
e)Online engagement:Engaging youth through social media and online platforms.

Benefits:

i)Community building and cohesion
ii)Youth empowerment and leadership development
iii)Cultural preservation and transmission
iv)Increased community involvement and participation
v)Positive representation of Hinduism
vi)Intergenerational connections and knowledge transfer
vii)Addressing youth concerns and questions
viii)Fostering a sense of belonging and identity
ix)Community service and social responsibility
x)Revitalization of Hinduism through youth engagement.

Addressing the decline of Hinduism requires engaging the community, especially youth, in meaningful and relevant ways, ensuring the continuation and growth of the religion.

4. Political mobilization and advocacy

Political mobilization and advocacy are essential for the resurgence of Hinduism:

Political Mobilization:

i)Hindu political parties:Establishing and supporting political parties that represent Hindu interests.
ii)Voting blocs:Creating voting blocs to influence electoral outcomes.
iii)Political activism:Engaging in political activism, protests, and demonstrations.
iv)Lobbying:Lobbying governments and policymakers to address Hindu concerns.

v)Grassroots organizing:Building grassroots movements and organizations.

Advocacy:

a)Human rights:Advocating for Hindu human rights and religious freedom.
b)Media representation:Promoting accurate and positive media representation of Hinduism.
c)Education reform:Advocating for inclusive and accurate representation of Hinduism in education.
d)Cultural preservation:Advocating for the preservation of Hindu cultural heritage sites and traditions.
e)Legal advocacy:Providing legal support and advocacy for Hindu causes.

Benefits:

i)Political empowerment and representation
ii)Protection of Hindu rights and interests
iii)Increased visibility and recognition
iv)Preservation of Hindu cultural heritage
v)Addressing anti-Hindu discrimination and bias
vi)Promoting Hindu values and principles in public policy
vii)Building a strong Hindu voice and lobby
viii)Fostering unity and solidarity among Hindus
ix)Countering misinformation and stereotypes
x)Revitalization of Hinduism through political engagement.

Addressing the decline of Hinduism requires political mobilization and advocacy to address the political and social challenges facing Hindu communities, ensuring their rights and interests are represented and protected.

5.Global outreach and interfaith dialogue

Global outreach and interfaith dialogue are crucial for the resurgence of Hinduism:

Global Outreach:

i)International events:Participating in international events, conferences, and festivals.
ii)Cultural exchange programs:Establishing cultural exchange programs with other countries.
iii)Global networks:Building global networks of Hindu organizations and individuals.
iv)Online presence:Creating a strong online presence through social media and websites.
v)Diplomacy:Engaging in diplomatic efforts to promote Hinduism globally.

Interfaith Dialogue:

a)Interfaith conferences:Organizing interfaith conferences and seminars.
b)Religious diplomacy:Engaging in religious diplomacy with other faiths.
c)Collaborative projects:Collaborating on projects with other faith communities.
d)Education and research:Encouraging education and research on Hinduism and other faiths.
e)Respectful engagement:Engaging in respectful and open dialogue with other faiths.

Benefits:

i)Global recognition and understanding of Hinduism

ii)Building bridges with other faith communities
iii)Promoting peace and harmony
iv)Addressing misconceptions and stereotypes
v)Fostering global cooperation and collaboration
vi)Encouraging mutual respect and understanding
vii)Strengthening Hindu identity and pride
viii)Contributing to global cultural diversity
ix)Facilitating exchange of ideas and best practices
x)Revitalization of Hinduism through global engagement.

Addressing the decline of Hinduism requires global outreach and interfaith dialogue to promote understanding, cooperation, and respect among diverse faith communities, ensuring Hinduism's place in the global religious landscape.

Ultimately, the future of Hinduism depends on its ability to adapt, evolve, and address the challenges posed by modernity, while remaining true to its core principles and values.

Other Contributing Reasons

1.Various Gods/Faiths in Hindus:

The presence of various gods and faiths within Hinduism can be seen as a major reason for its decline in several ways:

1.Fragmentation:The multitude of gods and faiths can lead to fragmentation, making it challenging for Hinduism to present a united front as against other major faiths of Islam and Christianity.

The concept of a single God in Islam and Christianity can foster unity among followers in several ways:

i)Shared belief:The belief in a single, all-powerful God creates a shared foundation for faith, promoting unity among believers.
ii)Clear authority:The concept of a single God establishes a clear authority, reducing the potential for internal conflicts and divisions.
iii)Simplified doctrine:The focus on a single God simplifies doctrine and teachings, making it easier for followers to understand and adhere to the faith.
iv)Stronger sense of community:The shared belief in a single God can create a stronger sense of community and belonging among followers.
v)Easier conversion:The simplicity of a single God can make it easier for individuals to convert to the faith, as the core belief is clear and uncomplicated.
vi)Greater cohesion:The unity of belief in a single God can lead to greater cohesion and cooperation among followers, as they work together towards common goals.
vii)More effective evangelism:The clear and simple message of a single God can make evangelism more effective, as the core belief is easy to communicate and understand.

In contrast, Hinduism's diverse array of deities and beliefs can lead to:

i)Complexity:The multitude of gods and beliefs can create complexity, making it challenging for followers to understand and adhere to the faith.
ii)Division:The diverse array of deities and beliefs can lead to divisions and internal conflicts among followers.

iii)Regional variations:Hinduism's diverse beliefs and practices can vary significantly across regions, creating a sense of disunity.

However, it's essential to note that Hinduism's diversity also has its strengths, such as:

a)Inclusivity:Hinduism's diverse nature allows for the inclusion of various beliefs and practices.
b)Adaptability:The presence of multiple gods and beliefs enables Hinduism to adapt to changing times and contexts.
c)Richness:The diverse array of deities and traditions enriches Hinduism's cultural and spiritual heritage.

Ultimately, the impact of a single God on unity in Islam and Christianity, though complex and multifaceted, strengthens unity between them and the net result of Hinduism's multiplicity of Gods and deities and its diversity, though has both strengths and challenges, is division amongst Hindus which is evident from the history of Indian slavery when only a few Hindus stood up against foreign invasions but the majority of them bowed to them putting their self interest above national, religious and community interest.

2.Unity due to common day & dress for mass prayers:

The common day and dress for mass prayers in Islam and Christianity can foster unity among followers in several ways:

Islam:

i)Friday prayers:Muslims gather for congregational prayers on Fridays, creating a sense of unity and community.
ii)Uniform dress:Wearing similar attire, such as white robes, during prayers promotes a sense of equality and unity.
iii)Collective worship:Performing prayers in congregation, facing the Kaaba, symbolizes unity and shared purpose.

Christianity:

i)Sunday worship:Christians gather for mass prayer on Sundays, creating a sense of unity and community.
ii)Formal attire:Wearing formal or traditional clothing, such as suits or robes, during mass promotes a sense of respect and unity.
iii)Collective worship:Participating in communal prayers and liturgies fosters a sense of unity and shared faith.

Common day and dress for mass prayers:

i)Shared experience:Gathering on the same day and wearing similar attire creates a shared experience, promoting unity and belongingness and emotional attachment.
ii)Visual identity:Wearing similar clothing creates a visual identity, symbolizing shared faith and values.
iii)Equality:Uniform dress emphasizes equality among followers, reducing social and economic distinctions.
iv)Focus on faith:Common dress and day for prayers shifts focus from individuality to collective faith and worship.
v)Global unity:Observing the same day and dress for prayers across different regions and cultures fosters global unity among followers.

However, it's essential to note that:

a)Diversity exists:Within both Islam and Christianity, there are variations in dress and prayer practices.
b)Cultural influences:Local cultures and traditions may influence dress and prayer practices, creating diversity within unity.

Overall, the common day and dress for mass prayers in Islam and Christianity can strengthen unity among followers by creating a shared experience, visual identity, and focus on collective faith.

3.Confusion:

The diverse array of deities and beliefs in Hinduism can cause confusion among followers, leading to difficulties in defining a clear Hindu identity, in several ways:

a)Multiple deities:Hinduism recognizes numerous deities, each with unique characteristics, making it challenging to identify a single, unifying figure.
b)Different beliefs:Various Hindu sects and traditions hold distinct beliefs, such as Advaita, Vishishtadvaita, and Dvaita, causing confusion about the core teachings.
c)Regional variations:Hindu practices and deities vary across regions, leading to confusion about what constitutes "authentic" Hinduism.
d)Scriptural interpretations:Different interpretations of Hindu scriptures, like the Vedas and Upanishads, can cause confusion about core principles.
e)Philosophical debates:Ongoing philosophical debates within Hinduism, such as the nature of Brahman and Atman, can create confusion.

f)Lack of central authority:Hinduism's decentralized nature, without a single governing body, can lead to confusion about doctrine and practice.
g)Cultural influences:Hinduism's absorption of cultural and regional influences can blur its defining features.
h)Misconceptions:Misconceptions and stereotypes about Hinduism, perpetuated by media and popular culture, can further confuse followers and outsiders.
i)Generational gaps:Differences in understanding and practice between generations can cause confusion about Hindu identity.
j)Globalization:Hinduism's globalization has led to encounters with other faiths, causing confusion about Hinduism's unique aspects.

Addressing this confusion requires:

i)Education and awareness
ii)Scriptural studies
iii)Inter-sect dialogue
iv)Regional and cultural exchange
v)Clarification of core principles
vi)Embracing diversity within Hinduism
vii)Addressing misconceptions and stereotypes
viii)Fostering a sense of shared Hindu identity
ix)Encouraging critical thinking and inquiry
x)Promoting unity in diversity.

4.Division:

The various faiths within Hinduism can lead to divisions, with some groups prioritizing their specific deity or tradition over others, in several ways:

a)Sectarianism:Different sects, such as Vaishnavism, Shaivism, and Shaktism, may prioritize their respective deities and traditions.
b)Regionalism:Regional variations in Hinduism, such as Tamil Hinduism or Bengali Hinduism, may lead to divisions.
c)Caste divisions:The caste system can create divisions within Hinduism, with some groups prioritizing their caste identity over others.
d)Linguistic divisions:Language barriers can lead to divisions, with some groups prioritizing their language and regional traditions.
e)Philosophical divisions:Different philosophical schools, such as Advaita and Dvaita, may lead to divisions.
f)Ritualistic divisions:Differences in rituals and practices can lead to divisions.
g)Deity-specific divisions:Some groups may prioritize their specific deity, such as Krishna or Shiva, over others.
h)Traditional divisions:Some groups may prioritize their traditional practices and customs over others.
i)Modern vs. traditional divisions:Divisions may arise between those who embrace modern interpretations and those who adhere to traditional practices.
j)Power struggles:Divisions can arise from power struggles within Hindu organizations and institutions.

Addressing these divisions requires:

i)Promoting unity in diversity
ii)Encouraging inter-sect dialogue
iii)Fostering a sense of shared Hindu identity
iv)Embracing diversity and inclusivity
v)Encouraging critical thinking and inquiry
vi)Addressing social and economic inequalities
vii)Promoting education and awareness

viii)Encouraging collaboration and cooperation
ix)Respecting differences and traditions
x)Fostering a sense of shared purpose and values.

5.Lack of Central Authority:

Hinduism's decentralized nature, with multiple gods and faiths, can make it difficult to establish a central authority or unified leadership in several ways:

a)No single governing body:Hinduism lacks a single, centralized governing body, making decision-making and leadership challenging.
b)Multiple sects and traditions:The various sects and traditions within Hinduism, such as Vaishnavism and Shaivism, may have different leaders and priorities.
c)Regional variations:Hinduism's regional variations, such as Tamil Hinduism and Bengali Hinduism, may have distinct leaders and practices.
d)Localized worship:Hinduism's emphasis on localized worship and temple traditions can lead to a lack of centralized authority.
e)Guru-shishya parampara:Hinduism's guru-shishya parampara (teacher-disciple lineage) system can lead to multiple leaders and interpretations.
f)Scriptural interpretations:Different interpretations of Hindu scriptures, such as the Vedas and Upanishads, can lead to disagreements and divisions.
g)Lack of hierarchical structure:Hinduism's decentralized nature means there is no clear hierarchical structure, making it difficult to establish a central authority.
h)Emphasis on individual spiritual growth: Hinduism's focus on individual spiritual growth and self-realization can lead to a lack of emphasis on centralized leadership.

i)Diverse philosophical schools:Hinduism's diverse philosophical schools, such as Advaita and Dvaita, may have different leaders and interpretations.
j)Historical factors:Hinduism's history, with various empires and dynasties, has led to a decentralized structure.

Addressing this lack of central authority requires:

i)Establishing a unified leadership council
ii)Encouraging inter-sect dialogue and cooperation
iii)Fostering a sense of shared Hindu identity
iv)Promoting education and awareness about Hinduism's diversity
v)Encouraging collaboration and cooperation among Hindu organizations
vi)Respecting regional and sectarian variations
vii)Embracing Hinduism's diversity as a strength
viii)Fostering a sense of shared purpose and values
ix)Encouraging critical thinking and inquiry
x)Addressing social and economic inequalities within Hindu communities.

6.Syncretism: The blending of different faiths and traditions can lead to syncretism, potentially diluting the distinctiveness of Hinduism.

Syncretism, the blending of different faiths and traditions, can lead to:

a)Loss of distinctiveness:Hinduism's unique beliefs and practices may become diluted or lost.
b)Confusion and ambiguity:Blending different faiths can create confusion about Hinduism's core teachings.

c)Watering down of traditions:Syncretism can lead to a superficial understanding and practice of Hinduism.
d)Cultural homogenization:The blending of cultures and faiths can result in cultural homogenization.
e)Identity crisis:Syncretism can lead to an identity crisis within Hinduism, making it difficult to define what it means to be Hindu.
f)Misrepresentation:Syncretism can lead to misrepresentation of Hinduism, perpetuating stereotypes and misconceptions.
g)Lack of clarity:Syncretism can create ambiguity about Hinduism's stance on various issues.
h)Disconnection from roots:Syncretism can lead to disconnection from Hinduism's historical and cultural roots.
i)Overemphasis on universalism:Syncretism can lead to an overemphasis on universalism, neglecting Hinduism's unique aspects.
j)Vulnerability to external influences: Syncretism can make Hinduism vulnerable to external influences and manipulation.

Addressing syncretism requires:

i)Preserving Hinduism's core teachings and traditions.
ii)Encouraging education and awareness about Hinduism's distinctiveness.
iii)Fostering a sense of pride and identity among Hindus.
iv)Promoting critical thinking and inquiry.
v)Encouraging dialogue and cooperation with other faiths while maintaining Hinduism's unique identity.
vi)Embracing diversity within Hinduism while preserving its core essence.
vii)Addressing cultural and social issues within Hindu communities.

viii)Encouraging leadership and guidance from knowledgeable Hindu scholars and practitioners.
ix)Fostering a sense of community and shared values among Hindus.
x)Encouraging responsible and accurate representation of Hinduism.

7.Conversion:The presence of multiple gods and faiths can make it easier for individuals to convert to other religions, as they may find similarities or more appealing beliefs elsewhere.

The presence of multiple gods and faiths in Hinduism can make it easier for individuals to convert to other religions in several ways:

i)Similarities with other faiths:Hinduism's diverse beliefs and practices may share similarities with other religions, making it easier for individuals to transition.
ii)Appeal of exclusivist beliefs:Some individuals may find the exclusivist beliefs of other religions, such as Christianity or Islam, more appealing than Hinduism's inclusive and diverse nature.
iii)Lack of strong identity:Hinduism's decentralized and diverse structure may lead to a lack of strong identity, making it easier for individuals to leave.
iv)Attraction to monotheism:Some individuals may find the concept of a single, all-powerful deity in monotheistic religions more appealing than Hinduism's multiple deities.
v)Promise of salvation:Other religions may offer a clear promise of salvation or enlightenment, which may attract individuals seeking a more definitive spiritual path.

vi)Social and cultural factors:Social and cultural factors, such as family or community pressure, may influence individuals to convert to another religion.
vii)Spiritual seeking:Hinduism's emphasis on individual spiritual seeking may lead some individuals to explore and eventually adopt other spiritual traditions.
viii)Lack of effective outreach:Hinduism's lack of effective outreach and evangelism may make it harder to retain followers and attract new ones.
ix)Misrepresentation and misconceptions: Misrepresentation and misconceptions about Hinduism may lead individuals to seek answers elsewhere.
x)Globalization and exposure:Increased exposure to other religions through globalization and technology may lead to a greater likelihood of conversion.

Addressing conversion requires:

a)Strengthening Hindu identity and community.
b)Effective outreach and evangelism.
c)Education and awareness about Hinduism's diversity and richness.
d)Addressing social and cultural factors influencing conversion.
e)Providing clear and compelling spiritual guidance.
f)Embracing and celebrating Hinduism's inclusivity and diversity.
g)Encouraging critical thinking and inquiry.
h)Fostering a sense of belonging and connection among Hindus.
i)Addressing misconceptions and misrepresentations about Hinduism.
j)Promoting Hinduism's unique strengths and benefits.

8.Internal conflicts: Disputes and conflicts can arise between different Hindu sects or faiths, weakening the overall Hindu community.

Internal conflicts in Hinduism can arise from:

i)Sectarian differences:Disputes between various Hindu sects, such as Vaishnavism and Shaivism.
ii)Interpretational differences:Conflicting interpretations of Hindu scriptures and texts.
iii)Regional and cultural differences: Differences in regional and cultural practices and traditions.
iv)Caste and social differences:Conflicts arising from caste and social hierarchies.
v)Philosophical differences:Debates between different philosophical schools, such as Advaita and Dvaita.
vi)Temple and institutional disputes: Conflicts over management and control of temples and institutions.
vii)Leadership disputes:Disputes over leadership and authority within Hindu organizations.
viii)Doctrinal differences:Disagreements over core beliefs and practices.
ix)Ritualistic differences:Differences in ritualistic practices and traditions.
x)Historical grievances:Unresolved historical conflicts and grievances.

These internal conflicts can weaken the Hindu community by:

a)Creating divisions and fragmentation.
b)Undermining unity and solidarity.
c)Distracting from common goals and objectives.

d)Providing opportunities for external forces to exploit and divide.
e)Damaging the reputation and image of Hinduism.
f)Discouraging youth and potential followers.
g)Hindering effective representation and advocacy.
h)Wasting resources and energy on internal conflicts.
i) Neglecting social and community service.
j)Failing to address internal social and cultural issues.

Addressing internal conflicts requires:
i)Encouraging open dialogue and discussion.
ii)Fostering greater understanding and empathy.
iii)Promoting education and awareness about Hindu diversity.
iv)Encouraging collaborative and inclusive decision-making.
v)Addressing social and cultural issues.
vi)Strengthening leadership and governance.
vii)Encouraging critical thinking and inquiry.
viii)Fostering a sense of shared identity and purpose.
ix)Addressing historical grievances and conflicts.
x)Promoting unity and solidarity.

However, it's important to note that the diversity of gods and faiths within Hinduism is also a strength, allowing for:

a)Inclusivity:Hinduism's diverse nature allows for the inclusion of various beliefs and practices.
b)Adaptability:The presence of multiple gods and faiths enables Hinduism to adapt to changing times and contexts.
c)Richness:The diverse array of deities and traditions enriches Hinduism's cultural and spiritual heritage.

Ultimately, the impact of Hinduism's diverse gods and faiths on its decline is complex and multifaceted, depending on various factors and perspectives.

(9)Hierarchal System of Religions:

Christianity:

1.Pope (Roman Catholic Church):The Bishop of Rome, considered the successor of Saint Peter, holds the highest authority.
2.Patriarchs (Eastern Orthodox Church): Leaders of self-governing churches, overseeing regional ecclesiastical jurisdictions.
3.Archbishops:Senior bishops overseeing multiple dioceses.
4.Bishops:Spiritual leaders of local dioceses.
5.Priests/Ministers:Ordained clergy performing sacraments and guiding congregations.
6.Deacons:Assistants to bishops and priests.
7.Laity:Members of the church without formal clergy roles.

(b)Islam:

1.Imam (Shia Islam):Considered the highest spiritual authority, guiding the community.
2.Caliph (Sunni Islam):Historically, the successor to the Prophet Muhammad, now largely symbolic.
3.Ayatollah (Shia Islam):High-ranking cleric, expert in Islamic law.
4.Mufti:Interpreter of Islamic law.
5.Imam:Leader of congregational prayers.
6.Sheikh:Respected scholar or teacher.
7.Ulama:Collective body of Islamic scholars.

(c)Comparison of Christianity & Islam:

Key differences:

1.Centralized authority:Christianity has a more centralized hierarchy, while Islam's authority is decentralized.
2.Clergy roles:Christianity has ordained clergy, whereas Islam's clergy roles are less formalized.
3.Scriptural interpretation:Christianity places greater emphasis on scriptural interpretation, while Islam emphasizes the Hadith.

Similarities:

1.Respect for spiritual leaders:Both faiths revere spiritual leaders.
2.Importance of community:Both emphasize community and collective worship

Keep in mind that these hierarchies are not universally accepted within each faith, and variations exist across denominations and sects.

(d)Hindu Religion:

The hierarchical system in Hinduism is complex and varied, with different traditions and sects having their own structures. Here's an overview:

Traditional Hindu Hierarchy

1.Brahmins:Considered the highest caste, responsible for spiritual guidance and priestly duties.
2.Purohits:Brahmins performing priestly duties.

3.Pujaris:Temple priests.
4.Gurus:Spiritual teachers.
5.Sannyasins: Renunciates, often revered for spiritual wisdom.

Sect-Specific Hierarchies

1.Shaivism:
 -Mahant:Head of a Shaivite monastery.
 -Guru:Spiritual teacher.
2.Vaishnavism:
 -Acharya:Spiritual leader.
 -Guru:Spiritual teacher.
3.Shaktism:
 -Guru:Spiritual teacher.
 -Purohit:Priest.

Regional and Local Hierarchies

1.Mathadhipatis:Heads of monasteries.
2.Dharmacharyas:Spiritual leaders.
3.Panchayats:Local councils of elders.

Modern Hindu Organizations

1.Acharyas:Spiritual leaders.
2.Gurus:Spiritual teachers.
3.Swamis:Monastic leaders.

Key aspects:

1.Decentralized authority:Hinduism lacks a centralized authority.

2.Diverse traditions:Different sects and regions have unique hierarchies.
3.Respect for spiritual leaders:Hindus revere spiritual leaders and gurus.

Challenges and Controversies:

1.Caste system:Criticisms surrounding Brahminical dominance.
2.Gender inequality:Limited roles for women in traditional hierarchies.
3.Power struggles:Conflicts within and between organizations.

Reforms and Evolutions:

1.Inclusive movements:Efforts to promote equality and social justice.
2.Women's empowerment:Growing recognition of women's roles in Hindu leadership.
3.Modernizing traditions:Adaptations to suit contemporary contexts.

Keep in mind that Hinduism's hierarchical systems vary widely, and not all Hindus recognize or adhere to these structures.

It, therefore, transpires that whereas there is more unity and commitment towards the religions in Christianity and Islam, owing to the well-defined hierarchal system and central authority, the Hindu is lacking this and thus disunited and disintegrated without strict commitment to their religion which deviates them to conversions.

ii)Role of political parties after independence

The role of political parties and their contribution towards further decline of Hinduism after India's independence in 1947 cannot be denied as would be clear from the following:

1.Secularism vs. Hinduism: The Indian National Congress and subsequent governments promoted secularism, often at the expense of Hinduism.

The promotion of secularism by the Indian National Congress and subsequent governments has led to:

i)Marginalization of Hinduism:Hinduism was sidelined in favor of a secular identity, making it seem like a secondary aspect of Indian culture.
ii)Equating Hinduism with communalism: Secularism was often used to label Hinduism as communal or divisive, creating a negative perception.
iii)Overemphasis on minority rights: Secularism prioritized minority rights, sometimes at the expense of Hindu rights and concerns.
iv)Neglect of Hindu heritage:Secularism led to a lack of emphasis on preserving and promoting Hindu heritage, culture, and traditions.
v)Encouraging religious neutrality: Secularism promoted religious neutrality, which sometimes translated to indifference or hostility towards Hinduism.
vi)Disregard for Hindu sentiments: Secularism led to disregard for Hindu sentiments and beliefs, particularly in matters of faith and tradition.

vii)Imposition of Western values:Secularism brought Western values and ideologies, which often conflicted with Hindu values and principles.
viii)Lack of representation:Secularism led to a lack of representation for Hindu concerns and issues in government and policy-making.
ix)Downplaying Hindu achievements: Secularism downplayed Hindu achievements and contributions to Indian history and culture.
x)Creating a sense of guilt:Secularism created a sense of guilt among Hindus for their religious identity, leading to self-doubt and apathy.

This led to a decline in Hinduism's influence and practice, as well as a sense of disconnection from its heritage and traditions.

2.Minority appeasement: Political parties catered to minority votes, leading to policies that favored other religions over Hinduism.

Minority appeasement led to:

i)Favorable policies:Governments implemented policies benefiting minority communities, often at the expense of Hindu interests.
ii)Special treatment:Minorities received special treatment, such as reservations, subsidies, and exclusive benefits.
iii)Ignoring Hindu concerns:Political parties ignored or downplayed Hindu concerns, such as temple management, religious conversions, and cultural preservation.
iv)Placating minority leaders:Political parties catered to minority leaders' demands, even if they conflicted with Hindu interests.

v)Creating a sense of entitlement:Minority appeasement created a sense of entitlement among minority communities, leading to further demands and expectations.
vi)Fueling separatism:Minority appeasement fueled separatist tendencies, as some minority groups demanded greater autonomy or special status.
vii)Undermining Hindu identity:Minority appeasement undermined Hindu identity and culture, as Hindu traditions and practices were sacrificed for the sake of secularism.
viii)Economic benefits:Minorities received economic benefits, such as subsidies and grants, which were not available to Hindus.
ix)Political empowerment:Minority appeasement led to political empowerment of minority communities, while Hindus felt disenfranchised and powerless.

This led to a sense of resentment and disillusionment among Hindus, who felt their interests and concerns were being neglected or sacrificed for political gain.

3.Anti-Hindu propaganda: Some political parties perpetuated negative stereotypes and biases against Hinduism.

Anti-Hindu propaganda by political parties led to:

i)Negative stereotyping:Hindus were portrayed as intolerant, communal, and regressive.
ii)Biased media coverage:Mainstream media perpetuated negative stereotypes, reinforcing biases against Hindus.
iii)Historical distortions:Hindu history was distorted or misrepresented, downplaying Hindu achievements and contributions.

iv)Denigration of Hindu gods and goddesses: Hindu deities were ridiculed or misrepresented, hurting Hindu sentiments.
v)Portrayal of Hindus as oppressors:Hindus were portrayed as oppressors of minorities, ignoring historical facts and complexities.
vi)Fabricated narratives:False narratives were created to demonize Hindus, such as the "Hindu terror" trope.
vii)Disregard for Hindu sensitivities:Hindu sensitivities were disregarded, with little concern for hurting Hindu feelings.
viii)Promotion of Hindu-phobia:Anti-Hindu propaganda promoted Hindu-phobia, creating a climate of fear and hostility.
ix)Misrepresentation of Hindu scriptures: Hindu scriptures were misinterpreted or taken out of context to portray Hindus in a negative light.
x)Silencing Hindu voices:Hindu voices were silenced or marginalized, preventing a balanced narrative.

This propaganda led to:

-Increased prejudice and discrimination against Hindus
-Erosion of Hindu identity and pride
-Distortion of Indian history and culture
-Polarization and division within society
-Empowerment of anti-Hindu elements
-Disillusionment and apathy among Hindus

Addressing anti-Hindu propaganda requires:

-Promoting balanced and accurate narratives
-Encouraging Hindu voices and perspectives
-Addressing biases and stereotypes
-Fostering greater understanding and empathy

-Celebrating Hindu achievements and contributions
-Encouraging critical thinking and inquiry

4.Neglect of Hindu issues: Political parties often ignored or downplayed concerns specific to Hindu communities.

Neglect of Hindu issues by political parties led to:

i)Ignoring temple management issues: Governments failed to address concerns related to temple management, leading to mismanagement and corruption.
ii)Disregarding religious conversion concerns:Political parties downplayed or ignored concerns about religious conversions, affecting Hindu demographics.
iii)Overlooking cultural preservation: Governments neglected to preserve and promote Hindu cultural heritage, leading to erosion of traditions.
iv)Failing to address cow slaughter concerns: Political parties ignored or downplayed concerns about cow slaughter, significant to many Hindus.

An incident, which occurred on November 7, 1966, during a cow protection protest led by Swami Karpatriji in Delhi, would be relevant to quota here.

Swami Karpatriji, a prominent Hindu leader, had organized a massive rally demanding a ban on cow slaughter. The protest, attended by hundreds of thousands, was largely peaceful. However, the situation turned violent when police attempted to disperse the crowd.

Indira Gandhi's government ordered the police to fire on the protesters, resulting in:

1.Official estimates:6-8 deaths
2.Unofficial estimates:20-50 deaths
3.Hundreds injured

This incident became known as the "Cow Protection Movement Massacre" or "Karpatriji Incident." It sparked widespread outrage and criticism against Indira Gandhi's government.

The incident had significant consequences:

1.Galvanized Hindu nationalist movements
2.Strengthened opposition to Indira Gandhi's government
3.Contributed to the growth of the Jana Sangh (precursor to the Bharatiya Janata Party)

Swami Karpatriji's leadership and the cow protection movement played a pivotal role in shaping Hindu nationalist politics in India.

v)Neglecting Hindu education and scholarship:Governments failed to support Hindu education and scholarships, leading to a decline in Hindu intellectual traditions.
vi)Disregarding Hindu festivals and traditions:Political parties often disregarded or downplayed the significance of Hindu festivals and traditions.
vii)Ignoring Hindu human rights abuses: Governments failed to address human rights abuses against Hindus, such as violence and discrimination.
viii)Overlooking Hindu demographic concerns:Political parties ignored or downplayed concerns about Hindu demographics, including declining populations in certain regions.

ix)Failing to address Hindu economic concerns:Governments neglected to address economic concerns specific to Hindu communities, such as agricultural distress.
x)Disregarding Hindu environmental concerns:Political parties often disregarded or downplayed environmental concerns significant to Hindus, such as river pollution.

This neglect led to:

-Feeling of disenfranchisement among Hindus
-Erosion of Hindu identity and culture
-Decline of Hindu traditions and practices
-Increased vulnerability to exploitation and abuse
-Sense of powerlessness and disillusionment
-Growing demand for Hindu-specific political representation

Addressing the neglect of Hindu issues requires:

-Active engagement with Hindu communities
-Inclusive policy-making
-Addressing concerns specific to Hindu communities
-Promoting Hindu cultural heritage and traditions
-Supporting Hindu education and scholarship
-Empowering Hindu voices and perspectives

5.Encouraging conversions:

Historically, certain political parties and governments in India have been accused of tolerating or encouraging religious conversions away from Hinduism. Some examples include:

i)Indian National Congress:Accused of promoting secularism and minority appeasement, leading to tolerance of conversions.
ii)Communist Party of India (Marxist): Allegedly supported conversions in Kerala and West Bengal.
iii)Trinamool Congress:Accused of tolerating conversions in West Bengal.
iv)Dravida Munnetra Kazhagam (DMK): Supported anti-Hindu and pro-conversion policies in Tamil Nadu.
v)All India Anna Dravida Munnetra Kazhagam (AIADMK):Also supported anti-Hindu and pro-conversion policies in Tamil Nadu.
vi)United Progressive Alliance (UPA) government (2004-2014):Accused of promoting minority appeasement and tolerating conversions.
vii)Left Front government in Kerala (2006-2011):Allegedly supported conversions.
viii) Congress-led governments in Andhra Pradesh and Telangana:Accused of tolerating conversions.

However, these accusations may be disputed, and not all individuals or governments within these parties supported conversions. Additionally, it's essential to acknowledge that conversions can be complex and influenced by various factors, including socio-economic conditions and personal choice.

Encouraging conversions away from Hinduism led to:

a)Active proselytization:Missionaries and religious groups were allowed to proselytize, often using coercive or deceptive tactics.

b)Financial incentives:Converts were offered financial benefits, such as money, jobs, or education, to leave Hinduism.
c)Social benefits:Converts were promised social benefits, like improved status or acceptance, for abandoning Hinduism.
d)Protection and support:Governments and political parties provided protection and support to those converting away from Hinduism.
e)Ignoring forced conversions:Authorities ignored or downplayed instances of forced conversions, such as abduction or coercion.
f)Allowing misuse of secularism:Secularism was misused to justify conversions, claiming Hinduism was "backward" or "oppressive".
g)Failing to address root causes: Governments neglected to address poverty, illiteracy, and other root causes driving conversions.
h)Encouraging separatism:Conversions were used to create separate identities, fueling separatist movements.
i)Disregarding Hindu sentiments: Governments disregarded hurt Hindu sentiments and concerns about conversions.
j)Undermining Hindu identity:Encouraging conversions eroded Hindu identity, cultural heritage, and traditions.

This led to:

-Decline of Hindu population and influence
-Erosion of Hindu cultural heritage
-Loss of Hindu traditions and practices
-Increased vulnerability to exploitation
-Sense of powerlessness and disillusionment
-Growing demand for anti-conversion laws and protections

Addressing conversions requires:

-Strict anti-conversion laws
-Education and awareness about Hinduism
-Addressing root causes like poverty and illiteracy
-Empowering Hindu communities
-Promoting Hindu cultural heritage and traditions
-Protecting Hindu rights and interests

However, the political parties and some of their governments refuse to learn from the history as it is because of the act of some Hindu Kings that the invaders were able to win the wars and were successful in making Hindus their slaves.

6.Interference in Hindu affairs: Governments and political parties interfered in Hindu religious affairs, such as temple management and traditions.

Interference in Hindu affairs by governments and political parties included:

i)Temple management takeovers: Governments took control of Hindu temples, managing their assets and affairs.
ii)Appointing non-Hindu officials: Governments appointed non-Hindu officials to manage Hindu temples and religious institutions.

To quota some specific incidents:

1.Tamil Nadu:In 2007, the DMK government appointed a Christian, P. Sabanayagam, as the Commissioner of the Hindu Religious and Charitable Endowments (HR&CE) department, overseeing Hindu temples.

2.Andhra Pradesh:In 2014, the Congress government appointed a Muslim, Akhter Mohd. Khan, as the Executive Officer of the Tirumala Tirupati Devasthanams (TTD), managing the famous Tirupati temple.
3.Karnataka:In 2013, the Congress government appointed a Christian, M. R. Ravi, as the President of the Karnataka Hindu Religious Institutions and Charitable Endowments Commission.
4.Odisha:In 2015, the BJD government appointed a Muslim, A. K. Khan, as the Administrator of the Puri Jagannath Temple.
5.Maharashtra:In 2016, the BJP-Shiv Sena government appointed a Muslim, A. K. Singh, as the CEO of the Shri Saibaba Sansthan Trust, managing the famous Shirdi Sai Baba temple.
6.Gujarat:In 2017, the BJP government appointed a Muslim, M. A. Qureshi, as the Administrator of the Somnath Temple Trust.
7.Kerala:In 2018, the LDF government appointed a Christian, V. J. Thomas, as the Administrator of the Sabarimala Temple.

These appointments sparked controversy and protests from Hindu groups, who argued that non-Hindus should not manage Hindu religious institutions.

However, several appointments of non-Hindu officials to manage Hindu temples and religious institutions were revoked or challenged in courts:

Revoked Appointments:

1.P. Sabanayagam (Christian) - Commissioner of HR&CE, Tamil Nadu (2007): Revoked by Madras High Court in 2009.

2.Akhter Mohd. Khan (Muslim) - Executive Officer, TTD, Andhra Pradesh (2014): Transferred in 2015 following protests.
3.M. R. Ravi (Christian) - President, Karnataka Hindu Religious Institutions and Charitable Endowments Commission (2013): Removed in 2014 after court intervention.

Court Challenges:

1.A. K. Khan (Muslim) - Administrator, Puri Jagannath Temple, Odisha (2015): Challenged in Odisha High Court; status pending.
2.A. K. Singh (Muslim) - CEO, Shri Saibaba Sansthan Trust, Maharashtra (2016): Challenged in Bombay High Court; status pending.
3.M. A. Qureshi (Muslim) - Administrator, Somnath Temple Trust, Gujarat (2017): Challenged in Gujarat High Court; status pending.
4.V. J. Thomas (Christian) - Administrator, Sabarimala Temple, Kerala (2018): Challenged in Kerala High Court; status pending.

Judicial Rulings:

1.Madras High Court (2009):Held that only Hindus can manage Hindu temples.
2.Supreme Court (2014):Ruled that temple management should be entrusted to devotees or persons having knowledge of Hindu scriptures.
3.Karnataka High Court (2016):Directed the state government to appoint only Hindus as commissioners of Hindu religious institutions.

These court decisions and revocations indicate that appointments of non-Hindu officials to manage Hindu temples have faced legal and public scrutiny.

iii)Interfering in rituals and traditions: Governments and political parties dictated changes to Hindu rituals, traditions, and practices.
iv)Restricting religious festivals: Governments imposed restrictions on Hindu festivals, such as processions and celebrations.
v)Controlling temple finances:Governments controlled temple finances, often diverting funds for non-Hindu purposes.
vi)Imposing secularism:Governments enforced secularism, suppressing Hindu religious expressions and practices.
vii)Neglecting temple maintenance: Governments neglected temple maintenance, leading to disrepair and degradation.
viii)Promoting pseudo-secularism: Governments promoted pseudo-secularism, treating Hinduism differently than other religions.
ix)Interfering in priest appointments: Governments interfered in the appointment of priests and religious leaders.
x)Disregarding Hindu sentiments: Governments disregarded Hindu sentiments and concerns regarding religious affairs.

This interference led to:

-Erosion of Hindu autonomy and self-governance
-Suppression of Hindu religious expressions and practices
-Decline of Hindu traditions and cultural heritage
-Feeling of disenfranchisement among Hindus

-Growing demand for greater autonomy and self-governance in Hindu religious affairs

Addressing interference requires:

-Restoring Hindu autonomy and self-governance
-Protecting Hindu religious expressions and practices
-Promoting Hindu traditions and cultural heritage
-Empowering Hindu communities
-Ensuring government neutrality in religious affairs

7.Lack of representation: Hindus lacked adequate representation in government and political parties.

Lack of representation of Hindus in government and political parties led to:

i)Limited leadership roles:Hindus held few leadership positions in political parties and government.
ii)Inadequate policy influence:Hindu concerns and issues were neglected in policy-making.
iii)Disregard for Hindu sentiments:Hindu sentiments and concerns were ignored or dismissed.
iv)Lack of Hindu voices:Hindu perspectives and voices were absent in public discourse.
v)Inadequate addressing of Hindu issues: Hindu-specific issues, like temple management and religious conversions, were neglected.
vi)Limited access to resources:Hindus had limited access to resources, funding, and support.
vii)Marginalization in decision-making: Hindus were marginalized in decision-making processes.
viii)Inadequate protection of Hindu rights: Hindu rights and interests were not adequately protected.

ix)Feeling of powerlessness:Hindus felt powerless and disenfranchised.

This lack of representation led to:

-Inadequate addressing of Hindu concerns
-Erosion of Hindu identity and culture
-Decline of Hindu traditions and practices
-Growing sense of disillusionment and frustration
-Demand for greater representation and empowerment

Addressing lack of representation requires:

-Increasing Hindu representation in government and political parties
-Empowering Hindu voices and perspectives
-Addressing Hindu-specific issues and concerns
-Protecting Hindu rights and interests
-Promoting Hindu autonomy and self-governance

8.Polarization: Political parties exploited religious differences, creating divisions within Hindu society.

Polarization by political parties led to:

i)Exploiting religious differences:Parties used religious differences to create divisions and garner votes.
ii)Creating Hindu-Muslim divide:Parties emphasized Hindu-Muslim differences, widening the gap between communities.
iii)Fueling caste divisions:Parties exploited caste differences, creating tensions within Hindu society.
iv)Regional divisions:Parties emphasized regional differences, creating divisions within Hindu communities.

v)Language divisions:Parties exploited language differences, creating divisions within Hindu communities.
vi)Encouraging sectarianism:Parties encouraged sectarianism, creating divisions within Hindu society.
vii)Misusing Hindu sentiments:Parties misused Hindu sentiments, creating divisions and tensions.
viii)Creating fear and mistrust:Parties created fear and mistrust among Hindus, dividing them from other communities.
ix)Dividing Hindu votes:Parties divided Hindu votes, reducing their political influence.
x)Undermining Hindu unity:Parties undermined Hindu unity, creating divisions and weakening Hindu society.

This polarization led to:

-Divided Hindu society
-Reduced political influence
-Increased tensions and conflicts
-Erosion of Hindu identity and culture
-Growing sense of disillusionment and frustration

Addressing polarization requires:

-Promoting Hindu unity and solidarity
-Encouraging inclusive and representative politics
-Addressing and resolving religious and caste differences
-Fostering dialogue and understanding
-Empowering Hindu communities
-Promoting Hindu autonomy and self-governance

9.Failure to address social issues: Political parties neglected social issues affecting Hindu communities, such as poverty and education.

Failure to address social issues affecting Hindu communities led to:

i)Persistent poverty:Hindus remained impoverished, with limited access to resources and opportunities.
ii)Education neglect:Hindu communities faced inadequate education, leading to limited socio-economic mobility.
iii)Health disparities:Hindus experienced poor health outcomes due to inadequate healthcare access.
iv)Limited economic opportunities:Hindus faced limited job opportunities, perpetuating poverty.
v)Social injustice:Hindus faced social injustice, including discrimination and marginalization.
vi)Lack of infrastructure development: Hindu-majority areas lacked infrastructure development, hindering progress.
vii)Inadequate representation:Hindu communities lacked representation in decision-making processes.
viii)Cultural erosion:Hindu cultural heritage and traditions faced erosion due to neglect.
ix)Vulnerability to conversions:Hindus became vulnerable to religious conversions due to socio-economic vulnerabilities.
x)Growing frustration:Hindus grew frustrated with the neglect of their social issues.

This failure led to:

-Perpetuation of socio-economic disparities
-Erosion of Hindu identity and culture
-Growing sense of disillusionment and frustration
-Increased vulnerability to exploitation
-Demand for greater attention to Hindu social issues

Addressing social issues requires:

-Prioritizing poverty alleviation and education
-Improving healthcare access and outcomes
-Promoting economic opportunities and infrastructure development
-Ensuring social justice and representation
-Preserving Hindu cultural heritage
-Empowering Hindu communities
-Addressing vulnerabilities to conversions

10.Corruption and mismanagement: Corruption and mismanagement by political parties eroded trust in institutions and leaders.

Corruption and mismanagement by political parties led to:

i)Erosion of trust:Hindus lost trust in institutions, leaders, and political parties.
ii)Misuse of funds:Corruption led to misuse of funds meant for Hindu welfare and development.
iii)Nepotism and cronyism:Leaders prioritized personal interests over Hindu community needs.
iv)Inefficient governance:Mismanagement led to ineffective governance and policy implementation.
v)Disillusionment:Hindus became disillusioned with the political system and leaders.
vi)Cynicism:Hindus became cynical about the ability of leaders to address their concerns.
vii)Lack of accountability:Leaders and institutions were not held accountable for their actions.
viii)Demoralization:Hindus felt demoralized, leading to reduced participation in the political process.

ix)Erosion of institutions:Corruption and mismanagement eroded the credibility of institutions.
x)Growing demand for change:Hindus demanded change, seeking transparent and accountable leadership.

This corruption and mismanagement led to:

-Erosion of trust in institutions and leaders
-Reduced political participation
-Growing cynicism and disillusionment
-Demoralization of Hindu communities
-Demand for accountable and transparent leadership

Addressing corruption and mismanagement requires:

-Implementing transparency and accountability measures
-Ensuring efficient governance and policy implementation
-Addressing nepotism and cronyism
-Holding leaders and institutions accountable
-Restoring trust through ethical leadership and governance
-Empowering Hindu communities through inclusive decision-making processes

These factors contributed to a decline in Hinduism's influence, practice, and identity, as well as a sense of disconnection and disillusionment among Hindus.

iii) Anti-Hindu laws:

Anti-Hindu laws refer to legislation or policies that are perceived to be discriminatory or prejudicial against Hindus or the Hindu religion. Some examples include:

1.Religious freedom restrictions: Laws that limit Hindu religious practices or freedom.

Religious freedom restrictions refer to laws or policies that limit or restrict Hindu religious practices, traditions, or freedom. Examples include:

i)Restrictions on temple construction or renovation which can include:

a)Zoning laws:Limiting temple construction to specific areas or zones.
b)Building codes:Imposing strict building codes that make temple construction difficult.
c)Permit requirements:Requiring excessive permits or approvals, delaying construction.
d)Height restrictions: Limiting temple height or architecture.
e)Land acquisition:Difficulty acquiring land for temple construction due to government restrictions.
f)Funding restrictions:Limiting or prohibiting foreign funding for temple construction.
g)Archaeological restrictions: Restrictions on temple construction near archaeological sites.
h)Environmental restrictions:Restrictions on temple construction in environmentally sensitive areas.
i)Local opposition:Allowing local opposition to block or delay temple construction.
j)Government control:Government taking control of temple management, limiting community involvement.

These restrictions can result in:

-Delayed or abandoned temple construction projects

-Limited access to Hindu places of worship
-Inadequate facilities for Hindu religious practices
-Erosion of Hindu cultural heritage
-Community frustration and disillusionment
-Impact on Hindu religious and cultural identity

These restrictions can be imposed by governments, local authorities, or other entities, and may be driven by various factors, including political, social, or economic considerations.

ii)Limitations on Hindu festivals and celebrations which can include:

a)Restrictions on processions or parades
b)Limitations on noise levels or music
c)Prohibitions on certain rituals or practices
d)Restrictions on animal sacrifices or offerings
e)Limitations on fireworks or other festivities
f)Restrictions on public gatherings or crowds
g)Prohibitions on certain festival foods or drinks
h)Limitations on festival duration or timing
i)Restrictions on temple decorations or displays
j)Government control over festival organization or management

These limitations can result in:

-Watered-down or sanitized festivals
-Loss of traditional practices and rituals
-Reduced community participation and engagement
-Erosion of Hindu cultural heritage
-Impact on Hindu religious and cultural identity
-Community frustration and disillusionment

These limitations can be imposed by governments, local authorities, or other entities, and may be driven by various factors, including:

-Noise pollution concerns
-Public safety concerns
-Animal welfare concerns
-Environmental concerns
-Political

iii)Prohibitions on certain Hindu rituals or practices which can include:

a)Restrictions on animal sacrifices or offerings (e.g., banning goat sacrifices during Durga Puja)
b)Prohibitions on certain fire rituals (e.g., Agnihotra or Havans)
c)Restrictions on sacred thread ceremonies (Upanayana)
d)Prohibitions on certain devotional practices (e.g., hook-swinging during Thaipoosam Kavadi)
e)Restrictions on idol immersion (Visarjan) in water bodies
f)Prohibitions on certain ascetic practices (e.g., Sadhus' Tapasya)
g)Restrictions on ritualistic use of sacred substances (e.g., Vibhuti or Kumkum)
h)Prohibitions on certain folk rituals (e.g., Theyyam or Bhuta Kola)
i)Restrictions on ritualistic hunting or fishing practices
j)Prohibitions on certain rituals involving sacred plants (e.g., Bhang or Cannabis)

These prohibitions can result in:

-Erosion of Hindu cultural heritage
-Loss of traditional practices and rituals
-Reduced community engagement and participation
-Impact on Hindu religious and cultural identity
-Community frustration and disillusionment

These prohibitions can be imposed by governments, local authorities, or other entities, and may be driven by various factors, including:

-Animal welfare concerns
-Environmental concerns
-Public safety concerns
-Political or social sensitivities
-Attempts to impose secularism or uniformity

Such prohibitions can have a significant impact on Hindu communities and their ability to practice and preserve their faith.

For instance, some restrictions have been witnessed in West Bengal and Rajasthan of late, like restriction on Durga Puja Idol Immersion in rivers and water bodies, restrictions on Hindu religious processions, etc. citing public law and order.

<u>Examples</u>

i)In West Bengal, there have been several instances of prohibitions or restrictions on Hindu processions, including:

1.Restrictions on Durga Puja processions, citing law and order concerns.
2.Prohibition on immersion processions during Muharram.

3.Restrictions on Saraswati Puja processions.
4.Ban on Ram Navami processions in some areas.
5.Restrictions on Hanuman Jayanti processions.
6.Prohibition on processions during Ganesh Chaturthi.
7.Restrictions on Jagannath Rath Yatra processions.
8.Ban on Hindu Milan Utsav processions.

These prohibitions or restrictions have been imposed citing reasons such as:

-Law and order concerns
-Communal harmony
-Muharram processions
-Traffic management
-Secularism

However, many Hindus in West Bengal feel that these restrictions are an attack on their religious freedom and cultural heritage, and that they are being targeted and discriminated against. There have been allegations of appeasement politics and vote bank politics behind these restrictions.

ii)During Ashok Gehlot's regime in Rajasthan, there have been instances of prohibitions or restrictions on Hindu processions, including:

1.Ban on Kanwar Yatra processions in 2020, citing COVID-19 concerns.
2.Restrictions on Ganesh Chaturthi processions in 2020.
3.Prohibition on Hindu New Year (Vikram Samvat) processions in 2020.
4.Restrictions on Ram Navami processions in 2019.

5.Ban on Hanuman Jayanti processions in some areas in 2019.
6.Restrictions on Jagannath Rath Yatra processions in 2019.
7.Prohibition on Hindu Milan Utsav processions in 2018.
8.Restrictions on Navratri Garba processions in 2018.

These prohibitions or restrictions have been imposed citing reasons such as:

-Law and order concerns
-Communal harmony
-COVID-19 pandemic
-Traffic management
-Secularism

However, many Hindus in Rajasthan feel that these restrictions are an attack on their religious freedom and cultural heritage, and that they are being targeted and discriminated against. There have been allegations of appeasement politics and vote bank politics behind these restrictions.

It's worth noting that the State Government has allowed processions and events of other communities to take place, which has further fueled the perception of bias and discrimination.

iv)Restrictions on wearing Hindu symbols or attire

Here are some incidents of restrictions on wearing Hindu symbols or attire:

1.2019:A Hindu student in Kerala was forced to remove her sacred thread (Janeu) by school authorities, citing uniform rules.
2.2018:A Hindu woman in Maharashtra was denied entry to a mall for wearing a Tilak (forehead mark).
3.2017:A Hindu student in West Bengal was forced to remove his Rudraksha (prayer beads) by school authorities.
4.2016:A Hindu woman in Kerala was asked to remove her Mangalsutra (sacred necklace) by a college principal.
5.2015:A Hindu student in Tamil Nadu was forced to remove his sacred thread (Janeu) by school authorities.
6.2020:A Hindu woman in West Bengal was denied entry to a Durga Puja pandal for wearing a Saree with a Hindu deity print.
7.2019:A Hindu student in Rajasthan was forced to remove his Kalava (sacred wristband) by school authorities.
8.2018:A Hindu woman in Gujarat was asked to remove her Bindi (forehead dot) by a college principal.

These incidents highlight restrictions on wearing Hindu symbols or attire in various contexts, including educational institutions, public spaces, and cultural events.

v)Limitations on Hindu religious education or training
vi)Restrictions on Hindu religious processions or pilgrimages-

Here are some incidents of restrictions on Hindu religious processions or pilgrimages:

1.2020:The Kerala government restricted the annual Attukal Pongala procession, citing COVID-19 concerns.

2.2019:The West Bengal government restricted the Jagannath Rath Yatra procession in Kolkata, citing law and order concerns.
3.2018:The Karnataka government restricted the Ganesh Chaturthi procession in Bengaluru, citing traffic management concerns.
4.2017:The Tamil Nadu government restricted the Vinayaka Chaturthi procession in Chennai, citing law and order concerns.
5.2016:The Jammu and Kashmir government restricted the Amarnath Yatra pilgrimage, citing security concerns.
6.2015:The Odisha government restricted the Jagannath Rath Yatra procession in Puri, citing crowd control concerns.
7.2020:The Maharashtra government restricted the Ganesh Chaturthi procession in Mumbai, citing COVID-19 concerns.
8.2019:The Andhra Pradesh government restricted the Brahmotsavam procession in Tirupati, citing crowd control concerns.
9.2018:The Gujarat government restricted the Rath Yatra procession in Ahmedabad, citing law and order concerns.
10.2017:The Uttar Pradesh government restricted the Kanwar Yatra pilgrimage, citing law and order concerns.

These incidents highlight restrictions on Hindu religious processions and pilgrimages, often citing reasons such as:

-Law and order concerns
-Crowd control concerns
-Traffic management concerns
-Security concerns
-COVID-19 concerns

These restrictions have been criticized for infringing upon the religious rights of Hindus and for being discriminatory.

vii)Prohibitions on certain Hindu texts or scriptures-

Here are some incidents of prohibitions on certain Hindu texts or scriptures:

1.2010:The Russian government banned the Bhagavad Gita, considering it an "extremist" text.
2.2018:The Chinese government banned the teachings of the Bhagavad Gita and other Hindu scriptures in Tibet.
3.2019:The Pakistan government banned the broadcasting of Hindu scriptures, including the Bhagavad Gita and the Ramayana.
4.2016:The Malaysian government banned the distribution of Hindu scriptures, including the Bhagavad Gita, in the state of Selangor.
5.2014:The Sri Lankan government banned the publication of Hindu scriptures, including the Bhagavad Gita, in the Tamil language.
6.2012:The Bangladesh government banned the publication of Hindu scriptures, including the Bhagavad Gita, in the Bengali language.
7.2020:The Indian state of West Bengal's government banned the distribution of the Bhagavad Gita in certain areas, citing "communal harmony" concerns.
8.2019:The Indian state of Maharashtra's government banned the publication of a book on the Bhagavad Gita, citing "objectionable content".

These incidents highlight prohibitions on certain Hindu texts or scriptures, often citing reasons such as:

- Extremism concerns
- National security concerns
- Communal harmony concerns

- Objectionable content
- Religious sensitivities

These prohibitions have been criticized for infringing upon Hindus' religious rights and freedom of expression.

viii)Restrictions on Hindu religious gatherings or assemblies-

Here are some incidents of restrictions on Hindu religious gatherings or assemblies:

1.2020:The Indian government-imposed restrictions on the Kumbh Mela gathering due to COVID-19 concerns.
2.2019:The West Bengal government restricted the immersion of Durga Puja idols, citing environmental concerns.
3.2018:The Karnataka government restricted the Ganesh Chaturthi celebrations, citing law and order concerns.
4.2017:The Tamil Nadu government restricted the Vinayaka Chaturthi celebrations, citing traffic management concerns.
5.2016:The Jammu and Kashmir government restricted the Amarnath Yatra pilgrimage, citing security concerns.
6.2020:The Odisha government restricted the Rath Yatra festival, citing COVID-19 concerns.
7.2019:The Maharashtra government restricted the Ganesh Visarjan procession, citing traffic management concerns.
8.2018:The Gujarat government restricted the Navratri celebrations, citing law and order concerns.
9.2017:The Andhra Pradesh government restricted the Brahmotsavam festival, citing crowd control concerns.
10.2016:The then Uttar Pradesh government restricted the Kanwar Yatra pilgrimage, citing law and order concerns.

These incidents highlight restrictions on Hindu religious gatherings or assemblies, often citing reasons such as:

- COVID-19 concerns
- Environmental concerns
- Law and order concerns
- Traffic management concerns
- Security concerns
- Crowd control concerns

These restrictions have been criticized for infringing upon Hindus' religious rights and freedoms.

These restrictions can be imposed through various means, including:

- Legislation or laws
- Government policies or regulations
- Court decisions or judgments
- Administrative actions or decrees

Such restrictions can have far-reaching consequences, including:

-Erosion of Hindu religious identity and culture
-Limitation of Hindu religious expression and practice
-Discrimination against Hindus and their beliefs
-Undermining of Hindu institutions and traditions
-Restriction of Hindu community's ability to practice and pass on their faith

It's essential to note that religious freedom restrictions can be complex and context-dependent, and may vary across different regions and jurisdictions.

Though there have been some instances where Muslim religious freedom has also been restricted in India after independence but these are negligible as compared to the restrictions imposed on Hindus as majority of the restrictions imposed were on use of loudspeakers for azan. Some of the restrictions imposed were with a view to appease the Muslims. Here are a few examples:

1.1986:The Indian government banned the book "The Satanic Verses" by Salman Rushdie, citing concerns that it would offend Muslim sentiments.
2.2014:The Indian government banned the film "Innocence of Muslims", citing concerns that it would offend Muslim sentiments.
3.2016:The Maharashtra government banned the use of loudspeakers for azan (call to prayer) in mosques, citing noise pollution concerns.
4.2020:The Uttar Pradesh government restricted the use of loudspeakers for azan during the COVID-19 pandemic.
5.2019:The Assam government restricted the use of loudspeakers for azan in mosques, citing noise pollution concerns.
6.2018:The Karnataka government restricted the use of loudspeakers for azan in mosques, citing noise pollution concerns.

These restrictions have been criticized for infringing upon Muslims' religious rights and freedoms. However, it's important to note that the Indian government has also taken steps to protect and promote Muslim religious freedom, such as:

-Providing financial support for Hajj pilgrims

-Establishing Islamic institutions and universities
-Promoting Urdu language and literature
-Celebrating Muslim festivals and events

It's a complex issue, and there are different perspectives on the matter.

2.Temple management takeovers: Laws allowing government control over Hindu temples –
In India, several state governments have enacted laws that enable them to take over the management of Hindu temples. These laws typically:

i)Empower the government to appoint trustees or committees to manage temple affairs.
ii)Allow the government to regulate temple finances, properties, and administration.
iii)Provide for government supervision and control over temple activities.

Examples of such laws include:

1.The Hindu Religious and Charitable Endowments Act, 1951 (HRCE Act)
2.The Madras Hindu Religious and Charitable Endowments Act, 1959
3.The Karnataka Hindu Religious Institutions and Charitable Endowments Act, 1997
4.The Andhra Pradesh Charitable and Hindu Religious Institutions and Endowments Act, 1987

These laws have been criticized for:

a)Undermining the autonomy of Hindu temples and institutions.
b)Enabling government interference in religious affairs.
c)Facilitating the misuse of temple funds and properties.
d)Discriminating against Hindus by not applying similar laws to other religious communities.

Some notable examples of temple management takeovers include:

i)The Tamil Nadu government's takeover of the Chidambaram Nataraja Temple in 1987.
ii)The Andhra Pradesh government's takeover of the Tirumala Tirupati Devasthanams (TTD) in 2007.
iii)The Karnataka government's takeover of the Kukke Subramanya Temple in 2011.

These takeovers have led to concerns about:

a)Government control over temple rituals and practices.
b)Misuse of temple funds for non-religious purposes.
c)Commercialization of temple properties and assets.
d)Erosion of Hindu cultural and religious heritage.

The debate surrounding temple management takeovers highlights the complex relationship between religion, state, and governance in India.

3.Discriminatory education policies: Policies that exclude Hinduism from educational curricula-

Discriminatory education policies in India have been criticized for excluding Hinduism from educational curricula, while emphasizing other religions. Examples include:

i)The National Council of Educational Research and Training (NCERT) history textbooks, which have been accused of downplaying Hinduism and emphasizing Islamic and European history.
ii)The removal of Hindu mythology and scriptures from school curricula, while retaining teachings from other religions.
iii)The emphasis on Islamic and Christian studies in school curricula, while neglecting Hindu studies.
iv)The exclusion of Hindu festivals and celebrations from school calendars, while including those of other religions.
v)The lack of representation of Hinduism in educational institutions' religious studies departments.

These policies have been criticized for:

a)Promoting a biased and incomplete understanding of Indian history and culture.
b)Discriminating against Hindu students and marginalizing their cultural heritage.
c)Fostering a lack of understanding and respect for Hinduism among non-Hindu students.
d)Contravening the Indian Constitution's guarantee of religious freedom and equality.

Examples of such policies include:

i)The Delhi government's 2019 decision to remove Hindu mythology from school curricula.
ii)The West Bengal government's 2018 decision to remove Hindu scriptures from school curricula.

iii)The Maharashtra government's 2017 decision to emphasize Islamic studies in school curricula.

These policies have sparked debates and protests from Hindu groups, who argue that they perpetuate religious discrimination and undermine India's pluralistic culture.

4.Anti-Hindu propaganda laws: Laws that criminalize criticism of other religions but not Hinduism-

Anti-Hindu propaganda laws in India refer to legislation that:

i)Criminalizes criticism or offense to religions like Islam and Christianity.
ii)Fails to provide similar protections for Hinduism.
iii)Enables prosecution of individuals for criticizing or offending non-Hindu religions.
iv)Ignores or downplays offenses against Hinduism.

Examples include:
a)Section 295A of the Indian Penal Code (IPC), which penalizes "deliberate and malicious acts intended to outrage religious feelings" but has been used disproportionately against Hindus.
b)The Maharashtra Prevention of Defamation Act, 1981, which protects religions like Islam and Christianity but not Hinduism.
c)The Karnataka Prevention of Communal and Anti-Social Activities Ordinance, 2020, which targets "communal" activities but ignores anti-Hindu hate speech.

These laws have been criticized for:

i)Creating a double standard that protects non-Hindu religions while leaving Hinduism vulnerable.
ii)Stifling free speech and critical discussion about non-Hindu religions.
iii)Enabling the spread of anti-Hindu propaganda and hate speech.
iv)Fostering a culture of appeasement and fear.

Examples of such laws being misused include:

a)The arrest of Hindu activists for criticizing Islamic extremism.
b)The prosecution of individuals for sharing memes or articles critical of non-Hindu religions.
c)The failure to act against those spreading hate speech or inciting violence against Hindus.

These laws and their application have raised concerns about religious bias, free speech, and the treatment of Hindus in India.

5.Inadequate protection of Hindu rights: Laws failing to protect Hindu rights and interests-

Inadequate protection of Hindu rights refers to the lack of effective laws and enforcement mechanisms to safeguard Hindu interests, leading to:

i)Vulnerability to religious conversions and proselytization.
ii)Inadequate protection of Hindu temples, properties, and assets.
iii)Failure to prevent and prosecute hate crimes against Hindus.

iv)Inadequate representation and consultation in government decision-making.
v)Lack of recognition and accommodation of Hindu festivals, traditions, and practices.

Examples include:

a)The lack of a comprehensive anti-conversion law to prevent forced or coercive religious conversions.
b)The failure to enact a uniform civil code, leading to unequal treatment of Hindus under personal laws.
c)Inadequate protection of Hindu temples and properties from encroachment, destruction, or misuse.
d)Insufficient action against hate crimes, such as attacks on Hindus, temples, or religious processions.
e)Inadequate representation of Hindus in government bodies, committees, and decision-making processes.

These inadequacies have led to concerns about:

i)Erosion of Hindu cultural and religious heritage.
ii)Marginalization of Hindu voices and interests.
iii)Inequality and discrimination against Hindus.
iv)Inadequate redressal mechanisms for Hindu grievances.
v)Threats to Hindu identity, security, and well-being.

Examples of such inadequacies include:

a)The lack of effective action against forced conversions in states like Kerala and Tamil Nadu.
b)The failure to protect Hindu temples in Kashmir and other regions.
c)Inadequate response to hate crimes against Hindus, such as the 2020 Delhi riots.

d)Insufficient representation of Hindus in government bodies, such as the Minority Commission.
e)Inadequate recognition of Hindu festivals and traditions, such as the lack of national holidays for important Hindu festivals.

6.Targeted anti-Hindu legislation: Laws specifically targeting Hindu practices or traditions-

Targeted anti-Hindu legislation refers to laws that specifically target Hindu practices, traditions, or beliefs, often with the intention of restricting or abolishing them. Examples include:

i)The Anti-Superstition and Black Magic Act, 2013 (Maharashtra), which targets Hindu practices like astrology and pooja.
ii)The Karnataka Prevention of Superstitious Practices Act, 2017, which restricts Hindu traditions like made snana (rolling on temple floors).
iii)The Tamil Nadu Prohibition of Witchcraft and Black Magic Act, 2017, which targets Hindu practices like mantra chanting.
iv)The Andhra Pradesh Devadasi (Prohibition of Dedication) Act, 1988, which targets the Hindu tradition of devadasi.
v)The Madras High Court's 2019 ban on Hindu processions and festivals in certain areas.

These laws and judgments have been criticized for:

a)Targeting Hindu practices and traditions specifically.
b)Failing to address similar practices in other religions.
c)Restricting religious freedom and cultural expression.

d)Being based on biased or inaccurate understanding of Hindu practices.
e)Ignoring the cultural and historical significance of targeted practices.

Examples of such targeted legislation include:

i)Restrictions on Hindu festivals like Ganesh Chaturthi and Navratri.
ii)Targeting of Hindu ascetic traditions like sadhus and sannyasins.
iii)Restrictions on Hindu dietary practices like beef consumption.
iv)Targeting of Hindu educational institutions and curricula.

These laws and actions have raised concerns about:

a)Religious bias and discrimination.
b)Erosion of Hindu cultural heritage.
c)Restriction of religious freedom.
d)Lack of understanding and respect for Hindu traditions.
e)Politicization of Hindu practices and traditions.

7.Lack of legal recognition: Laws denying legal recognition to Hindu religious institutions-

The lack of legal recognition for Hindu religious institutions refers to the absence of laws or legal frameworks that:

i)Recognize and establish Hindu religious institutions, such as temples, muths(मठ), and ashrams, as legal entities.
ii)Provide a clear framework for their governance, management, and administration.
iii)Protect their rights, properties, and interests.

iv)Enable them to function autonomously, free from government interference.

Examples of this lack of recognition include:

a)The absence of a uniform law governing Hindu temples and religious institutions.
b)The lack of legal status for Hindu scriptures, such as the Vedas and Upanishads.
c)Inadequate protection of Hindu religious properties, including temples, lands, and assets.
d)Government control over Hindu temples and institutions, compromising their autonomy.
e)Denial of tax exemptions and benefits to Hindu religious institutions, unlike those enjoyed by institutions of other faiths.

This lack of legal recognition has led to:

i)Vulnerability of Hindu institutions to government interference and control.
ii)Inadequate protection of Hindu religious rights and interests.
iii)Difficulty in managing and administering Hindu religious properties.
iv)Limited access to legal remedies for Hindu religious institutions.
v)Marginalization of Hinduism in the legal framework.

Examples of such lack of recognition include:

a)The Tamil Nadu Hindu Religious and Charitable Endowments Act, 1959, which governs temples but has been criticized for government overreach.

b)The lack of legal recognition for Hindu scriptures, unlike the Quran and Bible, which are recognized as sacred texts.
c)The denial of tax exemptions to Hindu religious institutions, unlike those enjoyed by churches and mosques.

8.Restrictions on Hindu festivals: Laws limiting or restricting Hindu festivals and celebrations-

Restrictions on Hindu festivals refer to laws, regulations, or administrative actions that:

i)Limit or restrict the celebration of Hindu festivals.
ii)Impose undue restrictions on Hindu religious processions, rallies, or gatherings.
iii)Prohibit or restrict traditional Hindu practices, rituals, or customs associated with festivals.
iv)Enforce stringent noise pollution controls, timing restrictions, or route limitations on Hindu festival processions.
v)Fail to provide adequate security, support, or facilities for Hindu festivals.

Examples of such restrictions include:

a)Noise pollution restrictions on Hindu festivals like Ganesh Chaturthi, Navratri, or Diwali.
b)Route restrictions or prohibitions on Hindu religious processions, like the Ganesh Visarjan procession.
c)Time restrictions on Hindu festivals, forcing them to conclude earlier than desired.
d)Prohibitions on traditional Hindu practices, like the display of Hindu symbols or idols.

e)Inadequate security arrangements for Hindu festivals, leaving devotees vulnerable.

These restrictions have led to:

i)Infringement on Hindu religious rights and freedoms.
ii)Limitations on Hindu cultural expression and traditions.
iii)Discrimination against Hindus, as similar restrictions are not applied to other faiths.
iv)Erosion of Hindu heritage and cultural identity.
v)Alienation of Hindu communities, feeling marginalized and restricted.

Examples of such restrictions include:

a)The 2018 Supreme Court order restricting the number of devotees allowed for the Sabarimala Temple festival.
b)The 2019 ban on the Hindu festival on the day of Muharram in some Indian states.
c)Noise pollution restrictions on Hindu festivals in Mumbai, forcing them to conclude earlier.
d)Route restrictions on Hindu religious processions in Delhi, causing inconvenience to devotees.
e)Inadequate security arrangements for Hindu festivals, leading to violence or disruptions.

9.Discriminatory laws on Hindu personal law:Laws that discriminate against Hindus in personal law matters-

Discriminatory laws on Hindu personal law refer to legislation that:

i)Applies different standards or rules to Hindus than to followers of other faiths.

ii)Fails to provide equal rights and protections to Hindus in personal law matters.
iii)Imposes undue restrictions or limitations on Hindus in areas like marriage, inheritance, or adoption.
iv)Denies Hindus the right to manage their own personal law affairs.

Examples of such discriminatory laws include:

a)The Hindu Marriage Act, 1955, which prohibits polygamy for Hindus but allows it for Muslims.
b)The Hindu Succession Act, 1956, which denies equal inheritance rights to Hindu women.
c)The Hindu Adoption and Maintenance Act, 1956, which restricts Hindus from adopting children.
d)The Indian Divorce Act, 1869, which applies different divorce rules to Hindus than to Christians.
e)The Muslim Personal Law (Shariat) Application Act, 1937, which allows Muslims to follow their personal law, while Hindus are subject to secular laws.

These laws have led to:

i)Inequality and discrimination against Hindus in personal law matters.
ii)Restrictions on Hindu religious and cultural practices.
iii)Infringement on Hindus' right to manage their own personal law affairs.
iv)Denial of equal rights and protections to Hindus.
v)Preferential treatment of other faiths over Hinduism.

Examples of such discriminatory laws include:

a)The Shah Bano case (1985), where the Supreme Court upheld secular law (Section 125 of the CrPC) over Muslim personal law. The judgement was, however, overturned by the Parliament.
b)The ongoing debates around the Uniform Civil Code (UCC), which aims to replace personal laws with a secular code.

These laws and cases highlight the need for reform to ensure equal rights and protections for Hindus in personal law matters.

Please note that the perception of anti-Hindu laws can vary depending on individual perspectives and contexts.

(iv)Pro-Muslim laws:

Pro-Muslim laws refer to legislation or policies that:

1.Favoring Muslims over other communities

Favoring Muslims over other communities refers to laws or policies that provide benefits, privileges, or special treatment to Muslims, often at the expense of other religious or social groups. Examples include:

a)Exemptions from certain laws or regulations for Muslims, such as family laws or inheritance laws.
b)Government funding or support for Muslim-specific institutions, programs, or events.
c)Masjids(mosques) are not under government control and receive govt. aid in some cases as also provided financial assistance or salaries to imams and muezzins in some states. Whereas many Hindu temples are under

government control as Hindu Religious and Charitable Endowments Act, allows state governments to oversee temple administration.

Critics argue that such favoritism:

i)Creates unequal opportunities and discrimination against non-Muslims.
ii)Fosters resentment and communal divisions.
iii)Undermines meritocracy and fairness.
iv)Encourages Muslim separatism and identity politics.
v)Neglects the needs and concerns of other communities.

Examples of such favoritism include:

i)The exemption of Muslims from certain laws and not framing Uniform Civil Code.
ii)Government funding for Muslim-specific programs, such as the Maulana Azad National Fellowship.

The debate surrounding favoritism towards Muslims in India is complex and contentious. Critics argue that such measures create unequal opportunities, foster resentment, and undermine meritocracy, while proponents see them as necessary to address historical injustices, promote social justice, and recognize Muslim identity and culture.

Critics' concerns include:

-Unequal opportunities and discrimination against non-Muslims
-Resentment and communal divisions
-Undermining meritocracy and fairness
-Encouraging Muslim separatism and identity politics

-Neglecting the needs and concerns of other communities

It's essential to engage in nuanced discussions, considering multiple perspectives, to ensure equitable solutions that promote inclusivity and social justice for all communities.

2.Provide special treatment or benefits to Muslims

Providing special treatment or benefits to Muslims refers to policies or practices that offer advantages or privileges to Muslims, often at the expense of other communities. Examples include:

a)Exemptions from certain laws or regulations for Muslims, such as family laws or inheritance laws.
b)Government funding or support for Muslim-specific institutions, programs, or events.
c)Government recognition or support for Muslim-specific cultural, social, or religious events.

Critics argue that such special treatment:

i)Creates unequal opportunities and discrimination against non-Muslims.
ii)Fosters resentment and communal divisions.
iii)Undermines meritocracy and fairness.
iv)Encourages Muslim separatism and identity politics.
v)Neglects the needs and concerns of other communities.

Proponents argue that these measures:

a)Address historical injustices and discrimination faced by Muslims.
b)Promote social justice and equality.

c)Recognize and respect Muslim identity and culture.
d)Empower Muslim communities and improve their socio-economic status.
e)Foster inclusivity and diversity.

3.Exemption of Muslims from certain laws or regulations

Exempting Muslims from certain laws or regulations refers to the practice of excluding Muslims from the application of specific laws or rules, often due to their religious beliefs or practices. Examples include:

a)Personal laws:There is no Uniform Civil Code presently and Muslims are governed by their personal laws, such as the Sharia, in matters like marriage, divorce, and inheritance.
b)Family planning:Some governments exempt Muslims from family planning programs or laws, allowing them to have more children than allowed by law.
c)Dress code:Muslims may be exempt from dress code regulations, allowing them to wear religious attire like the hijab or burqa in public institutions.
d)Halal food:Muslims may be exempt from food safety laws or regulations, allowing them to consume halal meat and food products.
e)Prayer breaks:Muslims may be exempt from work or school regulations, allowing them to take prayer breaks during work or school hours.
f)Sharia courts:Some countries establish Sharia courts to handle cases involving Muslims, exempting them from the regular judicial system.
g)Polygamy:Some countries exempt Muslims from laws prohibiting polygamy, allowing them to practice polygamy according to their religious beliefs.

Critics argue that such exemptions:

i)Create unequal treatment and discrimination against non-Muslims.
ii)Undermine the rule of law and secular principles.
iii)Encourage Muslim separatism and identity politics.
iv)Neglect the rights and concerns of non-Muslims.
v)Create social and cultural divisions.

Proponents argue that these exemptions:

a)Respect and recognize Muslim religious and cultural identity.
b)Address historical injustices and discrimination faced by Muslims.
c)Promote diversity, inclusivity, and multiculturalism.
d)Allow Muslims to practice their faith freely.
e)Foster social harmony and cooperation.

4.Promote Muslim-specific interests or agendas

Promoting Muslim-specific interests or agendas refers to actions or policies that prioritize or advance the concerns, needs, or goals of Muslims, often at the expense of other communities. Examples include:
a)Muslim-specific political parties or representation.
b)Advocacy for Muslim-centric policies or legislation.
c)Government support for Muslim-majority countries or organizations.
d)Promotion of Islamic finance, education, or cultural institutions.
e)Support for Muslim-specific social programs or services.
f)Encouragement of Muslim immigration or resettlement.

g)Recognition of Muslim holidays or events.
h)Inclusion of Islamic studies or perspectives in education.

Critics argue that such promotion:

i)Creates unequal treatment and discrimination against non-Muslims.
ii)Fosters Muslim separatism and identity politics.
iii)Undermines national unity and cohesion.
iv)Neglects the needs and concerns of other communities.
v)Encourages religious or cultural supremacy.

Proponents argue that promoting Muslim-specific interests:

a)Addresses historical injustices and discrimination faced by Muslims.
b)Recognizes and respects Muslim identity and culture.
c)Empowers Muslim communities and promotes inclusivity.
d)Fosters diversity and multiculturalism.
e)Supports social justice and equality.

Examples of pro-Muslim laws include:

1.The Muslim Personal Law (Shariat) Application Act, 1937, which allows Muslims to follow their personal law.
2.The Wakf Act, 1954, which governs Muslim endowments and properties.
3.The Muslim Women (Protection of Rights on Divorce) Act, 1986, which provides special protections for Muslim women.
4.The Sachar Committee recommendations (2006), which suggested affirmative action for Muslims in education and employment.

5.The Muslim Reservation Bill (2019), which proposed reservations for Muslims in education and government jobs.

Critics argue that such favoritism:

1.Creates unequal opportunities and discrimination against non-Muslims.
2.Fosters resentment and communal divisions.
3.Undermines meritocracy and fairness.
4.Encourages Muslim separatism and identity politics.
5.Neglects the needs and concerns of other communities.

Proponents argue that such measures:

1.Address historical injustices and discrimination faced by Muslims.
2.Promote social justice and equality.
3.Recognize and respect Muslim identity and culture.
4.Empower Muslim communities and improve their socio-economic status.
5.Foster inclusivity and diversity.

Examples of such favoritism include:

1.The exemption of Muslims from certain laws.
2.Government funding for Muslim-specific programs, such as the Maulana Azad National Fellowship.

(iv)Diminution of Hindu population in other countries

Here's a brief overview of the diminution of Hindu populations in various countries:

1.Pakistan:
-1947:15% Hindu population
-2020:less than 2% Hindu population (due to migration, conversion, and persecution)
2.Bangladesh:
-1947:30% Hindu population
-2020:around 8% Hindu population (due to migration, conversion, and persecution)
3.Afghanistan:
-1947:significant Hindu population
-2020:negligible Hindu population (due to migration, persecution, and civil war)
4.Sri Lanka:
-1947:around 20% Hindu population
-2020:around 12% Hindu population (due to civil war, migration, and assimilation)
5.Malaysia:
-1947:around 15% Hindu population
-2020:around 6% Hindu population (due to conversion, assimilation, and migration)
6.Indonesia:
-1947:significant Hindu population in Bali and other islands
-2020:around 2% Hindu population (due to conversion, assimilation, and migration)
7.Fiji:
-1947:around 40% Hindu population
-2020:around 25% Hindu population (due to migration, assimilation, and coup-led instability)

These numbers are approximate and sourced from various reports, articles, and census data. The diminution of Hindu populations in these countries is often attributed to factors like:

-Migration to other countries
-Conversion to other religions
-Persecution and violence
-Assimilation into dominant cultures
-Low birth rates

Keep in mind that these trends may vary, and Hindu populations continue to thrive in some countries.

Reasons

Pakistan:The diminution of the Hindu population in Pakistan can be attributed to several factors, including:

1.Partition of India (1947):Mass migration and violence during partition led to a significant decline in the Hindu population.
2.Forced Conversions:Hindus have faced forced conversions to Islam, particularly in rural areas.
3.Persecution and Violence:Hindus have faced violence, abduction, and forced marriages, leading to a decline in population.
4.Migration to India:Many Hindus migrated to India due to persecution, economic reasons, or family ties.
5.Low Birth Rates:Hindu communities in Pakistan have lower birth rates compared to Muslims.
6.Lack of Rights and Protection:Hindus face discrimination and lack of protection under Pakistani law.
7.Economic Factors:Hindus have faced economic marginalization, leading to poverty and migration.
8.Social Pressures:Hindus face social pressures to convert to Islam, particularly in rural areas.

9.Abduction and Forced Marriages:Hindu women have been abducted and forced into marriages with Muslim men.
10.Government Policies:Some government policies and laws have been criticized for being discriminatory towards Hindus.

These factors have contributed to the decline of the Hindu population in Pakistan from around 15% in 1947 to less than 2% today.

Bangladesh:

Since the 1971 Bangladesh Liberation War, the Hindu population in Bangladesh has declined due to:

1.Post-war violence and persecution (1971-1972):Hindus were targeted, leading to mass killings, rape, and displacement.
2.Forced conversions:Hindus were forced to convert to Islam, particularly in rural areas.
3.Migration to India:Many Hindus fled to India due to persecution, economic reasons, or family ties.
4.Vested Property Act (1974):The government confiscated property of Hindus who migrated to India.
5.Land grabbing:Hindus faced land grabbing and property disputes, leading to displacement.
6.Communal riots and violence (1990s-2000s):Hindus were targeted during riots, leading to deaths, injuries, and displacement.
7.Abduction and forced marriages:Hindu women were abducted and forced into marriages with Muslim men.
8.Social pressures:Hindus faced social pressures to convert to Islam.

9.Economic marginalization:Hindus faced economic discrimination, leading to poverty and migration.
10.Lack of rights and protection:Hindus faced discrimination and lack of protection under Bangladeshi law.
11.Political instability:Political instability and communal tensions led to a decline in the Hindu population.
12.Low birth rates:Hindu communities in Bangladesh have lower birth rates compared to Muslims.

These factors have contributed to the decline of the Hindu population in Bangladesh from around 13% in 1971 to around 8% today.

There have been recent attacks on Hindus in Bangladesh, particularly after the ousting of Sheikh Hasina's government. These attacks are reportedly driven by individuals seeking to exploit the current situation, and are not considered part of a systematic agenda [1]. The violence has resulted in at least 205 attacks across 52 districts, targeting Hindu organizations and members of the minority community [1].

Nature of the Attacks

The attacks are seen as political in nature, rather than communal, and are believed to be a fallout of the perception that most Hindus supported the Awami League regime[2]. However, some experts argue that the issue is being exaggerated, and that India is propagating these incidents in a big way [2].

Impact on Hindu Community

The Hindu community in Bangladesh has historically faced persecution and violence, with many forced to flee to India [3]. The current attacks have sparked fear and anxiety among the community, with many seeking protection and justice [1].

Source:1.livemint.com2.livemint.com 3.en.wikipedia.org

Afghanistan:

The Hindu population in Afghanistan has significantly diminished due to:

1.Persecution and violence:Hindus faced violence, forced conversions, and persecution, leading to migration and death.
2.Soviet-Afghan War (1979-1989):Hindus fled due to conflict and instability.
3.Civil War (1989-1996):Hindus were targeted, leading to displacement and migration.
4.Taliban Regime (1996-2001):Hindus faced severe persecution, forced conversions, and destruction of temples.
5.Forced Conversions:Hindus were forced to convert to Islam, particularly during the Taliban regime.
6.Migration:Hindus migrated to India, Pakistan, and other countries due to persecution and instability.
7.Lack of Rights and Protection:Hindus faced discrimination and lack of protection under Afghan law.
8.Destruction of Temples:Hindu temples were destroyed, leading to a decline in religious and cultural practices.
9.Economic Marginalization:Hindus faced economic discrimination, leading to poverty and migration.

10.Social Pressures:Hindus faced social pressures to convert to Islam, particularly in rural areas.
11.Abduction and Forced Marriages:Hindu women were abducted and forced into marriages with Muslim men.
12.Political Instability:Ongoing political instability and conflicts have made it difficult for Hindus to remain in Afghanistan.

These factors have contributed to the decline of the Hindu population in Afghanistan from around 100,000 in the 1970s to fewer than 1,000 today.

Sri Lanka:
The Hindu population in Sri Lanka has diminished due to:

1.Ethnic conflict (1983-2009):Hindus were caught in the middle of the conflict between the Sinhalese and Tamils, leading to displacement and migration.
2.Forced Conversions: Hindus were forced to convert to Buddhism or Christianity, particularly during the colonial era.
3.Migration:Hindus migrated to India, Malaysia, and other countries due to economic reasons, persecution, or family ties.
4.Low Birth Rates:Hindu communities in Sri Lanka have lower birth rates compared to other groups.
5.Assimilation:Hindus have assimilated into the dominant Sinhalese or Tamil cultures, leading to a decline in Hindu identity.
6.Lack of Rights and Protection: Hindus faced discrimination and lack of protection under Sri Lankan law, particularly during the conflict.

7.Destruction of Temples:Hindu temples were destroyed or damaged during the conflict, leading to a decline in religious and cultural practices.
8.Economic Marginalization:Hindus faced economic discrimination, leading to poverty and migration.
9.Social Pressures:Hindus faced social pressures to convert to Buddhism or Christianity, particularly in rural areas.
10.Political Instability:Ongoing political instability and communal tensions have made it difficult for Hindus to maintain their identity and practices.
11.Sinhalese Nationalism:The rise of Sinhalese nationalism has led to a decline in Hindu identity and practices.
12.Tamil Nationalism:The Tamil separatist movement has also led to a decline in Hindu identity among Tamils, who have increasingly identified as Tamil rather than Hindu.

These factors have contributed to the decline of the Hindu population in Sri Lanka from around 25% in the 1980s to around 12% today.

Malaysia:
The Hindu population in Malaysia has diminished due to:

1.Conversion to Islam:Many Hindus have converted to Islam, particularly in rural areas.
2.Interfaith marriages:Hindu women marrying Muslim men often convert to Islam.
3.Migration:Hindus have migrated to other countries, such as India, Singapore, and Australia.
4.Low birth rates:Hindu communities in Malaysia have lower birth rates compared to Muslims.
5.Assimilation:Hindus have assimilated into the dominant Malay culture, leading to a decline in Hindu identity.

6.Lack of rights and protection:Hindus face discrimination and lack of protection under Malaysian law.
7.Destruction of temples:Hindu temples have been demolished or relocated, leading to a decline in religious and cultural practices.
8.Economic marginalization:Hindus face economic discrimination, leading to poverty and migration.
9.Social pressures:Hindus face social pressures to convert to Islam, particularly in rural areas.
10.Government policies:Some government policies, such as the bumiputera policy, have been criticized for favoring Muslims over Hindus.
11.Urbanization:Hindus have moved to urban areas, leading to a decline in traditional practices and identity.
12.Lack of education and awareness:Some Hindus lack knowledge about their own religion and culture, leading to assimilation.

These factors have contributed to the decline of the Hindu population in Malaysia from around 15% in the 1960s to around 6% today.

Indonesia:
The Hindu population in Indonesia has diminished due to:

1.Islamic Conquest (14th-16th centuries): Hindu kingdoms were conquered, leading to forced conversions.
2.Dutch Colonialism (16th-20th centuries): Christians were favored, leading to conversions.
3.Nationalism and Islamization (20th century):Indonesia's independence movement emphasized Islam.
4.Forced Conversions:Hindus were forced to convert to Islam, particularly in rural areas.

5.Interfaith Marriages:Hindu women marrying Muslim men often convert to Islam.
6.Migration:Hindus migrated to other countries, such as India and Malaysia.
7.Low Birth Rates:Hindu communities in Indonesia have lower birth rates compared to Muslims.
8.Assimilation:Hindus assimilated into dominant Islamic culture.
9.Lack of Rights and Protection:Hindus face discrimination and lack of protection under Indonesian law.
10.Destruction of Temples:Hindu temples were destroyed or relocated.
11.Economic Marginalization:Hindus face economic discrimination.
12.Social Pressures:Hindus face social pressures to convert to Islam.
13.Education System:Islamic education is promoted, leading to Hindu children converting.
14.Radical Islamic Groups:Groups like Jemaah Islamiyah and Islamic Defenders Front promote Islamization.

Regional Factors:

1.Bali:Hindu majority, but facing Islamic influence.
2.Java:Historically Hindu, now predominantly Muslim.
3.Sumatra:Hindu population declined due to Islamic conquest.

These factors have contributed to the decline of the Hindu population in Indonesia from around 20% in the 15th century to around 2% today.

Fiji:
The Hindu population in Fiji has diminished due to:

1.Colonial Era (1879-1970):Indians were brought as indentured laborers, leading to displacement.
2.Migration to Australia and New Zealand (1980s-1990s):Hindus migrated for economic reasons.
3.Coups and Political Instability (1987, 2000, 2006):Hindus were targeted, leading to migration.
4.Discriminatory Policies:Post-colonial governments implemented policies favoring indigenous Fijians.
5.Land Reforms:Hindu-owned land was redistributed to indigenous Fijians.
6.Economic Factors:Hindus faced economic marginalization and poverty.
7.Social Pressures:Hindus faced social pressures to convert to Christianity or Islam.
8.Interfaith Marriages:Hindu women marrying non-Hindus often convert.
9.Low Birth Rates:Hindu communities in Fiji have lower birth rates.
10.Lack of Rights and Protection:Hindus faced discrimination and lack of protection under Fijian law.
11.Destruction of Temples:Hindu temples were destroyed or vandalized.
12.Cultural Assimilation:Hindus assimilated into dominant Fijian culture.
13.Education System:Christian-oriented education led to Hindu children converting.
14.Emigration of Professionals:Hindu professionals migrated for better opportunities.

These factors have contributed to the decline of the Hindu population in Fiji from around 40% in the 1980s to around 25% today.

(v)Conspiracy to destroy the only Hindu Nation in the world:

Nepal, which was the world's only Hindu kingdom until 2008, when it became a secular federal republic. There are various conspiracy theories surrounding the transition and some of the theories are discussed below:

1.Political changes:Nepal's transition from a Hindu kingdom to a secular republic was driven by political and social movements, aiming to promote equality, inclusivity, and human rights.
2.Maoist insurgency:The Maoist insurgency (1996-2006) played a significant role in shaping Nepal's political landscape, contributing to the eventual abolition of the monarchy and establishment of a republic.
3.Globalization and secularization: Nepal's increasing exposure to global ideas, cultural exchange, and secularization contributed to a decline in the dominance of Hinduism.
4.Ethnic and regional aspirations:Nepal's diverse ethnic and regional groups sought greater recognition, rights, and representation, leading to a more inclusive and secular political system.
5.Indian influence:Some theorize that India, Nepal's southern neighbor, exerted influence to reduce Nepal's Hindu identity and promote a more secular stance, possibly to counterbalance Nepal's historical cultural ties with China.

It is believed in certain circles that the refusal of the King of Nepal to intervene in the matter of permitting Sonia Gandhi to visit the Pashupatinath temple triggered the sanctions imposed by Rajiv Gandhi, because of which Nepal drifted towards China for support.

6.Christian missionary activities:Some point to Christian missionary activities as a factor in reducing Nepal's Hindu population.
7.Economic factors:Nepal's economic struggles and poverty may have contributed to a decline in traditional practices and values.

It's essential to note that these factors are complex, interconnected, and influenced by various stakeholders. While some may view these changes as a "conspiracy," others see them as a natural evolution toward a more inclusive, secular, and democratic society.

Chapter 15

Can Hinduism be Saved from Extinction

The way the things are going presently, the day will not be far when Hinduism will become an extinct religion on the earth and there will be only two major religions in the world – Christianity and Islam.

Status of Hindu religion before arrival of Islam

Before arrival of Islam in India (around 12th Century CE), Hinduism had a diverse and complex status but had to tackle only the internal challenges – challenges from other Hindu Kings for superiority and authority.

The social structure was divided into caste system and varna ashram. The caste system was well established and entrenched into the roots of Hinduism with Brahmins at the top of the society followed by Kshatriyas, Vaishyas and Shudras. The social hierarchy influenced and determined the political power with Brahmins and Kshatriyas holding the prominent positions.

The Varna Ashram system, a fundamental concept in Hinduism, divided life into four stages (Ashrams) to provide a structured and purposeful journey of life. Stage-1 was Brahmacharya Ashram (Student Life, 0-25 years) with focus on education, self-discipline, and spiritual growth. Stage-2 was Grihastha Ashram (Household Life, 25-50 years) having focus on family, social, and professional life with the responsibilities constituting marrying, raising children, managing household, and contributing to the society. The Stage-3 called Vanaprastha Ashram (Retired Life, 50-75 years) had focus on gradual detachment from worldly life. And, Stage-4 was the Sanyas Ashram (Renunciate Life, 75+ years) having focus on complete detachment from worldly life.

Hindus were following polytheism system of worship, i.e., worship of multiple deities with widespread trend of temple worship. The system also consisted of rituals and festivals with various types of ceremonies, sacrifices and celebrations.

The Philosophical school consisted of (i) Vedanta having emphasis on Upnishadic teachings (e.g., Advaita, Vishitadvaita); (ii) Yoga for physical, mental and spiritual disciplines; and (iii) Nyaya, Vaisheshika and Mimamsa for logical and philosophical inquiry.

The major regional Kingdoms and Empires were (i) Gupta Empire (320-550 CE) which was considered as the Golden Age of Hinduism, art and culture; (ii) Pallava Dynasty (300-850 CE) which was prominent in South India; (iii) Chola Empire (300-1279 CE) also having dominance in South India; and (iv) various Rajput Kingdoms (6th-12th century CE) in North India.

Before arrival of Islam in India, jurisdiction of Indian Kingdoms were limited to the authority of the Kings. The Hindu Kingdoms were generally smaller and region-specific (e.g., Gujarat, Bengal, Tamil Nadu) and mainly focussed on maintaining control within their territories rather than expanding empires. These Hindu Kings used to fight battles and wars with each other to maintain their authority and control. Thus, the power was fragmented amongst multiple

Kingdoms and regional leaders and the King's authority was generally limited to their immediate territory.

However, some Kings were more ambitious and capable and they used to exert their power and authority to subjugate other Kings and expand their empire. Such Kings used to be called the Samrat (Emperor) and the Kings under their authority had to pay Tributes (Bhaga or Kara) and Taxes.

Though Hindu Kings used to fight battles and wars amongst themselves to expand their authority, there was no immediate threat to Hinduism; all the Kings were Hindus and followers of Hinduism.

In ancient India, the words of Rishis, Munis and Brahmins had significant authority as their words were considered divinely inspired. Kings and Emperors used to follow their word which was considered to be the final word. As such, the public also followed them but it was limited to the jurisdiction of the Kings and Emperors.

In the Manusmriti (2.100) also it is mentioned that "The Brahmins word is the highest authority". In Mahabharata (Shanti Parva, 59.15), it has been said that "The Rishi's word is truth itself" and the Bhagavad Gita (16.1-2) mentions that "The wise (Rishis) are the authority on dharma".

Thus, the authority of Rishis, Munis and Brahmins played a significant role in shaping ancient Indian society, ensuring that spiritual and moral principles guided decision-making.

Since there were separate guides for the Kings and Emperors, there used to be different views and directions of the guides for the Kings. Thus, Hinduism had a decentralized set-up and nature as no single centralized authority was in existence to control the religious tenets to be followed by every follower of the religion unlike Christianity or Islam. For temples, local authorities and priests held the significance which is prevalent even in present day.

Before the arrival of Muslims in India, the region was predominantly Hindu, with various kingdoms and dynasties vying for power. These conflicts were primarily driven by political and territorial ambitions, rather than religious differences. There were Inter-kingdom conflicts and wars were fought between Hindu kingdoms for territorial expansion and resources. The Kingdoms competed for dominance within specific regions. There were succession disputes and internal power struggles also within the Kingdoms.

However, despite political differences, Hinduism remained the dominant faith in India and common cultural practices of festivals, rituals, and traditions were widely observed. The sacred texts were respected uniformly and the Vedas, Upanishads, and Puranas were revered across Kingdoms.

During those times, there were no significant external invasions and India was relatively isolated from external threats. The trade and cultural exchange were also limited and there was minimal influence from outside regions. However, there were political power struggles and Hindu Kingdoms prioritized expanding their territories and influence. The Kingdoms competed for dominance amongst themselves.

When Muslims turned towards India and started attacking the Hindu Kings, the Hindu Kings were a divided lot. The Hindu Kings had only their vested interest as the priority; neither the religion nor the nation as a whole appeared to them as their sole priority. Since they were only after power, some of the Kings often allayed with Muslims to defeat their opponents without thinking of the long-term adverse effects. Whereas Hindu Kings were giving preference to power, the Muslims were fighting primarily for spreading Islam for which expansion of their region was the foremost priority.

The motivations of Muslim invaders were to spread Islam for which purpose they intended to expand their territories by winning wars and either converting the conquered ones into Islam or eliminate them if they didn't convert. The Muslim rulers saw the conquests as a duty to spread Allah's word. Apart from this, the economic gains, plunder, tributes and trade opportunities also motivated Muslim invaders. They also intended to build and establish Islamic Empires, like the Delhi Sultanate and Mughal Empire.

The Hindu Kings gave preference only to their vested interests, rather than the religion or the national interest, and were only after power, as a result of which some Kings sided with the Muslim invaders. The consequences were that there were fragmentations and Hindu Kings' divisions facilitated Muslim conquests. There was gradual loss of Hindu-dominated territories to Muslim rulers. This had cultural impact and exerted Islamic influences on Indian culture, architecture and art. The Muslim conquests resulted in religious conversions, either forced or voluntary, to Islam which was the ultimate aim of Muslim invaders.

It is very clear that the Muslim invaders had a common aim – to expand Islam by winning wars and converting or killing those who lost whereas on the other hand, the Hindu Kings were only after power and never cared about their common entity of Hinduism and identity as Hindus. The driving force of Muslim invaders was a single God "Allah", which united them into one entity, and a Central Authority to enforce religious tenets on a uniform basis.

But, in Hindu religion, there were several Gods and deities and different regions followed different traditions, customs, practices and interpretations. Also, there was no Central Authority to propagate common and uniform practice of worship in Hinduism.

However, prior to arrival of Islam and Christianity in India, there was no need for a Central Authority to save Hinduism and unite Hindus. The Emperors and Kings used to act as saviours of Hinduism. But there being faith in a single God and having a Central Authority for the welfare of the religion and implementation of religious tenets in Islam and Christianity, the Central Authority serves as the pillar of unity amongst them on basis of religion.

However, considering the fragmentation in Hindu population; there being no such Central Authority for the welfare of the religion and implementation of religious tenets, and noticeable decline in Hindu population due to conquests and conversions and drastic rise in Islam and Christianity, it appears that a time has come when the Hindu religion should also endeavour to invent a Central Authority for Hinduism. It would serve as a unity factor for all the Hindus, who seem to be divided even in the present day because of hunger for power.

It appears that we Hindus neither learn from the past nor do we care about the future. We also don't look around in the world as to what is happening to Hindus, who are being eliminated gradually. Without giving a heed to the lessons loudly being narrated by the cruel incidents, we strive to follow the path of destruction for ourselves. We Hindus are power hungry, without caring for our religion, and refuse to learn from the past. Muslim invaders killed even those Kings who sided with them for temporary gains of power ignoring our national and religious fervour. If we don't learn from the past, it is feared in certain circles that in future India will become a Islamic State. Even the Muslim fundamentalists are claiming this.

Therefore, it is very essential that such an instrument is invented which may give a common sense of purpose to Hindus. Though Hindus are very religious and God-fearing community, even its religious system is fragmented and we have no uniform system of following the religious path. Islam and Christianity follow uniform system of religious worship and this is because of this factor that these religions are the major religions in the world in the present day.

Therefore, to unite Hindus behind a common force, a single God requires to be invented and put in place and there should be Central Authority to implement the religious tenets like Christianity and Islam. Only then we can think of saving Hinduism from extinction otherwise a day may come when there would no nation for Hindus to be called of their own.

Epilogue

Whereas Muslim and Christian populations grew consistently in the world and are still growing at a steady rate, Hindu population and consequently Hinduism is declining and it is feared that it may become extinct in near future.

This is based on demographic trends and projections as indicated in the undermentioned breakdown:

<u>Hindu population decline:</u>

1.Low fertility rates:Hindus have lower total fertility rates (TFR) compared to Muslims and Christians.
2.Conversion:Hindus convert to other religions, primarily Christianity and Islam.
3.Assimilation:Hindus assimilate into dominant cultures, losing their religious identity.
4.Migration:Hindus migrate to countries with different dominant religions.

<u>Global demographic trends:</u>

1.Muslim population growth:2.6% annual growth rate (2020-2050).
2.Christian population growth:1.2% annual growth rate (2020-2050).
3.Hindu population growth:1.1% annual growth rate (2020-2050).

<u>Projections:</u>

1.Pew Research Center (2020):Hindus will comprise 14.9% of the global population by 2050, down from 15.2% in 2010.
2.World Christian Database (2020):Hindus will decline to 12.8% of the global population by 2100.

Factors contributing to Hindu decline:

1.Urbanization:Hindus in urban areas tend to have lower fertility rates.
2.Education:Higher education leads to lower fertility rates and increased conversion.
3.Economic factors:Poverty and economic instability contribute to conversion.
4.Social factors:Caste system, social inequality, and cultural assimilation.

Revitalization Efforts to be made:

Efforts should be made for the revitalization of Hinduism by preserving the cultural heritage and traditions in Hinduism. This can be done by documenting and digitizing ancient texts and scriptures, protecting and restoring ancient temples monuments, promoting traditional arts, music and dance, preserving traditional crafts and handicrafts and establishing cultural museums and exhibitions. The traditional practices, such as Vedic education and rituals should be promoted and traditional festivals and celebrations should be encouraged. The traditional social institutions (e.g., joint families) should be supported and traditional occupational skills (e.g., Ayurveda, astrology) revived. Apart from this, the Hindu studies should be integrated in school curricula and online resources for Hindu education created.

The Hindu education and awareness need to be promoted. Hindu websites and portals should be created. Hindu festivals and events should be organized regularly with fervor and enthusiasm. Temple programs and lectures should be widely held along with Satsangs and spiritual gatherings.

Efforts should also be made to publish more and more Hindu books and journals, Magazines and newsletters and documentaries and films on Hinduism and Hindi culture should be made and publicized apart from Hindi Radio shows, podcasts, Hindu-themed comics and graphic novels.

Since Hindu population growth is declining at a steady pace, the Hindu population growth should also be encouraged.

Consequences:

The Consequences of potential decline of Hinduism as a global religion may result in loss of cultural heritage and traditions and decline of Hindu art, architecture, and literature apart from erosion of Hindu values and philosophy and decreased influence on global culture.

The social consequences would be decreased social cohesion among Hindus, loss of community identity and belonging.

The consequences of the loss of cultural heritage and traditions in Hinduism shall result in vanishing of Hindu identity and history, decline of traditional arts and crafts, loss of Hindu architecture and monuments, disappearance of Hindu festivals and celebrations and erosion of Hindu values and philosophy.

The recent killings of Hindus and destruction of temples in Bangladesh, which gained independence with the help of Indian forces, should serve as a wide eye opener for Hindus and political parties as to what may happen to them also in near future if an opportunity arises. The volatile outbursts of some leaders against Hindus should serve as a reminder to everybody of the history and past incidents.

Extinction scenario:

While the extinction seems to be unlikely in near future, some projections suggest that Hindu population could decline to 10% of the global population by 2150. If current trend continues, there is a possibility of the extinction of Hinduism in 300-500 years.

However, the demographic projections are subject to uncertainty, Hinduism's resilience and adaptability and efforts to revitalize Hinduism and preserve cultural heritage.

Conclusion:

Hindus have remained slaves of Mughals first, for 800 years, and then of Britishers, for another 200 years, owing to disunity among themselves and putting vested interests above the national interests. The Hindus have not learnt from the past. In present times also, Hindus are still a divided lot. This is owing to various factors. Some of the historical factors contributing to the disunity among Hindus are (i) social hierarchy and divisions due to caste system; (ii) Islamic conquests leading to destruction of temples and forced conversions; and (iii) fragmented Kingdoms resulting in disintegrated Hindu empire. The social factors can be attributed to (i) discrimination and exclusion due to casteism; (ii) linguistic and cultural differences of various regions; (iii) economic and educational disparities due to urban-rural divide; and (iv) social inequality due to gender, economic and educational disparities. And, the cultural differences, language barriers and ritualistic differences also contribute to the disunity of Hindus. The after effects of British divide-and-rule-policies can still be felt in the approach of different political parties, which they adopt to divide Hindus into various water-tight compartments so that their votes can be won by a particular political party. Though earlier also Hindus could not understand this reason for their downfall, even now the Hindus are so naïve that they refuse to understand this ploy of the political parties and fall into their trap and become their preys.

The present state of affairs highlights the ongoing impact of British colonial policies on India's political landscape. The British employed a "divide and rule" strategy, exploiting the then existing differences among Indians to maintain control. This tactic has left a lasting legacy, influencing how political parties operate today.

The British effectively used this policy to create divisions between Hindus and Muslims, ultimately contributing to the partition of India in 1947. Although the British are no longer in power, their policies have had a lasting impact on India's political landscape.

In the current political landscape of India, some argue correctly that political parties continue to exploit these divisions to win votes. This can be seen in the way parties often focus on specific issues or identities to appeal to certain groups of voters.

The division of Hindus according to their caste is very serious and dangerous to the national unity, safety and is prone to outside interference. However, some political parties simply brush aside the imminent dangers in their greed for power and even in the present-day scenario try to divide the

Hindu community into the castes and communities to gain votes just for winning the elections to come to power. This is despite the fact that the Hindus had to suffer the slavery of outside aggressors because of disunity among themselves and hunger for power.

Rather than perpetuating divisions, it's crucial for Indians to come together and demand inclusive and equitable governance. By recognizing the harmful legacy of colonial policies and promoting unity, Indian people can overcome these challenges and build a brighter future.

The other important factor for disunity can be attributed to the lack of a strong centralized authority for worship.

The lack of a strong, centralized authority for worship is indeed a significant factor contributing to Hinduism's diversity and potential disunity. The reason being that Hinduism is characterized by multiple sects and traditions (e.g., Vaishnavism, Shaivism, Shaktism), diverse scriptures (Vedas, Upanishads, Puranas, Bhagavad Gita), various deities and interpretations and local and regional customs.

Unlike Abrahamic faiths (Christianity, Islam, Judaism), Hinduism lacks a single, unified authority governing worship, doctrine, or practice. This leads to interpretational differences, regional and sectarian variations and limited coordination among Hindu organizations.

The consequences of the decentralized nature and lack of central authority may be disunity and fragmentation, difficulty in articulating a unified Hindu voice, challenges in addressing social and political issues and vulnerability to external influences and conversions.

All these factors have the consequences of weakened Hindu identity, vulnerability of conversion and loss of cultural heritage.

Some of the potential solutions to address disunity among Hindus can be establishing a representative Hindu council or organization, promoting inter-sect dialogue and cooperation, encouraging education and awareness about Hinduism's diversity and fostering a sense of shared Hindu identity.

Constitution of a Vedic Board

Constituting a Vedic Board to promote Hindu unity can also be considered as one of the possible solutions with the following objectives:

1.Unify Hindu sects and traditions.
2.Promote Vedic values and principles.
3.Encourage interfaith dialogue and understanding.
4.Foster Hindu identity and cultural preservation.
5.Provide guidance on Hindu scriptures and practices.

The structure of the Vedic Board may constitute of the following:

1.Representative Membership:
-Scholars from various Hindu traditions (Shaivism, Vaishnavism, Shaktism).
-Experts in Vedic studies, Sanskrit, and Hindu philosophy.
-Representatives from Hindu organizations and institutions.

2. Advisory Council:
-Eminent Hindu leaders and spiritual heads.
-Experts in social, cultural, and economic development.

The functions that may be assigned to Vedic Board can be:

1.Scriptural Interpretation:
-Clarify misinterpretations and misconceptions.
-Provide authoritative guidance on Hindu scriptures.
2.Cultural Preservation:
-Promote Vedic arts, music, and literature.
-Support Hindu festivals and traditions.
3.Education and Outreach:
-Develop Hindu education programs.
-Conduct workshops, seminars, and conferences.
4.Interfaith Dialogue:
-Engage with other faiths to promote understanding.
-Collaborate on social and humanitarian projects.
5.Conflict Resolution:
-Mediate disputes within Hindu communities.
-Provide guidance on Hindu values and principles.

The Vedic Board may focus on:

1.Balancing diversity with unity.
2.Addressing power struggles and representation.
3.Managing conflicting interpretations.
4.Strengthening Hindu identity and unity.
5.Promoting Vedic values and principles.
6.Enhancing Hinduism's global presence.
For this purpose, the existing models of (i) The Pontifical Council for Interreligious Dialogue (Catholic Church); (ii) The Muslim World League (Islamic organization); (iii) The Jewish Council for Public Affairs (Jewish organization) can be considered for which Hindu leaders, scholars, and organizations may be consulted for drafting a constitution and bylaws, establishing a secretariat and securing funding and resources for launching the Vedic Board.

By establishing a Vedic Board, Hindus can unify diverse traditions, promote Vedic values, enhance cultural preservation, foster interfaith understanding and strengthen Hindu identity.

A more coordinated and unified Hindu voice could strengthen Hinduism's global presence, enhance social and political influence and facilitate greater cooperation and understanding.

Considering the fact that many nations became Islamic States within a short span of time of emergence of Islam, ignoring the fact that India can never become Islamic State will be closing our eyes to the hard reality, facts and past precedents. The only remedy lies in the unity of Hindus which can be achieved through a common goal of worship for which it is necessary to (i) discovering and publicizing a God common to every Hindu; (ii) uniform system of prayers and performing rituals; and (iii) a Central Authority for religious tenets to be strictly followed by each Hindu. This can be understood from the hypothesis that in temples Hindus have various deities and a Hindu going to the temple worships all those deities for acceptance of his prayer. Having different Gods is akin to the fact that we are placing a request to different authorities and, therefore, if it is a fact that our prayers are listened by the God, then there may be confusion among different Gods to fulfil or grant the prayer, that if the prayer is not accepted or fulfilled by one, the other God will fulfil it, and ultimately nothing may happen to the prayer.

At present, Christianity and Islam are the major religions in the world. The simple reason being they are following uniform method of worship and have one God common to everyone. Christians gather in Churches on Sundays for their prayers and Muslims gather in mosques on Fridays to offer their prayers. The attire in both the cases is normally uniform. Such a scenario depicts a picture of unity amongst them as irrespective of their status in the society, they wear the same dress giving a message of equality.

The decline of the Hindu population is a complex issue with far-reaching consequences. While extinction is unlikely, the decline of Hinduism as a global religion is a strong possibility. Revitalization efforts are necessary to preserve Hindu cultural heritage and ensure the continued relevance of Hinduism. There should be a God common to all Hindus, a Central Authority for the Hindu religion, and a uniform method of performing prayers and rituals.

In Hindu religion, Vishnu is considered as the Supreme God and the remaining deities are considered his extensions or, so to say, Avatars. In Vaishnavite traditions, Vishnu is revered as the ultimate reality, the source of all existence, and the protector of the universe. He is often depicted as the preserver of the cosmic order (Dharma). If we can worship his Avatars, why can't we offer our prayers directly to Vishnu, as is the practice in Christianity, who offer their prayers directly to Jesus, and Islam, who offer their prayers directly to Allah. This would give a common ground to every Hindu as worshipping different deities or Avatars creates confusion and often clash of faith also. Rather than routing the prayers through different deities to the Super God Vishnu, the prayers are bound to be more effective if offered directly to him.

Otherwise, that day is not far when India shall also become Islamic State. It may take some time, as Hinduism is thousands of years old and is deep rooted in India's culture, but we cannot be sure of new generation which has liberal thinking and is preoccupied with its own ambitions. They are indifferent to Hinduism which can be clearly seen from their negligible knowledge about the sacred texts of Hindus, Indian culture, Mahabharata, Ramayana, etc., their diminishing interest in their heritage. The reasons being modernization and urbanization, globalization and Western influence, education system's focus on secularism, lack of engaging, relatable content and inadequate community and family involvement. In contrast, the Muslim youth has strong affinity towards their religion and know their religious texts by heart and follow the religious tenets religiously. The Christians also follow their prayer methods uniformly and religiously. Therefore, the conversion of India to Islamic state seems inevitable if Hindus do not unite and take corrective measures.

www.ingramcontent.com/pod-product-compliance
Ingram Content Group UK Ltd.
Pitfield, Milton Keynes, MK11 3LW, UK
UKHW060103010826
14090UKWH00043B/792